Children's acquisition of language and their acc[...]
that have usually been studied separately. In [...]
connections between the two, this volume pr[...]
tegrated approach to the developmental study [...]

The volume focuses on the ways in which [...]
through language and socialized to use language in culturally specific ways.
The contribu[...] ith their
caregivers [...] owing
that these i [...] t is by
participatin [...] orien-
tations. The [...] others,
and show h [...] or and
cultural kn [...] phono-
logical, mc [...] rry so-
ciocultural [...] r con-
veying and [...] guage,
so they are

This inn[...] social-
ization will [...] , spe-
cialists in c

Studies in the Social and
Cultural Foundations of Language No. 3

Language socialization across cultures

Studies in the Social and Cultural Foundations of Language

The aim of this series is to develop theoretical perspectives on the essential social and cultural character of language by methodological and empirical emphasis on the occurrence of language in its communicative and interactional settings, on the socio-culturally grounded "meanings" and "functions" of linguistic forms, and on the social scientific study of language use across cultures. It will thus explicate the essentially ethnographic nature of linguistic data, whether spontaneously occurring or experimentally induced, whether normative or variational, whether synchronic or diachronic. Works appearing in the series will make substantive and theoretical contributions to the debate over the sociocultural–functional and structural–formal nature of language, and will represent the concerns of scholars in the sociology and anthropology of language, anthropological linguistics, sociolinguistics, and socioculturally informed psycholinguistics.

Language socialization across cultures

Edited by

BAMBI B. SCHIEFFELIN
New York University

and

ELINOR OCHS
University of Southern California

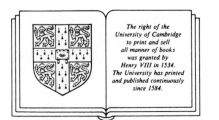

The right of the
University of Cambridge
to print and sell
all manner of books
was granted by
Henry VIII in 1534.
The University has printed
and published continuously
since 1584.

CAMBRIDGE UNIVERSITY PRESS

Cambridge
London   New York   New Rochelle
Melbourne   Sydney

Published by the Press Syndicate of the University of Cambridge
The Pitt Building, Trumpington Street, Cambridge CB2 1RP
32 East 57th Street, New York, NY 10022, USA
10 Stamford Road, Oakleigh, Melbourne 3166, Australia

First published 1986

Printed in the United States of America

Library of Congress Cataloging-in-Publication Data

Language socialization across cultures.

(Studies in the social and cultural foundations of language; no. 3)
Includes index.

1. Language acquisition. 2. Socialization. I. Schieffelin, Bambi B. II. Ochs,
Elinor. III. Series.
P118.L385   1986   401'.9   86–14798

British Library Cataloging-in-Publication Data

Language socialization across cultures. – (Studies in the social and cultural foundations of
language; 3)
1. Sociolinguistics
I. Schieffelin, Bambi B. II. Ochs, Elinor III. Series
401'.9   P40
ISBN 0 521 32621 4 hard covers
ISBN 0 521 33919 7 paperback

Contents

Part III   Expressing affect: input and acquisition

Contributors

Elaine S. Andersen Department of Linguistics, University of Southern California

Patricia M. Clancy Department of Linguistics, University of Southern California

Katherine Demuth African Studies Center, Boston University

Ann R. Eisenberg College of Behavioral and Cultural Sciences, University of Texas–San Antonio

Shirley Brice Heath Departments of English and Linguistics, Stanford University

Peggy Miller Department of Education, University of Chicago

Elinor Ochs Department of Linguistics, University of Southern California

Ann M. Peters and *Stephen T. Boggs* Department of Anthropology, University of Hawaii–Manoa

Martha Platt

Bambi B. Schieffelin Department of Anthropology, New York University

Karen Ann Watson-Gegeo Department of English as a Second Language, University of Hawaii–Manoa; and *David W. Gegeo*

1. Introduction

Elinor Ochs

Socialization

Socialization has been defined in a variety of ways, each reflecting theories of the individual and society. According to Wentworth (1980), theories of socialization have swung back and forth in terms of the role assigned to the individual in the process of becoming a member of society. Nineteenth-century theories followed Hobbes's notion of the individual as aggressive, selfish, and asocial by nature and saw socialization as the process of reshaping these natural impulses into pro-social feelings and desires (Ross 1896). Freudian theory in the early twentieth century also emphasized conflict between human nature (the id) and society (the superego) (Freud 1960). Then, with the rise of functionalism in the work of Parsons (1937, 1951) and Merton (1949), the individual is viewed as more passive and more socially directed. Through the process of socialization, individuals internalize the values of society, including those relating to personality and role behavior.

George Herbert Mead's theory of symbolic interactionalism (1956) also emphasized the impact of society on an individual's view of ''self''; individuals' perceptions of themselves are influenced by how interactional partners see them and treat them. However, for Mead, the individual is an active agent in his own socialization throughout life; individuals do not automatically internalize how others see them and the rest of the world but rather have the capacity to select images and perspectives. In this sense, individuals and society construct one another through social interaction. The selective, active role of individuals in constructing social order has been a theme of phenomenologists such as Schutz (1967) and Berger & Luckmann (1966). In this perspective, individuals acquire through socialization certain ''stock knowledge'' (rules, preferences for how to act appropriately, etc.), which they use in constructing contexts, in interpreting what is going on. Ethnometh-

1

odologists have adopted much of the phenomenological perspective and advocate examining closely the interactional procedures or methods that interactants (including older members of society interacting with young children) use to construct a sense of shared context or shared realities (Cicourel 1973; Garfinkel 1967; Mehan 1979; Mehan & Wood 1975; Sacks, Schegloff & Jefferson 1974).

The editors of this volume (Schieffelin and Ochs) consider socialization to be an interactional display (covert or overt) to a novice of expected ways of thinking, feeling, and acting (Becker et al. 1961; Wentworth 1980). Following Wentworth, we say that social interactions themselves are sociocultural environments (Wentworth 1980:68) and that through their participation in social interactions, children come to internalize and gain performance competence in these sociocultural defined contexts (Leontyev 1981; Vygotsky 1978). They learn to recognize and construct (with others) contexts and to relate contexts (and elements within contexts) to one another (Nelson 1981). We do not consider children to be passive participants in the process of socialization. First, like G. H. Mead, we see children and other novices as actively organizing sociocultural information that is conveyed through the form and content of actions of others. For example, the acquisition of sociocultural stock knowledge will be constrained by children's level of cognitive, social, and linguistic development. Second, children are active socializers of others in their environment. Even infants and small children have a hand in socializing other members of their family into such roles as caregiver, parent, and sibling. As such, second children enter a different social environment than do first children; often first children "break in" adults as caregivers. As older children, they may further socialize parents into modes of acting and communicating associated with their school and peer-group experiences. Currently this is vividly illustrated by children's role as socializers of computer literacy within their respective households.

Language socialization

Language socialization is a concept the editors take to mean both socialization through language and socialization to use language. In the perspective taken in this volume, children and other novices in society acquire tacit knowledge of principles of social order and systems of belief (ethnotheories) through exposure to and participation in language-mediated interactions. We take for granted the noncontroversial and obvious sense of this statement, that the development of intelligence and knowledge is facilitated (to an extent) by children's communication with others. Instead we pursue the nontrivial dimensions of this statement. Our approach is to examine closely the verbal interactions of infants and small children with others (older children, adults) for their sociocultural structure. Our perspective is that sociocultural information is generally encoded in the organization of conversational discourse and that discourse with children is no exception. Many formal and functional features of discourse carry sociocultural information, including phonological and morphosyntactic constructions, the lexicon, speech-act types, conversational sequencing, genres, interruptions, overlaps, gaps, and turn length. In other words, part of the meaning of grammatical and conversational structures is sociocultural. These structures are socially organized and hence carry information concerning social order (as has been demonstrated by Labov 1966, 1973). They are also culturally organized and as such expressive of local conceptions and theories about the world. Language in use is then a major if not the major tool for conveying sociocultural knowledge and a powerful medium of socialization. In this sense, we invoke Sapir (Mandelbaum 1949) and Whorf (1941) and suggest that children acquire a world view as they acquire a language.

Let us now turn to some illustrations of the acquisition of sociocultural knowledge through language.

Acquiring language and culture through interactional routines

Discourse is structured by speaker–hearer conceptions of the social activity or social event taking place. One critical area of social competence a child must acquire is the ability to recognize/interpret what social activity/event is taking place and to speak and act in ways sensitive to the context. Children must also have the competence to define activities/events through their language and nonverbal actions. In many cases, language is not simply responsive to the social activity/event; it *is* the social activity/event (Hymes 1974), as in teasing, negotiating, telling a story, tattletaling, explaining.

The importance of the activity/event in information processing has been emphasized by Bateson (1972), Minsky (1975), and Schank and Abelson (1977), among others. In this perspective, information is processed in a top–down fashion, with social event or activity being a primary information-organizing notion; objects, persons, and verbal and nonverbal behavior are given meaning vis-à-vis how one defines the activity or event in which they are embedded. Psycholinguists such as Nelson (1981) have argued that children acquire lexical knowledge in this manner; they come to understand lexical items first in terms of their role in particular situational contexts of use and later in terms of properties that generalize across contexts of use. Peters & Boggs (this volume) make the more sweeping claim that certain situational contexts are routinized in children's communication with others and that such routinization provides a language-learning environment for the child, "enabling her to perceive and analyze speech in a predictable and recurring context and to practice utterances with immediate reinforcement."

The Vygotskian or sociohistorical school of psychology has also emphasized the role of social activities in the development of the mind. Proponents of this perspective have argued that the organization of behavior in such activities affects cognitive growth (Cole & Griffin 1984; LCHC 1981; Leontyev 1981; Luria 1976; Scribner & Cole 1981; Vygotsky 1978). Of particular relevance here is the idea that cognitive skills are the outcome of using language for particular purposes associated with different activities. Language is seen as a tool that can be used to serve a number of ends; speakers will differ in the ends for which they use language and these differences will lead to the development of different cognitive skills.

Regardless of whether our readers assign the same importance to social activities/events as do those noted above, most would concur that tacit knowledge of these notions is critical to communication in a particular society and must be acquired by children and others entering the society (cf. Gumperz's [1983] discussion of native–foreigner crosstalk due to differing conceptions of the social activity in which native and foreigner are engaged [including goals and strategies for achieving them]). Language plays a major role in the acquisition of activity/event knowledge. Language, as noted, is both sensitive to and constructive of activities and events. In other words, language indexes situational context (Jakobson 1960). When caregivers and others use language to and in the presence of children, they are providing information or cues (Gumperz 1983) concerning what members are doing. As young children acquire tacit knowledge and competence in use of these cues, they are acquiring knowledge and competence in the social organization of activities and events. (We do not mean to suggest here that all of situational knowledge can be reduced to linguistic knowledge.)

There are many features of language and discourse that index activity/event (e.g. terms of address and reference, evidentials, tense/aspect, ellipsis, prosody, speech-act forms and sequences). Some activities and events may have (among certain social groups) highly predictable discourse structures (e.g. greetings, jokes, ritual insults, teasing, begging, tattletaling, clarification sequences, trick-or-treat routines), whereas others may have more variable discourse organization (e.g. gossip, negotiations, giving advice, explanations, instructions). In addition, in all societies activities and events are marked linguistically and nonverbally for the dimension of seriousness/playfulness (Bateson 1972; Goffman 1974). Goffman uses the term "keyings" to refer to the features that mark activities/events as playful or "not serious" or "not real." These keyings indicate to addressees how they should interpret what is being said and done. In many languages, prosody functions as a major keying device, distinguishing, for example, teasing from serious forms of speech activities such as insults, criticisms, or claims.

Heath (this volume) indicates ways in which communities organize events in which written language is used. She calls such occurrences "literacy events" and emphasizes that speech communities will differ in the kinds of literacy events that characterize their everyday lives. Children growing up in white middle-class, white working-class, and black working-class households in the Carolina piedmont area of the United States have different experiences with literacy and develop different expectations concerning behavior and attitudes surrounding reading and writing events. Conforming to these behaviors and attitudes establishes children as communicatively competent members of their households and communities. On the other hand, many children from non-middle-class environments experience difficulties in certain school literacy events that draw on areas of knowledge not part of their early interactions with literacy materials.

We are still in the early stages of research into the acquisition and language socialization of activity/event knowledge. What has been consistently observed across cultures, however, is the practice of caregivers providing explicit instruction in what to say and how to speak in a range of recurrent activities and events. In this volume, such practices are reported for the Kaluli of Papua New Guinea (Schieffelin), the Kwara'ae of the Solomon Islands (Watson-Gegeo & Gegeo), the Basotho of Lesotho (Demuth), white working-class Americans (Heath; Miller), black working-class Americans (Heath), and Mexican-Americans (Eisenberg). Explicit instruction in activity/event speech behavior has also been observed to be characteristic of white middle-class American (Grief & Gleason 1980), Samoan (Ochs 1982), and Wolof (Senegal) (Wills 1977) adult–child and child–child interactions.

Typically such instruction takes the form of explicit prompting by the caregiver or other member of a group. An older person will instruct a younger child in what to say by modeling each utterance for the child to repeat. The prompting routine is itself marked by characteristic linguistic features. For example, the routine is usually but not always initiated by an imperative verb form meaning "say" or "do," followed by the utterance to be repeated. Very often these utterances have a distinct voice quality and intonational contour, which mark them as components of the prompting activity. Young children will respond appropriately to utterances with these prosodic features, even when they are not preceded by an explicit directive to repeat (Schieffelin 1979 [now in press]). It may very well be that these prompting routines are some of the earliest verbal activities (along with, for example, greetings) children gain competence in.

There has been quite a bit written about other ways in which caregivers in certain societies facilitate children's participation in verbal activities/events (cf., among others, Bruner 1977; Bruner & Sherwood 1976; Greenfield & Smith 1976; Wertsch 1980; Zukow, Reilly & Greenfield 1982). Other verbal practices that assist children in understanding what is going on and/or helping them to perform include

- announcing to the child what activity/event is about to occur, is now occurring, should be or should not be occurring (e.g., "Let's look at a book"; "Those girls are teasing that little boy"; "He should tell the teacher what they did"; "The girls should not be teasing him"');
- providing leading questions that indicate what the child should say next (e.g., "What do you say?"; "How does the story end?"');
- simplifying the semantic content and grammatical structure of prompting directives, activity/event announcements, and the like;
- repeating utterances and/or entire verbal activities/events with the child as direct participant or observer;
- expanding the child's utterance into an activity/event-appropriate contribution (e.g., Child: "Trick treat"; Mother: "Trick or treat").

All of these practices provide a good environment for learning important linguistic and sociocultural structures. These practices illustrate what Bruner (1975, 1977) has called "scaffolding" and evidence support for Vygotsky's (1978) notion of "zone of proximal development" – that children develop social and cognitive skills through participating in structured cooperative interactions with more mature members of society. It is important to note here that *all societies do not rely on the very same set of language-socializing procedures. Indeed although prompting a child what to say appears widespread, expanding children's utterances, using leading questions, announcing activities/events for a child, and using a simplified lexicon and grammar to do so are cross-culturally variable.* These latter practices are not, for example, characteristic of adult–child or child–child interactions in traditional Western Samoan households, for example (Ochs 1982, in press).

Acquiring knowledge of status and role through language use

When members of a society interact with one another, their actions are influenced by their conceptions of their own and others' social status, i.e. their recognized position in society and/or in a particular social situation, and by the role behaviors associated with such statuses (Merton 1949; Mead 1956). These conceptions lead to expectations concerning their own and others' conduct. Included in these expectations are ones concerning language behavior. Languages have constructions at all levels of grammar and discourse that signal information concerning how interactants see their own and others' social positions and roles. As children acquire language, they are acquiring knowledge of this vital aspect of social order. Another way of putting this is to say that part of acquiring language is the acquisition of the social meaning of linguistic structures. Let us consider two examples of the link between social status/role expectations and language acquisition.

Platt (this volume) has shown that Samoan children display very early in their language behavior an understanding of the highly stratified nature of Samoan society. In her study of the acquisition of deictic verbs, Platt found that Samoan children used productively the semantically more complex verb "give" earlier and more frequently than the verb "come." This order is surprising from a cognitive perspective but not from a sociological one. Most of the deictic verbs appear in directives (e.g. "Come here!"; "Give me!") of which the use is socially constrained. In particular, it is appropriate for very small children to direct older siblings and adults to give them items but not to direct them to come; hence the more productive and earlier use of "give" over "come." The few cases of "come" are used primarily to animals and younger siblings, or to others when the child is speaking on behalf of an older person (as "messenger").

Andersen's study (this volume) indicates that young English-speaking American children have acquired sociolinguistic awareness at an early age as well. At the age of three, these children use status- and role-appropriate speech in role-playing interactions such as mother–father–child, teacher–student–student, and doctor–nurse–patient. Such sociolinguistic knowledge entails competence in the use of indirect and direct speech acts (e.g., women using more indirect requests than men), discourse markers (e.g., high status using more "well," "now"), referential alternatives to referring to speaker and addressee (e.g., doctor to patient: "Let's take a look at your throat now" versus "I'll take a look at your throat now"), tag questions, and prosody.

Not only the linguistic system but the organization of communication as well encodes cultural concepts of social status. For example, next speaker rights and communicative role rights (e.g., source, speaker, primary addressee, secondary addressee, audience) in a situation are embedded in and/or constitutive of conceptions of social status and role of co-present persons. As children engage in communicative interactions, they are acquiring information relevant to status and role. Indeed as children interact with others, they acquire a tacit understanding of their own social identities vis-à-vis others in their environment. The researcher as well can find in communication patterns ways in which caregivers and others perceive young children. One particularly revealing dimension of communication is the communicative roles children assume at different developmental points in time. Even before a child's first words, social order organizes the communicative interactions in which infants participate (Ochs & Schieffelin 1984). In some societies, such as the Anglo middle class, infants are treated as communicative partners within hours after birth (Bullowa 1979). In this social group, mothers and others will engage young infants in greeting exchanges. In other societies, such as the Kaluli of Papua New Guinea (Schieffelin 1979 [now in press], this volume), caregivers will talk about infants but not address them in the early weeks and months of life. On the other hand, Kaluli caregivers will hold up infants to face others (for example, siblings) and will speak for the infant (in a high-pitched voice) to these others. In other words, the Kaluli infant assumes the role of speaker. The important generalization is that although children the world over will ultimately assume all the basic communicative roles (speaker, addressee, referent, audience), societies will differ in the developmental point at which and the situations in which it is appropriate for children to assume particular roles, these differences being linked to their attitudes about children and their communicative competence.

Expressing affect: input and acquisition

An important component of sociocultural competence every child must acquire is the ability to recognize and express feelings in context. Every society has ways of viewing moods, dispositions, and emotions, including how they are to be displayed verbally and nonverbally and the social conditions in which it is preferable or appropriate to display them (cf. Levy 1984; Rosaldo 1980). Language accordingly is a major carrier of affective information. Among the features that convey affect are word order, dislocated structures, tense/aspect marking, mood, evidential and affect particles and affixes, phonological variation, and prosody (Ochs this volume). When children are exposed to language in use and begin to use language with older members of society, they are presented with an array of affective structures, a set of contexts, and a set of relations linking the two (e.g. markedness of affective forms vis-à-vis social identity of speaker/audience, social setting, activity, etc.).

Several articles in this volume consider the acquisition and socialization of affective language. Certain articles discuss speech acts and activities that are particularly affect-loaded. Miller, for example, discusses the value placed on masking hurt feelings in public among working-class families in Baltimore, Maryland. It is important that even young children be able to display emotional strength in the face of insult or other damaging acts. An important means of accomplishing this end is to successfully tease the other. Teasing in its more playful variety is also valued as a means of defusing a conflict. Mothers and others in this community often engage small children in teasing, and children acquire some competence in appropriate linguistic expression and contexts of use quite early in their language development. By 25 months, one child (Beth) had some competence, and by 28 months she had both the appropriate intonation and situations of use in her sociolinguistic repertoire.

Schieffelin (this volume) shows how Kaluli (Papua New Guinea) children as well are exposed to teasing and shaming in the first year of life, as they are considered crucial expressions of competence in Kaluli society. These speech activities are linguistically and cognitively complex. For example, one form of teasing includes use of a second person pronoun with a third person verb minus the final consonant. Further, such constructions are used to convey the opposite of what is literally expressed by the verb (e.g., "You eat" conveys "You don't eat"). Kaluli children get direct instruction in the use of this construction and by 30 months have acquired the form and knowledge of appropriate situations of use. This is only one of several forms of *bale to* 'turned-over words' that these children acquire in the course of learning to express and interpret affect.

Samoan language development (Ochs in press and this volume) also follows this pattern of intense socialization of affect through adult and older siblings' use of affect-loaded grammatical forms in speech acts such as teasing, shaming, challenging, and assertions of love and sympathy. And like the children observed in other societies, Samoan children acquire competence in these forms and contexts of use quite early in their language development. Indeed the Samoan data indicate that affect constructions may be particularly salient to the language-acquiring child. Samoan children acquire, for example, high affect forms before more neutral forms that identify the same object or have similar referential content (e.g. sympathy-marked first person pronoun before unmarked first person pronoun).

While the papers on working-class Baltimore, Kaluli, and Samoan language socialization focus on what Americans might call hot affect, Clancy's work on Japanese communicative style considers the socialization of an indirect, somewhat depersonalized mode of expression, which is highly valued in many contexts in Japanese society. Japanese mothers simplify the acquisition of this communicative style by following their own indirect directives and assertions to the child with more direct, explicit paraphrases and by following children's inappropriate direct utterances with the more appropriate indirect phrases. The endpoint of acquisition of Japanese is a subtle communicative style that demands a great deal of empathy on the part of the listener.

Cross-cultural patterns

This volume will attract researchers across several disciplines. For those relatively unfamiliar with cross-cultural research, a few orienting comments are in order. When one first discusses cross-cultural behaviors, the discussions dwell on phenomena that apparently never appear in the speaker's own society: "They do *x* and we don't." Though this characterization may have some truth, it usually warrants further thought. On further consideration, most cross-cultural differences turn out to be differences in *context* and/or *frequency of occurrence*. For example, as noted, in many of the societies represented in this volume (e.g., white working-class American, Kaluli, Kwara'ae, Basotho, Samoan), caregivers engage young children in lengthy elicited imitation routines. Probably in all societies such routines occur (see Gleason & Weintraub 1976; Grief & Gleason 1980 for an account of American middle-class caregiver–child imitative routines). What is different across societies is the extensiveness of these routines in terms of the semantic–pragmatic content covered (e.g. politeness phenomena, role instruction, teasing, shaming, insults, language correction), the number of interlocutors involved (dyadic, triadic, multiparty), the social relationship of interlocutors (e.g., caregivers, peers, strangers), the setting (e.g., inside/outside household dwelling, private/public, formal/informal distinctions in setting), the length of the imitative routines (e.g., number of turns, length of time), and the frequency of occurrence in the experience of young children. What is striking about Kaluli, Kwara'ae, and Basotho routines, for example, is the extraordinary length of these routines and the wide variety of topics and interlocutors they incorporate, relative to, say, imitative routines in which American middle-class children participate.

Another example of cultural differences in context and frequency concerns teasing in childhood. As discussed earlier, teasing occurs in many and probably all societies; however, its occurrence is distributed differently in different societies and its significance varies. Teasing among the Kwara'ae is always playful whereas white working-class Americans may use teasing to confront and insult as well. Teasing occurs pervasively in white, black, and Mexican-American working-class conversations with very young children, but is somewhat more restricted in white middle-class conversations with small children. It tends to occur in the speech of middle-class fathers more than mothers (Gleason 1973), in contrast to other social groups in which teasing characterizes the speech of a variety of persons (mothers, fathers, and other kin; friends; strangers) communicating with the developing child. Teasing is regarded as a vital component of a child's developing communicative competence in these working-class communities as well as among the Kaluli. Kaluli indeed say that the work of caregivers is to make the language of children "hard" the way their bones must be, and learning to tease and shame is part of the hardening process. The amount of overt socialization devoted to teasing reflects the importance of teasing in each of these speech communities.

Another point about cross-cultural research is that expectations, preferences, and belief systems are not necessarily shared by all members of society. This is obvious when reflecting upon complex societies, but we often forget to make this assumption in discussing lesser-known communities. To some extent this is a reflex of the researcher's style of analysis and presentation of generalizations. Most of us carrying out research on young children's speech behavior have limited ourselves to a handful of subjects because of the intense effort required to collect, transcribe, and analyze the data. We look first at what these studies have in common and from this evidence make generalizations about children's speech or caregivers' speech in the society as a whole. This procedure of course masks variation among members of a society. Watson-Gegeo & Gegeo (this volume) have transcended this orientation and have discussed differences in family communicative style. Watson-Gegeo & Gegeo have noted among Kwara'ae families distinct styles of child rearing, including procedures for instructing and making points. This variation appears related to both personal and social characteristics of family members. The extent to which orientations are shared or variable within society is a subject of considerable debate among anthropologists (cf. Geertz 1973; Leach 1982). The emphasis in this field has been more on presenting (hypothetical) cultural orientations than on assessing their scope within a society. In this volume as well, the emphasis is on presenting salient language behaviors of children and others and embedding these behaviors in broader patterns of social behavior and cultural knowledge. We take this to be a first step in understanding language in culture.

References

Bateson, G. 1972. *Steps to an ecology of mind*. New York: Ballantine.

Becker, H., Geer, B., Hughes, E. C., & Strauss, A. 1961. *Boys in white*. Chicago: University of Chicago Press.

Berger, P. & Luckmann, T. 1966. *The social construction of reality*. Harmondsworth: Penguin Books.

Bruner, J. 1975. The ontogenesis of speech acts. *Journal of Child Language* 2:1–19.
1977. Early social interaction and language acquisition. In H. R. Schaffer, ed., *Studies in mother–infant interaction*. London: Academic Press, pp. 271–289.

Bruner, J. & Sherwood, V. 1976. Peekaboo and the learning of rule structures. In J. Bruner, A. Jolly, & K. Sylva, eds., *Play: its role in development and evolution*. Harmondsworth: Penguin Books, pp. 277–285.

Bullowa, M., ed. 1979. *Before speech*. Cambridge: Cambridge University Press.

Cicourel, A. 1973. *Cognitive sociology*. London: Macmillan Press.

Cole, M. & Griffin, M. 1984. Re-mediation, diagnosis and remediation. Manuscript. Laboratory of Comparative Human Cognition, University of California, San Diego, Calif.

Freud, S. 1960. *The ego and the id*. New York: Norton.

Garfinkel, H. 1967. *Studies in ethnomethodology*. Englewood Cliffs, N.J.: Prentice-Hall.

Geertz, C. 1973. *The interpretation of culture*. New York: Basic.

Gleason, J. B. 1973. Code switching in children's language. In T. Moore, ed., *Cognitive development and the acquisition of language*. New York: Academic Press, pp. 159–167.

Gleason, J. B. & Weintraub, S. 1976. The acquisition of routines in child language. *Language in Society* 5:129–136.

Goffman, E. 1974. *Frame analysis.* New York: Harper & Row.

Greenfield, P. & Smith, J. H. 1976. *The structure of communication in early language development.* New York: Academic Press.

Grief, E. B. & Gleason, J. B. 1980. Hi, thanks, and goodbye: more routine information. *Language in Society* 9:159–166.

Gumperz, J. 1983. *Discourse strategies.* Cambridge: Cambridge University Press.

Hymes, D. 1974. *Foundations in sociolinguistics: an ethnographic approach.* Philadelphia: University of Pennsylvania Press.

Jakobson, R. 1960. Linguistics and poetics. In T. Sebeok, ed., *Style in language.* Cambridge: MIT Press, pp. 350–377.

Labov, W. 1966. *The social stratification of English in New York City.* Washington, D.C.: Center for Applied Linguistics.

1973. *Sociolinguistic patterns.* Philadelphia: University of Pennsylvania Press.

LCHC. 1981. Culture and cognitive development. Manuscript. Laboratory of Comparative Human Cognition, University of California, San Diego. To appear in W. Kessen, ed., L. Carmichael, *Manual of child psychology: history, theories, and methods.* New York: Wiley.

Leach, E. 1982. *Social anthropology.* Cambridge: Cambridge University Press.

Leontyev, A. N. 1981. *Problems of the development of mind.* Moscow: Progress Publishers.

Levy, R. 1984. Emotion, knowing, and culture. In R. Shweder & R. LeVine, eds., *Culture theory: essays on mind, self and emotion.* Cambridge: Cambridge University Press, pp. 214–237.

Luria, A. R. 1976. *Cognitive development: its cultural and social foundations.* Cambridge: Harvard University Press.

Mandelbaum, D. G., ed. 1949. *Selected writings of Edward Sapir.* Berkeley & Los Angeles: University of California Press.

Mead, G. H. 1956. *On social psychology.* Chicago: University of Chicago Press.

Mehan, H. 1979. *Learning lessons: social organization in the classroom.* Cambridge: Harvard University Press.

Mehan, H. & Wood, H. 1975. *The reality of ethnomethodology.* New York: Wiley.

Merton, R. 1949. *Social theory and social structure.* New York: Free Press.

Minsky, M. 1975. A framework for representing knowledge. In Winston, P., ed., *The psychology of computer vision.* New York: McGraw-Hill.

Nelson, K. 1981. Social cognition in a script framework. In J. Flavell & L. Ross, eds., *Social cognitive development.* Cambridge: Cambridge University Press.

Ochs, E. 1982. Talking to children in Western Samoa. *Language in Society* 11:77–104.

In press. *Culture and language acquisition: acquiring communicative competence in a Samoan village.* Cambridge: Cambridge University Press.

Ochs, E. & Schieffelin, B. 1984. Language acquisition and socialization: three developmental stories. In R. Schweder & R. LeVine, eds., *Culture theory: essays on mind, self and emotion.* Cambridge: Cambridge University Press, pp. 276–320.

Parsons, T. 1937. *The structure of social action.* New York: Free Press.

1951. *The social system.* Glencoe, Ill.: Free Press.

Rosaldo, M. 1980. *Knowledge and passion: Illongot notions of self and social life.* Cambridge: Cambridge University Press.

Ross, E. A. 1896. Social control. *American Journal of Sociology* 1:513–535.

Sacks, H., Schegloff, E., & Jefferson, G. 1974. A simplest systematics for the organization of turn-taking for conversation. *Language* 50:696–735.

Schank, R. C. & Abelson, R. P. 1977. *Scripts, plans, goals and understanding.* Hillsdale, N.J.: Erlbaum.

Schieffelin, B. 1979. How Kaluli children learn what to say, what to do, and how to feel: an ethnographic study of the development of communicative competence. Unpublished Ph.D. dissertation, Columbia University. In press, Cambridge: Cambridge University Press.

Schutz, A. 1967. *The phenomenology of the social world.* Evanston, Ill.: Northwestern University Press.

Scribner, S. & Cole, M. 1981. *The psychology of literacy.* Cambridge: Harvard University Press.

Vygotsky, L. 1978. *Mind in society.* Cambridge: Harvard University Press.

Wentworth, W. 1980. *Context and understanding: an inquiry into socialization theory.* New York: Elsevier North-Holland.

Wertsch, J. 1980. The significance of dialogue in Vygotsky's account of social, egocentric and inner speech. *Contemporary Educational Psychology* 5:150–162.

Whorf, B. L. 1941. The relations of habitual thought and behavior to language. In L. Spier, A. I. Hallowell, & S. S. Newman, eds., *Language, culture, and personality: essays in honor of Edward Sapir.* Menasha, Wis.: Banta.

Wills, D. 1977. Culture's cradle: social structural and interactional aspects of Senegalese socialization. Unpublished Ph.D. dissertation. University of Texas, Austin.

Zukow, P., Reilly, J., & Greenfield, P. 1982. Making the absent present: facilitating the transition from sensorimotor to linguistic communication. In K. E. Nelson, ed., *Children's language,* vol. 3. Hillsdale, N.J.: Erlbaum, pp. 1–90.

Part I

Acquiring language and culture through interactional routines

2. Calling-out and repeating routines in Kwara'ae children's language socialization

KAREN ANN WATSON-GEGEO AND
DAVID W. GEGEO

Growing interest among child-language researchers in how routines shape children's language acquisition has led to studies of individual routines, focused primarily on what aspects of communicative competence they teach and how they teach them.[1] Less attention has been paid to how individual routines in speakers' repertoires are interrelated. Yet, as Boggs (1985) points out, in order to interpret the meaning of a routine used in a particular instance, it is important to know both the content as understood by the speakers and why one routine rather than some other was selected. The latter concern is embodied in Hymes's (1974) concept of "speech economy," which has to do with the distribution of particular codes and modes of speech in the various relationships found within a speech community (Boggs 1985). The notion of speech economy directs the researcher's attention to several levels of analysis, including the degree to which routines are shared across a speech community, a routine's form and usage across situations and participants, what each routine is "for," contextual or other features (such as participation structure) that elicit a particular routine, and the life histories of routines.

Reflecting on these issues has been very useful in helping us to organize an analysis of routines engaged in by Kwara'ae caregivers and children. This paper focuses on two interrelated routines, calling out and repeating, which are key routines in Kwara'ae children's language socialization. Following a brief discussion of Kwara'ae people and culture and of the sample from which this work was drawn, we present a structural and descriptive account of calling out and repeating, and discuss the life histories of these routines.[2]

The sample

The Kwara'ae are a Melanesian people of Malaita in the Solomon Islands, speaking an Austronesian language. Our work was carried out in West

17

Kwara'ae in three Christian villages (Church of Melanesia – Anglican) whose populations are very poor and who support themselves primarily through subsistence gardening. Despite their proximity to the capital town of Auki (six miles away) and therefore to Western influences, West Kwara'ae people are conservative in their traditional values and in their desire for their children to both speak Kwara'ae well and know *falafala* (tradition).

Our analysis is based on three periods in the field: three months each in 1978 and 1979[3] and seven months in 1981. In 1981 we intensively observed and recorded a sample of five families in three villages; eighty hours of recordings were compiled from various times throughout the day for one to two hours per session, at intervals ranging from two to four weeks. In-depth interviews were conducted twice with the five families, and once with five other families, on child rearing, child care, family history, and language socialization. A total of twenty-four children ranging in age from 6 months to 15 years were recorded in the three villages; five other children 4–14 years of age in a fourth village were recorded once; and eight other children were observed as part of the village peer group. We therefore have data on a total of thirty-seven children and eleven families. For this paper, 162 examples of calling out and repeating were selected for close analysis.

Kwara'ae child rearing and socialization

Kwara'ae society is essentially egalitarian; unlike Polynesian societies, it lacks today a chiefdom system other than that imposed by the national government. Within the family, however, a hierarchical structure like that found in Hawaii (Boggs 1985) and Samoa (Ochs 1982) operates. Parents and other adults are senior in rank to children, and older siblings senior to younger. As in Hawaii, parents supervise an older child, usually a daughter, who then supervises younger ones in household work and infant caregiving. But parents are the main caregivers. In traditional times most caregiving responsibility went to mothers, who like the Kaluli (Schieffelin 1979) carried their infants about with them in a sling. But in the past two generations Kwara'ae fathers have taken over more childcare responsibility, and in West Kwara'ae they spend as much time babysitting as do mothers. Kwara'ae fathers are therefore deeply involved in their children's enculturation and language socialization.

From birth an infant's attention is directed away from its own feelings and towards the social group around it. Caregivers stimulate, talk to, and include infants in social conversation, with adults speaking for them and translating their vocalizations – which are seen as language – into Kwara'ae. Caregivers introduce simple routines to infants starting at about 6 months of age, speaking to them in a modified register of Kwara'ae that shares features of "baby-talk" or the caretaker speech register found in many other societies (Gleason

& Weintraub 1978). By 9 or 10 months of age, depending on its responses, parents shift into continuous talk with the infant structured by dozens of routines. This intensive level of interaction continues until the child is 3–4 years old. Between age 9 months and about 2½ years, heavy use of the caregiver speech register and repetitions of infant utterances and of the care-giver's own utterances characterize caregiver–infant interactions.

An important Kwara'ae child-rearing goal is to speed the child towards communicative competence and adult norms of behavior. Age 2½ to 3 years is a critical transition time for Kwara'ae children between infancy and respon-sible childhood. It is symbolized for girls, especially, by putting on clothes. Kwara'ae 3-year-olds are remarkably self-contained, independent, capable, and adult in behavior. Girls frequently participate in gardening, cooking, washing dishes and clothes, sweeping, carrying water and firewood, and babysitting with supervision. They can code-switch to the caregiver register used with small infants, but they are beyond babytalk themselves. Parents speak to them in an adult register, simplifying to some extent when they do not understand. Three-year-olds undergo intensive instruction on how to speak and behave, with heavy dosages of imperatives, corrections, and expla-nations for behavior, accompanied by praise for adultlike behavior and crit-icism for childish behavior. This intensive instruction ends before age 5 years. Thereafter children learn primarily through observation, practice, and coun-seling sessions held by the parents after dinner in the evenings (Watson-Gegeo & Gegeo 1983, in press).

Calling out

Calling out and repeating are routines found in Western Samoa and among the Kaluli, as well as in Kwara'ae. The two routines are also found in Lau (our observation) and To'abaita (Linda Simons, personal communication), Malaita neighbors of Kwara'ae. We suspect that calling out and repeating may occur throughout the Melanesian Central Solomons; on the Polynesian Eastern Sol-omons island of Tikopia, however, children are apparently restrained from calling out (Firth 1957:139–40). Calling out is used in three main ways in adult Kwara'ae discourse. First, people call out for practical reasons in run-ning a household, such as to locate a missing person or to bring a family member home for a meal. Secondly, a Kwara'ae man or woman working in the bush and hearing someone working nearby but out of sight will call out to seek identification of the other person. Thirdly, people call out from house to house, or as someone passes on the path, as a strictly social activity. They ask polite questions, or joke, tease, and engage in pleasant banter. Calling out, especially among women, is marked by a special intonation contour, by emphatic particles such as *ku* and *kwa* following the addressee's name, and by alternation of metathesized and underlying-form versions of names or words (see Table 2.2).

A tone of polite interest signals a strictly social intent. Adults meeting on the road, village path, in the gardens, or elsewhere engage in a series of polite questions about each other's activities and circumstances, even in cases where they already know the answers or the answers are obvious. Culturally, questions indicate that one is interested in the well-being, problems, needs, and conditions of others. Such social encounters are often marked by use of the same exaggerated intonation contours and stress that adults use in caretaker speech to children. In their most pronounced forms, these contours are found primarily in women's speech, but children, adolescents, and unmarried males can be heard to use them as well. Table 2.1 describes the conversational contour we call "polite interest," and contrasts it with other conversational contours in Kwara'ae. It would appear that the calling-out contour is an emphatic form of the "polite interest" contour, adjusted to be heard at a distance.

There are practical as well as social reasons, therefore, for teaching a child how to call out. Politeness strategies such as techniques of indirection, appropriate request and questions of information, and socially acceptable forms of teasing and banter are taught and practiced in calling-out routines with children.

Calling out is first introduced as one of three basic distracting routines used to help a child decenter when it is fussing, crying, or frightened. One of these is *lia,* in which a child is taken to a door or window in a caregiver's arms. The caregiver points to a butterfly, bird, flower, or other object while chanting *lia* 'look' in a low to middle pitch, and then describes the object, encouraging the infant to repeat its name or label. A second distracting routine involves asking the child a series of questions about the missing parent, beginning with "Where is *x?*" A third is calling out to the parent in the entertainment style. All three of these techniques direct an infant's attention outside itself, engage it in a speech activity, and are remarkably effective in calming infants, whose crying usually stops instantly when one of the routines is initiated.

The caregiver initiates the routine by the eliciting phrase *ako 'uana x* (*ako* 'call out'; *'uana* 'towards him/her/it'). The caregiver then demonstrates how to call out by calling in a light, high pitch. Calling out with preverbal infants employs a very soft voice, is joyous in tone with a relaxed often breathy voice, and at a higher pitch than real calling out. This sort of calling out is used to entertain or soothe a child, and sometimes to entertain the babysitting caregiver. The infant is often given sentences to repeat, sometimes prefaced by *'uri* (see below). The distinction between real calling out and calling out to entertain, therefore, is made by pitch and volume. In the following example, the mother appears to be calling out to her 5-year-old son, but is in fact soothing her sick 11-month-old infant Mosa, as indicated by her high, soft intonation contour:[4]

Example 1 – Namokalitau – 81.67

mo: Aok 'uan Sal/	Call out to Sala
call toward+3sg,poss Sala	[gentle, friendly, inviting].
"Sala! Sal! Sal ku!/	[Very softly, very high rise on *ku*]
"Lae mai' tua hain	"Come babysit Mosa."
go hither stay with+3sg,poss	
Mosa"/	
Mosa	

As in this example, caregivers often express what they suspect the child is feeling or wanting.

By 18 months of age children know how to call out and can repeat most of the phrases given to them in the routine. Calling out then takes on more uses. For example, adults may tease a child or another adult through a child by using the calling-out routine. Furthermore, children begin to call out spontaneously in appropriate ways. One afternoon in the Sulimaoma family, rice was dished out and members of the family sat down to eat it. But the grandfather had not arrived to join them. Two-year-old Fita put his rice aside, went to the door, and called out *Ko'! Hang!* 'Grandfather! Eat!' When there was no reply, he called out again. Then his father began giving him sentences to call out to his grandfather and Fita repeated them, echoed by a visiting cousin a few months younger than he.

For older children, caregivers may give the sentences to be repeated in an imperative or normal conversation tone (see Table 2.1), and the child provides calling-out intonation, pitch, and stress. In the following example from the Irosulia family, 3-year-old Susuli and her *'a'ai* or father's sister (fasi) are preparing food. The *'a'ai* gives sentences to the child in a normal conversational tone.[5]

Example 2 – Irosulia – 6.IX

fasi: Aok 'uan	Call out to grandpa.
call toward+3sg,poss	
koko'/	
rpl+grandfather	
S: Koko'!/	Grandpa! [calling out with high rise on
rpl+grandfather	final syllable]
[No answer]	
Koko'!/	
rpl+grandfather	
fasi: "Resi dua' na'"/	"The rice is done now" [matter-of-
rice cooked perf	fact, rapid, falling contour].

S:	Resi dua' na'!/	[Calling out, rise on final syllable]
	rice cooked perf	
fasi:	"Leak hang res"/	"Come and eat rice" [matter-of-fact,
	go eat rice	rapid, falling contour].
S:	Lak hang res!/	[Calling out, rise on final syllable]
	go eat rice	

Children this age also like to engage in calling out as a game with their caregivers. On one memorable occasion, Susuli's 'a'ai was in the house dishing up a late breakfast, and Susuli was playing in the outdoor kitchen a few feet away. The adult to be called was a visiting relative sitting in a house across the stream.

Example 3 – Irosulia – 21.1

fasi:	Susuli!/	Susuli! [calling out; rise on final syllable]
[No response]		
	Susuli:!/	[High rise on final syllable]
S:	Tae::/	What? [rise on final vowel; calling back]
	what	
fasi:	Aok 'uan sa Sene/	Call out to Sene.
	call toward+3sg,poss art,m Sene	
[No response]		
	Suil ku:!/	[Very high rise on ku]
S:	Tae:/	What? [rise on final vowel]
	what	
fasi:	Aok 'uan Sen 'a'an/	Call out to Sen senior/grownup (to distinguish him from a boy of the same name in the family).
	call toward+3sg,poss Sen senior	
S:	Aok 'uan Sen 'a'an?/	Call out to Sen senior? [parallels fasi's intonation except for interrogative rise– adult polite style]
	call toward+3sg,poss Sen senior	
fasi:	'Iu/	Yes [very high pitch convention signalling child she is importuning adult].
	yes	
S:	Sen 'a'an 'i hae?/	Sen senior is where? (She already knows the answer, of course.)
	Sen senior loc where	
fasi:	Lau'ba hear koko'/	Over there in grandpa's house.
	ovth,fr,e house rpl+grandfather	
S:	'I hae?/	Where?
	loc where	
fasi:	Lau'ba/	Over there [terminal rise].
	ovth,fr,e	
	Aok 'uan Sen 'ain res/	Call out to Sen to to come eat rice.
	call toward+3sg,poss Sen eat rice	
S:	'Ain tae?/	Eat what?
	eat what	
fasi:	'Ain res/	Eat rice.
	eat rice	
S:	Res 'i hae?/	Rice where?

rice loc where
fasi: Res 'i ne'e 'i luam/   Rice here in the house.
      rice loc here,e loc house
S: Hain   *tae*?   (Rice) with what?
      with+3sg,poss what
fasi: Hain   *mit*/   With meat.
      with+3sg,poss meat

Who knows how long this might have gone on had Sen not crossed the
stream, having heard it all from where he sat in his house. In this example an
instruction to call out is embedded in a calling-out routine itself. There are
several motives for Susuli wanting to prolong this interaction besides its
attraction as a game she frequently initiated with her *'a'ai*. Susuli was engaged in enjoyable play, and prolonging the routine was a technique to avoid
carrying out her *'a'ai*'s imperative. Even at age 3, however, Susuli has a
strong sense of seniority. Had she been instructed to call out to her father or
grandfather, she would have obeyed at once. But Sen is a visiting relative she
scarcely knows, and a very young man. Finally, Susuli was curious about
what they were all having to eat, especially whether a tin of meat would go
with the rice (both rice and meat being special treats). Two other aspects of
this example are important to note. First, a calling-out routine is interwoven
with a question-and-answer routine; the interweaving of routines marks the
child's progress towards adult norms of speech (see conclusion). Susuli demonstrated her competence at handling questions and her control over polite
intonation contours in calling them out. Secondly, the rhetoric of equality
(Boggs 1985) is displayed in this routine, demonstrating the almost egalitarian
relationship between this 3-year-old and her father's sister. Despite the strong
hierarchical nature of the family, adults encourage adult-style egalitarian relationships from age 3 in teaching children how to interact socially.[6] A 3-year-
old who demonstrates adultlike behavior is praised with "You are almost
sari'i 'a maiden'/*'alako* 'a young man' now." One who lapses into childish
behavior, such as whining and fussing, is criticized with the epithet *ma-
langela* 'childish/pseudo-child'.

When young children go out to the bush with their mothers to work and
become separated from them, calling out is a way to establish location, as it is
for adults. But when they go out in their peer groups calling out can again
become a game. A small distance between peers provides a context and an
excuse for calling out. Thus a group of girls of 3 to 5 years of age collecting
ngali (Pacific almond) nuts will call out, "How many have you collected so
far?" and reply, "Three. How about you?" and so on, even if they are
merely on different sides of the same tree.

Calling-out routines are important not only in teaching children appropriate
social behavior, but also in language acquisition. One significant area is in
teaching differences between the spoken and underlying form of the language.

In ordinary conversation, most Kwara'ae words are metathesized, with under-lying forms of words primarily used for emphasis or effect, to mark a pause or "comma" in a complex sentence or list of items, or to clarify a mishearing. Metathesis proceeds backwards from the final syllable of a word, but does not cross morpheme boundaries in the case of compound words. Thus, *leka* 'go' becomes *leak, daluma* (type of fish) becomes *daluam*, and *buriakalo* 'ward off' (*buri* = behind, *akalo* = spirit) becomes *buirakaol*. Words and phrases are further altered in speech by contraction, by habitually substituting an aspirated *h* for the fricative *f*, by raising diphthongs, and other processes. One question that intrigued us was how children learn to produce alternation of forms and to infer underlying forms from metathesized and contracted forms. We have found that calling out is an important routine in this regard. In calling out, the underlying form of a word is often used in alternation with the metathesized or contracted form, especially if the addressee does not hear the first time. For example, normally the word *'a'ai* is pronounced *'a'e* in speech. But in calling out, the speaker may shout *"'A'e!"*, then *"'A:'a:i:"*, produc-ing both forms together. Similarly, the word for father is *ma'a*, usually spoken as *ma'*. In calling out, the speaker may shout *"Ma'! Ma'a:::!"* In hearing others call out as well as in being shown how to call out themselves, children are exposed to both forms simultaneously. A shift in stress may help to underscore the contrast between metathesized and underlying form. As Exx. 1 and 3 illustrate in calling out *"Sala!"* or *"Susuli:!"*, in shifting primary stress to the final syllable in order to be heard (from the Kwara'ae point of view), the phonological shape of the underlying form is also empha-sized. We think stresses also call attention to certain aspects of grammar. In calling out, the sentence final position always receives primary or at the least secondary stress.

The portion stressed seems to be what an infant or child always manages to get right, in the case of a difficult or rapidly spoken calling-out segment:

Example 4 – Irosulia – 25.2

The *'a'ai* is holding the infant as they look out on a parrot eating papaya from a tree.

fasi: "No'o ne'e *ki–*"/ bird here,e pl	"These birds–" [high pitch, chanted, with very high rise on *ki*; calling out]
F: [mumbles] *ki–*/	[Same contour as fasi]
fasi: "–'ain kataoh *ki*"/ eat papaya pl	"–eat the papayas" [contour as above].
F: [mumbles] *ki*/	

In more complex examples with pronounced primary and secondary stress, and with secondary stress varying across the utterance, caregivers often draw the child's attention to an error by repeating the utterance and shifting the stress to the portion the child said correctly. This strategy is also used in correcting children in other repeating routines, to which we now turn.

Repeating

Telling a child what to say is a key strategy in Kwara'ae caregivers' organization of discourse with language-acquiring infants. The most typical form that the repeating routine takes in West Kwara'ae is for the adult to present a word, phrase, or sentence to be repeated, prefaced by the eliciting imperative *'uri*. The child then repeats whatever came after *'uri*. *'Uri* means "thus" or "like this" and, along with its past form *'unari* (referring back to something said or done earlier), fulfills most needs for "thus" in Kwara'ae discourse. The use of *'uri* to speak for someone also occurs occasionally with older children and even with adults. Schieffelin points out that in adult Kaluli discourse, one adult may speak for another who is not quick to respond to a humorous remark or challenge (1979:114). This is true of the Kwara'ae, too, but the Kaluli emphasis on assertion is absent from Kwara'ae. In fact, a Kwara'ae may speak for another as a way of showing compassion for one who has been criticized and wishes not to respond.

Speaking for someone in Kwara'ae, whether an infant, child, or adult, uses one of several conversational intonation contours, with *'uri* often being spoken rapidly at a very low pitch and at minimal volume. Table 2.1 displays three categories of conversational intonation contours in Kwara'ae speech. The categories are suggestive rather than exhaustive (for example, omitted are teasing, joking, speechmaking, and others). The purpose of Table 2.1 is to help illustrate the contrast between adult norms of speech and the special intonation contours used with infants and very young children, especially in repeating routine sequences. In eliciting speech with young children, adults use a variety of special contours, which we call *invitational intonation contours*. We chose the adjective "invitational" to emphasize that these contours are used from birth to stimulate infants to respond, and that they are light, happy, and affectionate. We have identified six such contours as occurring in calling-out and repeating routines. Table 2.2 displays the six invitational contours, briefly describes their characteristics, and gives an account of their main uses.

As we have seen with calling-out routines, getting a child to repeat starts very early. Although *'uri* is sometimes used to preface calling-out demonstrations, it is also used in other ways to show an infant what to say and do, as in the early routine of teaching a child how to *baebae* (wave goodbye).[7] Greetings and farewells are one example of early repeating sequences in which children learn how to repeat on command. By the time they are able to speak, the habit of trying to repeat has been established, the intonation contours for calling out and basic repeating (types 1–4 in Table 2.2) are familiar, and the ways a repeating sequence are initiated verbally are also well known. The child who will not repeat is said to be afraid (*ma'u*), or under some conditions

Table 2.1. *Conversational intonation contours*

Type	Description	Use
A. Polite-interest contour	Lightly serious tone; mid to high pitch with exaggerated pitch swings; strong stresses; clear, soft voice; often a terminal rise; friendly but emotionally detached	When meeting on the road or in the village, or for entertaining visitors/talking to hosts, to show interest and concern, demonstrate politeness, or exchange information on small matters
B. Normal conversational contours	Moderately serious to serious tone; middle pitch dominant; clear voice; an utterance tends to stay at one pitch with occasional rise or fall on emphasized words (especially those marking uncertainty, denial, agreement, or dawning realization) to mark pauses and sentence final, or on fixed formula segments appended at the end, such as *lea' na' nan* 'good now that there' – such falls or rises thus tend to be several syllables long *Focused discussion* – pace very rapid; utterance may be almost chanted in a monotone with terminal fall or rise *Casual conversation* – pace variable, with pronounced rises and falls	For most daily conversational uses within the home, village, and elsewhere
C. High-rhetoric contours	Grave, almost sacred tone; low pitch; melodic, rhythmic quality with easy, pronounced swings in pitch – almost singsong; low volume, quiet, relaxed voice and slow pace (to reflect confidence and knowledge of speaker, and because of a lack of need to compete for control of the floor); frequent within-utterance pauses before important verbs, nouns, or adjectives for emphasis or to show their connection to the preceding point; the frequent responses	All *falafala* contexts, including discussions of tradition-governed subjects (kinship, marriage, feasts, history, religion, politics, philosophy, values, etc.), dispute settling, speechmaking, planning, advising, counseling

Table 2.1. (*cont.*)

Type	Description	Use
	by listeners to show agreement (etc.) are in the same contour as the point or utterance they refer to	

Note: A and B are called *ala'anga kwalabasa;* C is called *ala'anga lalifu* (see note 9).

embarrassed (*'eke*), or simply *nia 'aila* 'he/she dislikes'. Words that elicit repeating, as well as commands when a child fails to repeat, are not used on every occasion. Often the caregiver will wave toward the person to be addressed by the child, give an upward nod of the head, and say what the child is supposed to say, looking at the child, then at the addressee, and then at the child again. Should the child respond appropriately by repeating, the caregiver will praise it with *le'a nai* 'good there'. Within the routine, if a number of phrases or sentences are to be repeated *'uri* will preface only the first one or two. Then if the child fails to repeat along the way, the adult may say the missed phrase or sentence again, or preface its repetition by *'uri*. The same strategy is followed if the child omits part of it or makes some other error.

Children become accustomed to repeating by listening for the intonation contour alone. As a result, they sometimes repeat spontaneously when adults are engaged in conversation with them or with other adults if a speaker happens accidentally to approximate a repeating routine invitational contour. Then, assuming the circumstances to be informal, the caregivers will usually turn to the infant at once and give it more sentences to repeat. Children are thus rewarded for voluntarily repeating. In fact, children must be continuously monitoring adult conversation in order to know when to repeat. With a 3-year-old, repeating contours are almost always conversational (type 5), and even if *'uri* is spoken it is done so rapidly, quietly, and at a very low pitch. Thus the habit of monitoring adult conversations to listen for invitational intonation contours that a young child has developed stands the 3-year-old, who must listen for very subtle cues for repeating, in good stead.

Dyadic (Schieffelin 1979) or two-person use of repeating is primarily associated with correcting and didactic drills. In addition to correcting phonology, morphology, syntax, or word choice, caregivers use dyadic repeating to teach social behavior such as table manners. Once an infant learns an instructional sequence, the caregiver can use it for yet other purposes. In the following example, a 15-year-old girl is trying to put Fita, her 27-month-old brother, to sleep. She is holding him and walking about the kitchen where they have just eaten, giving him familiar and contextually relevant sentences to repeat as a

Table 2.2. *Invitational intonation contours in calling out and repeating*

Type	Description	Use
(1) Calling out	Exaggerated pitch and stress, prolonging of syllables, terminal rise; very clear voice with bell-like quality; loud; mid to high pitch; tone of polite interest. Phrases to repeat are in type 4 intonation usually	For real calling out both by and to adults and children
(2) Calling out to entertain	Exaggerated pitch and stress, prolonging of syllables, terminal rise; very soft voice, joyous in tone, relaxed, often breathy; higher pitch than normal to very high	To entertain a child (or the caregiver), soothe a fussing child. Even when used only as a repeating routine, calling out is implied. If someone responds, it is replaced by type 1
(3) Straight invitation to repeat	Matter-of-fact, usually friendly tone, rise to mark phrases, or one in a series, or a "chunk" of speech; and fall to mark sentence final or routine final (may have other falls). Moderate to loud, usually middle pitch	For repeating with or without prefacing phrases (e.g., *'uri*)
(4) Imperative invitation to repeat	Same as in imperative routines: emphatic with strong stresses, usually loud, tending to have falling intonation for phrase and sentence final. Mid pitch to slightly higher. Sharp voice but often friendly tone	For imperative routines and behavioral commands. In calling out, this contour implies that a real message is to be delivered, when a child is to repeat. Used for didactic purposes, e.g., correcting a child's pronunciation or syntax or choice of statement. Also used without marked meanings, for a child to repeat
(5) Conversational contours for repeating	Contour et al. as appropriate in ordinary conversation – type A or B in Table 2.1. For type B, *'uri* often low and rapid; speed or tempo of phrase or sentence to be repeated may be very rapid	In repeating, type A used for teaching polite conversational style; type B used especially when one adult expresses opinion to an older child or another adult through a child; or with child of 3 years or older when teaching social conversational behavior/style

Table 2.2. (*cont.*)

Type	Description	Use
(6) *Nene* or lullaby[a]	Soft, lullaby-like talking with singing quality and terminal rise; gentle, soothing; exaggerated contours; very quiet voice; light but serious tone – taking the infant seriously	Putting a baby to sleep, including doing so by getting an infant who is tired to wind down through repeating; soothing a child who is in pain or afraid; talking to a child in a confidential manner (e.g., about someone's behavior in the village, raised by an incident or observation); cautioning a child not to interrupt when adults are in serious conversation; asking for something in a serious adult conversational situation, through a child repeating; discussing a sacred topic with or through a child

[a]*Nene* 'be quiet/silent' is our label, as are all the other labels given to intonation contours in these charts.

technique for lulling him to sleep. Her intonation contour is *nene* (type 6); the whole is tightly sequenced. Here is a portion of it:

Example 5 – Sulimaoma – 81.44

si: Go' 'aok   abus go'   Then when you're full you just speak
    then 2sg+2sg,sm full int   like this, "I don't want any more
    'aok   hat   na' 'uri   now."
    2sg+2sg,sm speak perf thus

    "Nauk   'aial   na' nai"/
    1sg+1sg,sm dislike perf there
F: / /————/   ⎤   [Whining, unclear]
si: / /"Go' 'aok   aul–"⎦ m/   "Just put–"
        then 2sg+2sg,sm put
F: Uh?/   What? [very high]
si: "Nauk   'aial   si   hang   "I don't want to eat any more now"
    1sg+1sg,sm dislike neg eat   [intonation as above].

    na' nai"/
    perf there
F: No' eal?/   I don't want? [high, rising]
    1sg dislike

si: Go' 'aok   hat   'unair#
    then 2sg+2sg,sm speak thus,p

    Then you just speak as I said, like this,
    "I don't want any more now."

    'uri "Nauk   'aial   na' nai"/
    thus 1sg+1sg,sm dislike perf there

F: No e ala/
    1sg dislike

    I don't want [mid high rise].

si: "Nauk   a:bus na'"/
    1sg+1sg,sm full   perf

    "I'm full now" [low rise to mid, fall;
    gently].

F: Amun na'/
    full perf

    Full now [mid, falling].

si: "Nauk–   nauk   abus
    1sg+1sg,sm 1sg+1sg,sm full

    "I'm–I'm full, I don't want to eat any
    more now" [*hang* rising, with rasp].

    nauk   'aial# si *hang*: na'"/
    1sg+1sg,sm dislike neg eat   perf

F: El   *ang* na'/
    dislike eat perf

    Don't want to eat any more now.

si: "Nauk   abus na'/
    1sg+1sg,sm full perf

    "I'm full now" [*abus* rising, with
    rasp].

    Go' 'aok   hat   na' 'uri–
    then 2sg+2sg,sm speak perf thus

    Then you speak like this–

    Go' 'aok   hat   'uri "Aul
    then 2sg+2sg,sm speak thus   put

    Then you speak like this, "Put it away
    now" [emphatic, gentle].

    na'"/
    perf

    Go' hat   na' 'uri "Aul na'
    then speak perf thus   put perf

    Then speak like this, "Put the stew away
    now.

    susuh ki/
    stew pl

    "Nauk   abus na'/
    1sg+1sg,sm full perf

    "I'm full now.

    "Nauk   'aial si hang
    1sg+1sg,sm dislike neg eat

    "I don't want to eat any more now"
    [singsong, exaggerated stress].

    na'"/
    perf

This is a lesson on what to say at the end of a meal when one is full. The teenage caregiver gives Fita socially appropriate sentences – frames – to repeat, and repeats them herself when he fails to respond. She also presents variations within frames: "I don't want any more now" is paired with "I don't want to eat any more now"; and "Put it away now" with "Put the stew away now." In doing so she is giving him important cues to how large segments of speech can be broken down into smaller segments (Peters 1983; see also conclusion below). When Fita produces only the second half of a long utterance, his sister repeats the first half, then offers a new sentence she originally attempted to introduce earlier ("Put it away"). This new frame is placed in the discourse context of the sentences Fita has repeated so far.

Correctional kinds of interactions with repeating often occur as side sequences (Jefferson 1972) in an ongoing interaction; so common are they that some interactions are almost evenly divided between ongoing talk and didactic side sequences. This is particularly true when children of 18 months to 2½ years are involved. The frequency of correctional side sequences may help explain why children repeat spontaneously when they hear an intonation contour that sounds invitational. In the following example, for instance, Fita's older sister is discussing with their parents the pork they are all at that moment eating, their share from a marriage feast.

Example 6 – Sulimaoma – 81.56   (Fita is 28 months old)

si:	Ni 'e'eor *liu*/	It's very greasy [lightly, rising].
	3sg fatty very	
mo:	Gwata ne' 'iar na'/	Pork's just like that [almost imperative
	pig here,e like that perf	tone type 3].
F:	(Gwata ne') 'iar na'/	Pork's just like that [like mo's contour].
	pig here,e like that perf	
fa:	'Uri "Gwata ne'–"/	Thus, "This pork–" [type 6, very
	thus pig here,e	gentle, almost whisperingly].
F:	Kwata ne'–/	This pork– [like fa's contour and tone]
	pig here,e	
fa:	–ādmia nam/	"–has to be eaten together with other
	eat+om together emph	food.
F:	–ādmia na'/	–has to be eaten together with other
	eat+om together perf	food.
fa:	"Sirai' ngwae ke–"	"Or else a person's stomach–" [as
	stomach+gen person sm	above]
F:	E ka ke'#	(or else a person's stomach–)
fa:	"–'aok'aok *liu:*"#	"–will become very hot."
	rpl+hot very	
F:	Lia ni *sil* na'/	Look, he/she has diarrhea now [louder,
	look 3sg diarrhea perf	high with very high rise].
fa:	M'/	Yes [very low, soft].

Fita repeated his mother's somewhat irritated rejoinder to his older sister because the mother unintentionally used a straight repeating intonation contour (in attempting to restrain her irritation). When his father saw that he was in the mood to repeat, he began a repeating side sequence on the Kwara'ae equivalent of a balanced diet, *ādami'anga*, eating a variety of foods together in any one meal. In Kwara'ae health theory, fatty meats like pork cause the stomach to get hot, leading to diarrhea. Fita has been taught the lesson embedded in this routine before in repeating and in overhearing adult conversations. He knows that if the dialogue continues, his father will next say that the person's hot stomach will cause him or her to have diarrhea. Rather than repeating, therefore, he hurries on to the conclusion, excitedly showing his knowledge. Notice that the father presents sentences that are basically parallel in length and structure. His segmenting of these sentences follows Kwara'ae intonational phrasing and points out to Fita the boundary between noun phrase and verb phrase.

Teaching interactions that lean on the repeating routine and a drill format include instructing a child in how to count and, in some families labeling drills prefaced by the eliciting phrase *tae nin?* 'What this here?' Counting drills are by far the most common kind of drill in West Kwara'ae. Labeling is an activity usually carried out through the *lia* 'look' routine mentioned earlier, and sometimes through *tae nin?* sequences. The following example began as a *lia* routine initiated by Talia, an 18-month-old girl. Her father's sister was sitting with Talia when the infant, who liked to do the *lia* routine as a game, began to point to items hanging on the wall of the house. The *'a'ai* responded to Talia's initiation by naming the items as Talia pointed to them. Then she turned to face Talia, changed to a type 4 imperative repeating contour, and said *'uri* – all of which signal a change of routine:

Example 7 – Irosulia – 15.3

fasi:	'Uri "ngwai'!"/ thus basket	Like this, "basket."
T:	Ai/ basket	Basket.
fasi:	'Uri "umbrel"/ thus umbrella	Like this, "umbrella" [European black nylon type, not the traditional pandanus].
T:	Wa/	Umbrella.
fasi:	'Uri "lam!"/ thus lamp	Like this, "lamp" [kerosene lamp].
T:	Du/ du'a = burn, burnt	(It is) burning/(it is) lighted.
fasi:	'Uri "gas"!/ thus gas	Like this, "lamp" [kerosene lamp].
T:	Be/	[In an irritated tone]
fasi:	"Gas!"/ lamp	"Lamp!" [strong imperative tone]

Talia's *'a'ai* perhaps began this routine because of the family concern over the slow progress the infant had made in learning to speak compared with her twin brother. Notice that when Talia failed to approximate *lam,* the *'a'ai* substituted *gas,* another term for kerosene lamp. However, Talia's *du* is not actually a failure to approximate *lam.* Close observation of Talia over several months showed that when she was unable to say the label (noun) presented to her, Talia frequently switched to a related, usually functional, term that she could say: in this case, the verbal adjective "lit/lighted" – what the lamp does. Her *'a'ai*'s failure to understand her caused Talia to become angry and resistant to trying to repeat correctly.

Another dyadic use of repeating routines is in teaching certain kinds of tasks. Showing and repeating together occur with steps in a task when the task is special – not performed every day – and the child is excited about learning to do it. In the following example 3-year-old Sila was being taught how to uncover and disassemble a traditional heated rock oven (*gwa'abi*) to separate the cooked potatoes and packages of *'ara* (a type of cassava pudding) from the hot rocks and leaves. As they worked Sila looked back and forth between what she was doing and what her mother was doing, synchronizing her movements and her speech with her mother's.

Example 8 – Alita – 81.12

mo: Ai'   taih   nauk
    emph move aside 1sg+1sg,sm
    ho'ea   na' nai/
    open+om perf there

> Okay, step aside so I can open it [rapidly, mid-high, cheerful, imperative emphatic tone].

S: *Ho*'ea   na'#
    open+om perf

> Open it.

mo: *Nauk*   ho'ea   'ar/
    1sg+1sg,sm open+om 'ara

> I open the pudding [mid pitch, type 4, for S to repeat].

S: *Ho*'ea   'ar/
    open+om 'ara

> Open the pudding [more softly].

mo: 'Arai'   bia/
    'ara+gen cassava

> Cassava pudding [low rise, mid fall].

S: 'Arai'   bia/
    'ara+gen cassava

> Cassava pudding [like mo's intonation].

mo: 'I*u*/
    yes

> Yes [mid pitch, slight rise].

S: Ho'ea   na'/
    open+om perf

> Open it [softly, mid pitch].

mo: *Ho*'ea   na' kwau/
    open+om now thither

> Go ahead and open it [rapid, low pitch, low fall].

    //Hoe' '*u*ri an/
    open thus of+3sg,poss

> Open like this [low; not to repeat but demonstrating].

S: //Ho'ea   na' kwau/
    open+om perf thither

> Go ahead and open it [very softly].

mo: //Hoe' '*u*ri an/
    open thus of+3sg,poss

> Open like this [low, softly].

S: Hoe' '*u*ri an/
    open thus of+3sg,poss

> Open like this [mid pitch, louder].

mo: Dau *lea'* an/
    hold good of+3sg,poss

> Hold it carefully [mid pitch].

[1.5-sec. pause]

    Tae'ea   na' '*u*ri/
    lift+om perf thus

> Lift it like this [loud, emphatic, correcting S's movements].

[1.5-sec. pause]

    Tae'ea *tai*'hau mal (:) 'ir
    lift+om together int   so that
    ni lea'/
    3sg good

> It works better if you lift all those leaves together.

S: Lea' go'/
    good int

> It's fine [slowly, adultlike as when praising a child].

Sila's tone and demeanor are those of excitement; *'ara* is a favorite treat. In special or seasonal events, or the first time they participate in a task, children repeat voluntarily or on command. Repeating introduces children to the language that accompanies the task (*'ara'i bia* and *ho'e, ho'ea* in this example) and to a new set of physical skills, as well as underscoring the steps of the task. Sila's mother praised her as she worked, saying "*ho'ea na' kwau*": *Kwau* 'in the direction away from the speaker' implies that the mother can step back and let Sila uncover the oven because she is working skillfully. Hidden in this praise is a tease to be understood by the observing adults – that children are always in a hurry to learn how to do things. At the end of the task, the mother summarized and demonstrated how to lift so that the *'ara* would come out properly. Sila's mother emphasized the linguistic aspects of the lesson through repetition of frames with variation and substitution (*ho'ea na', ho'ea 'ar*). When Sila repeated incorrectly, her mother shifted primary stress to the portion Sila missed.

Dyadic-structured repeating routines may be participated in by more than one person. Often two or three adults present during a dyadic repeating routine will contribute to it, such that together they create a single routine with an infant. Similarly, more than one infant may be given sentences to repeat in the course of the same routine.

Triadic (Schieffelin 1979) repeating involves telling a child what to say to a third person. One use is to teach names, nicknames, and kin terms, such as in calling-out sequences, as part of a longer repeating sequence, or in the course of teaching the child to report events. For instance, once 2-year-old Fita (Sulimaoma family) reported about riding on a truck to Auki. He was told to say the full name of the truck's owner and his village, which is the socially appropriate way of identifying people in Kwara'ae. Social interactional behavior as taught in repeating includes: the social uses of questions, how to ask and answer questions, greetings and leave-takings, making requests, responding appropriately in situations where food is offered, and carrying on polite conversations. Sometimes repeating on these topics is direct and short, but often these topics are embedded in more complicated interactional sequences, as will be shown by the examples below.

Repeating is frequently used to assist a child in conversing with another child or an adult. On a rainy Sunday morning, Fena came with his mother to visit his father's brother. She reported that someone's pigs had broken out during the night and eaten her new garden. The adults then went on to talk about a different subject, when Fena suddenly looked at his father's brother:

Example 9 – Irosulia – 37.2

F: Gwat 'ain kaman/   The pig ate the potato [child's word]
     pig   eat   potato

[No response as adults talk on among themselves, not hearing him]

Gwat 'ain kaman/	The pig ate the potato.
pig eat potato	

[Adults now turn to look at F]

mo:	Gwat 'ain kamān/	The pig ate the potato [invitational
	pig eat potato	contour; corrects F's pronunciation].
F:	Gwat 'ain kamān/	The pig ate the potato.
	pig eat potato	
fb:	Gwat 'ain kamān?/	The pig ate the potato? [polite,
	pig eat potato	invitational tone]
	Kamān kaum?/	Your (all) potato?
	potato 2p1h	
F:	Kamān . . ./	Potato . . . [hesitating, unsure of
	potato	pronoun]
mo:	Kamān *kaim*/	Our potato.
	potato 1plh,ex	
F:	Kamān *kaim*/	Our potato [same contour as mo].
	potato 1plh,ex	
fb:	'Iar/	I see/Is that so.
	as you say	
	Lalia 'ain kui/	Chase it with the dog.
	chase+om with dog	
F:	Kui *taih*/	The dog ran (that is, chased it).
	dog run	
mo:	Lalia kui *taih*/	Chase it, the dog runs/ran.
	chase+om dog run	
F:	Kui *taih*/	The dog ran.
	dog run	
mo:	Gwat 'ain kamān kami/	The pig ate our potato.
	pig eat potato 1plh,ex	
	Kui ka lalia/	(Then) the dog chased it.
	dog sm chase+om	

[Following the mother's statement, which was said in a matter-of-fact, summary rather than invitational tone, the interaction ended and the adults went on to talk about another topic. But later when the visit was nearing an end, the father's brother turned to Fena]:

fb:	Gwat 'ain kamān?/	The pig ate the potato?
	pig eat potato	
F:	Gwat 'ain ka*mān*/	The pig ate the potato.
	pig eat potato	
fb:	Kamān tai?/	Whose potato?
	potato who	
mo:	Kamān *kaim*/	Our potato.
	potato 1plh,ex	
F:	Kamān *kaim*/	Our potato.
	potato 1plh,ex	
fb:	Ka lalia na'/	(The dog) chased it already/Then (the
	sm chase+om perf	dog) chased it.
F:	Ka lalia na/	Then (the dog) chased it.
	sm chase+om perf	

Several processes are at work in this example. One is the use of invitational intonation contours to encourage a child who has initiated a topic. The mother corrected the child's pronunciation (a long vowel rather than a short one is required) of Fena's version of *kamāna,* the child's word for *kumara.* Secondly, the mother turned to her son as soon as her husband's brother signaled his availability as a conversational partner by the polite question, *Gwat 'ain kamān?* The mother assisted Fena by supplying the correct pronoun when he was unsure of it. In this case the boy was reporting on an event the adults have already discussed. Thirdly, Fena was assisted in segmenting and building utterances through: repetition with variation and substitution (*kamān kaum/kamān kaim*); expansion of his utterances (*kui taih/lalia kui taih*); and reworking of his and his caregivers' utterances (*gwat 'ain kamān, kamān kaim/gwat 'ain kamān kami; lalia ain kui, kui taih/kui ka lalia*). (Note the presence of both metathesized and underlying forms of *kaim* and *kami*.) Finally, the adults returned to the child's topic later and reviewed with him its salient points.

Teasing, criticizing someone's behavior, and giving imperatives to a child are frequent in triadic routines. The flavor of spontaneous teasing was illustrated when a teenage male caregiver was doing the counting routine with a 21-month-old infant. Just as the teenager said "six," the infant reached down to pick up a bit of old rice from the floor, dutifully repeating "six" as he did so. The teenager smoothly inserted *"siknis"* as the next number, with a teasing smile, and the infant repeated it. Then "seven" and so on. *Siknis* (Pijin from the English "sickness") is a reprimand used in a teasing way when an infant touches or tries to eat something dirty. Here the teenager was teasing the infant by getting him to repeat the word as if it were a number in the counting sequence. The child was thereby commenting on his own behavior unawares.

Adults often speak, express their opinions, or ask a question or favor of another adult through a child, or speak to one child through another. Sometimes an adult expresses an opinion to another while at the same time teaching a child how to respond, for example, to a tease. In the Irosulia family when Fena and Talia were being weaned at 19 months, the mother asked Talia if she wanted the breast. The father then teased Talia for wanting to nurse all the time. The mother told Talia to say in reply that breast milk is her and her brother's food, and that they eat it to get full just the way their father eats potato. This exchange reflects the tension at that time between the parents on when the infants ought to be weaned. In another example, a visiting relative taken with the cleverness of an infant in one of the families joked that he was going to set a very high brideprice when the infant married. The infant's mother, who strongly opposes high brideprices because of the important leadership role her family has taken in the district in getting them lowered, avoided a direct confrontation with the visitor by having the infant repeat a disapproving vocative. Teasing an adult is also frequent: In one case, a louse fell from the hair of a visiting woman, and she crushed it with an audible snap. An infant was told to repeat teasingly, "What was that you just broke? My goodness, your head is louse-infested just like a bush woman." Everyone laughed.

A significant role that children's repeating plays in adult social interaction has to do with requests. Suppose a group of adults is sitting in a room engaged in serious talk, possibly about land or a marriage, and speaking in high rhetoric (see note 9). One of the adults, say a woman, wants to ask for a betel fruit from a female relative across the room, but it would be inappropriate to interrupt the talk to make such a request. She can turn to a nearby child, however, and, using a *nene* (type 6) intonation contour, have the child repeat the request to the targeted adult from where they sit. The adult addressed will use another child to reply in the same way. The serious adult talk is not seen to have been interrupted by this exchange, and indeed may go on as if it is not occurring.

Other kinds of cultural knowledge besides ways of speaking are taught through repeating. We will take up just one example here. Example 10 is only a small portion (despite its apparent length) of a very long repeating routine that Susuli and her father engaged in on woman's role. Her father is teaching Susuli what she and her younger sister will do as adults, and in doing so he moves back and forth between straight repeating (type 3) and imperative repeating (type 4) intonation contours. The whole event is serious but animated and affectionate:

Example 10 – Irosulia – 81.8 (Susuli 3;3; Talia and Fena, 20 months)

S: *Mai'* 'ok maliu/ hither 2sg+2sg,sm sleep	Come here and be put to sleep (often said to a sleepy child) [to Talia; mid pitch, falling].
fa: Ai' *ru*rua/ emph rock+om	Okay, rock her [as S takes T in her arms].
'Uri "Ngeal kami maliu na' thus child 1plh,ex sleep perf 'amu" miv+2sg,poss	Like this, "Our child sleep now" (words of a well-known Kwara'ae lullabye) [wide pitch swings].
'Uri "Ngeal kami teo thus child 1plh,ex rest 'amu"/ miv+2sg,poss	Like this, "Our child rest yourself."
S: Ngeal kami teo 'amu child 1plh,ex rest miv+2sg,poss ne'e/ here,e	Our child rest yourself here.

fa: Ngeal kami   'i   *Talia?*/
    child 1plh,ex art,f Talia

Our child Talia? [sharp rise, interrogative fall]

S: M'#
    yes

Yes [very softly].

fa: 'Uri "*Ba*rat nai"/
    thus brother 1sg

Like this, "My brother" [type 4].

S: *Ba*lat   nai/
    brother 1sg

My brother.

fa: *Hem* nao/
    that's it

That's it (Pijin) [low falling, soft, slowly].

"*Ngwae huat* nau"
person   born 1sg

"Person born in my line" [type 4].

S: Ngwae *huat* nau/
    person born 1sg

Person born in my line.

fa: "Rorod   ni   *doe:–*"/
    tomorrow 3sg big

"When she grows up–" (tomorrow metaphorical for future, some day)

S: Ni *doe–*/
    3sg big

She grows up–

fa: "–kero' ka leak *kwai' soi'* "/
    1dl,ex sm go chop firewood

"–we two will go chop firewood" [rapidly to *kwai'* and low; then slowly with rise and fall stressed].

S: *Kwai'* soi'/
    chop firewood

Chop firewood [mid rise, then fall, mid volume].

fa: "'Okoa   ho' *soi:*'
    tie+om cl firewood
    huan"/
    for+3sg,poss

"(I'll) tie it into bundles for her" [rapid, low; *soi'* higher, *huan* falls to low].

S: 'Okoa ho' soi'*i:*   huan"/
    tie+om cl firewood for+3sg,poss

(I'll) tie it into bundles for her [as father but slowly].

fa: "Nik   *ho*ea"/
    3sg+sm carry on back+om

"She'll carry it on her back" [rising].

S: Ho*ea*/
    carry on back+om

Carry it on her back.

fa: "Leak hanoa"/
    go   village

"Go home/to the village."

T: [vocalization]

S: Leak *ha*noa/
    go   village

Go home/to the village.

[2-sec. pause]

T: Huh?/

[High]

fa: 'Ao' long Tal*ia?*/
    2sg+e also Talia

You too, Talia? [terminal high rise]

T: Huh?/

[High]

fa: 'Aeo' *long?*/
    2sg+e also

You too?

T: Uh 'uh#

S: Tae'an kia–   Talia kail   leak
    today 1plh,in Talia 1pl,ex go

    *ma*ket sean   tea'   nai
    market with+3sg,poss mother 1sg

Today we all– Talia we will go with mother to the market (S means "tomorrow"–when we are older. S wants to go but has been repeatedly

. ne/
there

fa: 'Io *hem*/
yes that's it

    told she's too young) [high, rapid, terminal rise].

Lea' nan/
good that th,df

    Yes, that's it [husky, high].

S: Na'/
perf

    That's good! [very high and rising]

fa: Kaulu ka leak (.) hain
2pl sm go with+3sg,poss

    Now [mid pitch].

ka 'il kum*ar* leak *ma*ket/
sm dig potato go market

    You'll all go with her to dig potatoes to take to the market [slow; terminal mid pitch].

S: Nau maket 'ain *ka*hisi
1sg market with cabbage

nauk–   nauk–
1sg+1sg,sm 1sg+1sg,sm

nauk–   nau leak *ngail*
1sg+1sg,sm 1sg go carry

nauk   maket *'ain ka*hisi/
1sg+1sg,sm market with cabbage

    I'll sell cabbage– I'll take (it) to the market– I'll sell cabbage [marked stresses and rises].

fa: –h/

    [Inbreath] Yes.

Kahisi ≠ ma gwai' bae'ear≠ ki≠
cabbage and cl ba'era pl

ma/
and

    Cabbages and *ba'era* (various leaves eaten as vegetables) and.

S: 'E:: noa' le/
emph no emph

    Hey, no! [rejecting *ba'era*]

fa: Se: ma han- han baear ki
emph and pana- pana that,p pl

ni' tau'ba re/
3pl,n upthfr emph

    Don't think that way! And the prickly yam up there (in the garden) [*Se*: scolding S for not wanting to sell other produce].

Han baear ki ba kor leak
pana that,p pl that,p 1dl,in go

hail 'ahi'/
weed around+3pln,om

    The pana that you and I went to weed [mid rise, then fall, rapid].

Ne' rorod 'ae leak maket
that tomorrow 2sg go market

'ani'/
with+3pln,om

    That tomorrow you'll take to the market [rapid, low; terminal rise].

[1.5-sec. pause]

Ba ko leleak
that,p 2dl,in rpl+go

saean kun
inside+3sg,poss swamp

aontol/
ground ridge

    Remember we had to cross the swamp to get to the ridge [low, quietly; referring to a time they weeded].

[1.5-sec. pause]

'Aok- (.) koroa' sui bain 2sg+2sg,sm 2dl,in compl that,df,p leak?/ go	Do you remember the time just the two of us went together? [mid rising, rapid]
Koroa' bain leak/ 2dl,in that,df,p go	It was the two of us who went.
Aos baear ba/ day that,p that,p	That day.

[F cries; fa turns to him]

'Uri "Talia–"/ thus Talia	Like this, "Talia–" [rising, type 3]
F: Ta/	Talia [very high].
fa: "–rorod–"/ tomorrow	"–tomorrow–" [mid rising]
F: 'Ud–/	[Mid, sustained]
fa: "–'ae leak–" 2sg go	"–you'll go–"

[Interrupted by unrelated side sequence]

fa: 'Uri# "Rorod nai leak# thus tomorrow 1sg go an# maket"/ to+3sg,poss market	Thus, "Tomorrow I'll go to the market" [to S, very rapidly].
S: Rorod nai leak an tomorrow 1sg go to+3sg,poss maket/ market	Tomorrow I'll go to the market [slowly].
fa: "Talia hai' kero' "/ Talia with 2dl,ex	"Talia and I together."
S: Talia hai' kelo'/ Talia with 2dl,ex	Talia and I together.
fa: "Kero' leak 'il kumar sa 2dl,ex go dig potato inside aontolo"/ ground ridge	"We'll go dig potato (at the garden) on the ridge."
S: Leak 'il kumar sa aontolo/ go dig potato inside ground ridge	Go dig potato on the ridge.
fa: "Kero' ka leak mai' "/ 2dl,ex sm go hither	"Then we'll come back" [rapid, low; high terminal rise].
S: Kelo' leak mai'/ 2dl,ex go hither	Then we'll come back.
fa: "Dao kero' ka tau'hin"/ arrive 2dl,ex sm wash+3pln,om	"Having arrived we'll wash them" [primary stress on tau'; low, rapid up to final word].
S: M leak na to'hin/ go sm wash+3pln,om	Go wash them [rapidly].
fa: "Tau'hi' ka sui–"/ wash+3pln,om sm compl	"After they're washed–" [terminal rise]

S: *Tau*'hi'   ka *sui*–/   After they're washed– [as fa's]
   wash+3pln,om sm compl

fa: "–*alui*'   sa   bae*ka*–"/   "–put them in a bag–" [terminal rise]
   put+3pln,om inside bag

S: –*alui*'   sa   bea*ka*–/   –put them in a bag–
   put+3pln,om inside bag

   Beak hao*lo*#   Clean bag [terminal rise].
   bag new

fa: Hem/   That's it [mid pitch; praise].
   that's it

   Ni lea' nan/   That's very good [high, rapid].
   3sg good that th,df

   "Beak– beak– beak haol"#   "Clean bag."
   bag   bag   bag new

   Ne ba?   Right? [rapidly, soft]
   there that,p

[Unrelated side sequence]
[1.5-sec. pause]

fa: 'Ira ma: (.)   'uri "Tal*ia*–"/   If that is the case (what we just said)
   if that is the case thus   Talia   then like this, "Talia–" [to S to repeat;
                                  terminal high rise]

S: Tal*ia*–/   Talia– [as fa's]

fa: "'Ae 'a'an   'ai'*ail*"/   "You had better grow up quickly."
   2sg grow up quickly   (Note: *'ai'ail* = slang form.)

S: 'A'an   'ail'*ail*/   Grow up quickly. (Note: *'ail'ail* =
   grow up quickly   correct metathesized form.)

fa: / /"Huan   kwae ⎤   "So that we two can go–" [low,
   for+3sg,poss 2dl,ex+sm ⎟   unstressed]
   leak–"/   ⎟
   go   ⎟

S: / /*Nauk*   'a'an   *na*'– ⎦   I'm grown up already– [low pitch]
   1sg+1sg,sm mature perf

   nauk   'a'an   na'/   I'm grown up already [softly].
   1sg+1sg,sm mature perf

fa: 'Uri "Huan   kwae   leak   Like this, "So that we two can go chop
   thus for+3sg,poss 2dl,ex+sm go   firewood for daddy" [low, rapid].
   kwai' soi'   'an
   chop firewood miv+3sg,poss
   ma*ma*"/
   rpl+father

S: *Kwai*' soi'   ma*ma*'/   Chop firewood (for) daddy.
   chop firewood rpl+father

fa: "Huan   rara'   "To warm him up" [low, middle pitch,
   for+3sg,poss warm   rapid].
   'an   ki"/
   miv+3sg,poss pl

S: Lala 'an   ki/   Warm him up.
   warm miv+3sg,poss pl

fa: "Kaidai nia'   gwairi''/ "When he's cold." (Correct form is
    time   3sg+e cold   *gwari.*)
S: Gwaili/   Cold.
  cold

fa: "Kaidai nia'   gwari''/   "When he's cold" [correcting earlier
    time   3sg+e cold   pronunciation].
S: Gwali/   Cold.
  cold

fa: Kaorao' ka leak kwai' soi'   You two will chop firewood for me.
   2dl   sm go chop firewood

  mai' huauk/
  hither for+1sg,poss

  Karao' ka ngail mai' auh   You'll carry the bundles of firewood
  2dl   sm carry hither cl   back here and put them on the *bara* (a

  soi'   ki kao' ka alui'   shelf built over the hearth)
  firewood pl 2dl sm put+3pln,om [conversational tone].

  sa   ba:r/
  inside shelf

  Ne # ba?/   Okay?
  there that,p

[2-sec. pause]

S: Keo'   Talia dodok le/   Talia and I are too short (to reach the
  2dl,ex+e Talia short emph   *bara*).
fa: Se! (.) 'iar   ber 'an   For goodness sakes! That's okay, when
  emph however but miv+3sg,poss you're grown up you'll be able to just
  'ao'   ngwae 'a'ana 'aoko   stand on the ground and throw them up
  2sg+e person mature 2sg+2sg,sm on the shelf [argumentative tone].
  ū   go' 'aok   'ui
  stand int 2sg+2sg,sm throw
  'ani'   sa   bar/
  with+3pln,om inside shelf

Susuli was first instructed how to rock her infant sister Talia to sleep with a
traditional lullaby. Susuli was observed several times to hold and rock Talia,
using a variety of Kwara'ae lullabying techniques. Her father then instructed
Susuli to refer to her sister as *barata,* the Pijin "brother" often used for either
sex.[8] When she repeated correctly, she was praised again in Pijin. Then the
father told her to repeat the Kwara'ae definition of sibling – a person born of
the same line as oneself. He went on to describe what Susuli and Talia will do
as adult women, speaking in the second person dual for Susuli to repeat on
behalf of herself and her sister. When Talia seemed to intrude into the conversation, she was at once included by her father. Susuli was praised for offering
sentences of her own about Talia and herself going to the market, though she
confused the metaphorical "today" with the metaphorical "tomorrow." In

fact her father expanded her point to include digging potatoes to take to market. When Fena – omitted from this discussion because he is male – cried for attention, his father immediately distracted him by giving him sentences to repeat to Talia. After a short break the father resumed the original repeating routine with Susuli, and went through the steps of harvesting potato and preparing it for market. After another break he had Susuli tell Talia that as adults they will cut firewood to warm their poor, cold father – one element in showing respect to one's parents. At the end, Susuli confused what will be with what is now when she argued that she and Talia are too short to lift the wood onto the shelf over the fire. Her father assured her that when she is grown up she will be able to throw wood up there.

The father accepted less than full repetitions from Susuli in this example, partly because it was late and she was tired. Caregivers are primarily concerned to have children repeat the most important elements of the phrase or sentence, particularly if they are tired or restless. This example shows how long repeating sequences may involve many different kinds of lessons presented together. In the complete version of this event, Susuli's father also corrected his daughter's phrasing of sentences she offered on her own.

One feature of repeating routines important for language acquisition is the way that caregivers do "chunking" – the size of the individual segments they give to infants to repeat. In Ex. 10 the father gave whole sentences and phrases, some of them rather complex, to his daughter to repeat. Repeating with 3-year-olds emphasizes rapid delivery of full sentences often much more complex than these children can spontaneously produce. If a child consistently fails to be able to reproduce an entire phrase or sentence at a time, the caregiver will break it down into smaller chunks. Sentences or phrases given to younger infants are broken down into two or three syllables per segment, according to word boundaries. Caregivers thus adjust the material to be repeated to fit the language development of the infant. Another kind of chunking is that involved in correcting a child's pronunciation of a word. In one example from the Alita family, Sila was asked to repeat a tease to her older sister about the girl's poor hearing. However, she pronounced *ailngauk* 'my ear' as *ainglauk* 'my crying'. When Sila repeated the word incorrectly on three tries, her mother broke it into two syllables and had her pronounce each separately.

Finally, conventionalized communicational forms are also taught through repeating routines. Variation of expression occurs in retellings of traditional stories, but this is not true of lullabies, rhymes, prayers, and songs, all of which are formulaic. These latter kinds of communications are rich in cultural information and high-rhetoric vocabulary and phrasing. Because of their frozen formats, however, it may be difficult for a language-learning child to extract much lexical or grammatical information from them (Peters 1983:64).

Life history of a routine

Here we will summarize the evolution of calling-out and repeating routines, drawing on what has been explicitly and implicitly said about them so far. Kwara'ae parents emphasize communicative and interactional competence as both a means to language acquisition and a sign that the child is becoming social. Skill in speaking and interaction is highly prized in Kwara'ae society, especially competence in high rhetoric, *ala'anga lalifu*.[9] However, competence in survival skills and in proper behavior is equally important, though we have touched only lightly on these areas because of our focus on language.

As we have seen, repeating routines are introduced to very young infants by 6 months of age through calling-out, *baebae,* and *lia* routines. In calling out the child is at first encouraged to make a vocalization in the correct intonation contour, and later to say vocatives. In *baebae* the child is first encouraged to wave, and later to say *baebae* with a correct intonation contour, perhaps adding a name or kin term. With *lia* the infant is first encouraged to look and then to point, and eventually to say the name of the object singled out.

Somewhere between 18 months and 2 years of age, depending on the infant's linguistic progress, there is a sudden increase in the frequency of all kinds of repeating routines. *Lia,* used at first to still a crying infant, evolves into a game played for fun, initiated by the infant as often as by the caregiver. In the families we studied, the eliciting term *lia* with its special intonation contour was dropped or said in a conversational tone only. *Ngwae ki* (person pl) became an alternative eliciting phrase because *lia* came to focus on photographs of people or actual people passing on the path or road. The caregiver would say *ngwae ki* in a rising contour, the infant would try to repeat, and if it did so successfully, the caregiver would add an additional word to repeat. Infants of this age come to initiate the *lia* routine with phrases they have already been taught to repeat.

It is also at about 18 months that repeating prefaced by *'uri* and involving behavior, teasing, or subject matter not directly observable (such as reporting or what the child will do tomorrow) is introduced. Calling out to entertain the child or to practice speaking continues; but real calling out is also introduced. Children at this age begin to call out on their own, too. Children begin to repeat spontaneously whenever they hear a seeming invitational intonation contour, and sometimes to pronounce words or phrases that particularly strike them. When this happens, caregivers not engaged in serious talk will turn to them and give them more sentences to repeat, thereby extending the language lesson.

By age 2, children can sometimes rework sentences given them to repeat – using transformation rules they have learned – or may add words or expressions to them. These creative efforts in repeating are highly praised by caregivers. In the Alita family, the mother was having 3-year-old Sila repeat a sentence teasing her 5-year-old sister. The mother said, ''Person's mouth –,'' her voice rising to indicate that a predicate was coming. Sila repeated it, automatically adding the subject marker *ka* at the end in expectation of a verb phrase. Her mother continued with the predicate, omitting *ka*. In this case Sila was not overtly praised for her sense of the overall form of an utterance, but her mother's omission of *ka* indicated that it had been heard and recognized. On another occasion, however, Sila repeated after her mother, addressing the cat who had sniffed at vegetable (*ba'era*) stew. ''You thought that it was meat,'' the mother said. Sila repeated it dutifully, but added ''rotten'' after meat. She was scolded sharply by her mother, as the implication is that Sila's family eats spoiled meat.

By age 3 years the entertainment calling-out routine has disappeared and has been wholly replaced with real calling out. Children also regularly call out on their own, and turn calling out into a game. Certain other repeating routines also disappear. *Baebae* is replaced by intensive instruction, in the form of repeating and imperative routines, on the adult way to greet and take leave, as well as to inquire after the health, well-being, and doings of others. *Lia* also disappears as a routine, though adults and children will point out and discuss objects or people as they walk about or sit relaxing. Discussing who owns which gardens or buildings is a very common activity when children accompany adults or older children in going along the paths. Other kinds of repeating seem to take up the gap left by the disappearance of entertainment calling out and *lia* routines. Repeating is often prefaced by *'uri* at this age, but instead may be indicated intonationally. Sentences to repeat are primarily given in straight repeating (type 3), imperative repeating (type 4), and conversational repeating (type 5) invitational intonation contours. Complex sentences are delivered in type 5 contour at an exceedingly rapid rate with the apparent expectation that a child of 3 years should be able to decode and repeat. In terms of voice contours at 3 years old, then, entertainment calling out (type 2) and *nene* or lullaby repeating (type 6) have disappeared. Serious talking with children now uses adult intonation. We found that high rhetoric is spoken to children of 3 years whenever a culturally important subject is broached, especially in counseling sessions. High-rhetoric intonation contours accompany all very serious talk to children of this age, even when the language itself is simplified.

The kinds of cultural lessons in repeating also change from age 18 months to 3 years. For young children, the focus is on simple drills like counting, simple games or poems, teasing and replying to teases, making requests and responding to favors or gifts, giving and sharing, table manners, and conversing with siblings. At age 3 children are taught hymns and traditional stories through repeating, but the main focus is on social role, household or garden work, and correct interactional behavior with adults.

In 1981 we hypothesized that the final stage of repeating routines involves teaching a child to report, which begins at 18 months but becomes strongly emphasized at 3 years. We hypothesized that once a child learns to report accurately and fully (between ages 5 and 6 years), repeating routines are phased out. However, in our 1984 restudy of the same Kwara'ae families, concentrating on children aged 3;6 to 6;6, we found that repeating routines are still used with 5- and 6-year-olds – although the frequency of occurrence of these routines has declined and their focus has shifted to school knowledge (for example, simple addition and subtraction) and traditional storytelling. Moreover, we found that it is the children themselves who phase out repeating routines. (How and why this occurs lies outside the scope of the present paper.) Corrections prefaced by *'uri* are made with older children, but there is no expectation that they should repeat. As a routine, then, *'uri*-prefaced statements become short examples of how to say something correctly – a usage consonant with the role of *'uri* in adult conversation, but no longer a repeating routine.

Conclusion

This paper has examined the role of calling-out and repeating routines in the speech economy of the Kwara'ae. As our account has indicated, Kwara'ae caregivers do these and other routines with their children as a way to control the behavior of infants by engaging them in predictable interactions, as a way for adults to have fun with young children, and to assist and guide children's language development and acquisition of sociocultural knowledge. The variety of routines available in the language serves well; Kwara'ae caregivers try many different techniques in teaching the child to speak and behave properly.

Peters (1983) effectively argues that learning syntactic rules is not the first order of structural business for the language-acquiring child. Rather the child first carries out "analyses of individual chunks into shorter recurrent segments," and arrives at units and structural patterns based on these (91–2). Input speech and caregiver expectations for the child's participation and production are among the factors affecting how the child accomplishes segmentation (ibid.:35–70). Kwara'ae caregiver speech and participation structures (Philips 1972) in caregiver–infant interactions seem designed to promote segmentation and structural analyses.

For one thing, Kwara'ae caregivers almost continuously engage their charges in routines that give a child a predictable way to participate in interaction, and provide it with large chunks of speech which can be memorized and then analyzed (Peters 1983:65–9). As we have seen, Kwara'ae caregivers use calling-out and repeating routines as "scaffolding" (Bruner 1978) to include an infant in interaction and to support its entry and continuation in conversation as soon as it begins to talk. Kwara'ae caregiver speech incorporates many of the techniques Peters discusses as important in aiding a child in segmentation and analysis: "chunking" utterances in various ways; honoring important boundaries, such as that between morphemes or words for very young infants or noun and verb phrases for older children (Exx. 6, 10), through chunking and marked stress (Ex. 1); repetition of frames with variation (Exx. 5, 7, 8, 9) and substitution (Ex. 9); correcting errors, often with marked stress (Exx. 9, 10); filling in omissions of parts or phrases in the child's utterance (Ex. 9); presenting metathesized and underlying forms together for comparison (Exx. 1, 3); reworking sentences in ways that help a child to recognize them as frames with slots (syntagmatic and paradigmatic structures) (Ex. 9); expansion of the child's utterances (Ex. 9); and providing positive reinforcement for the child's recognition of the overall form of an utterance and attempts to transform its caregiver's or own utterances. A complete treatment of Kwara'ae caregiver speech is beyond the scope of this paper; we only add here that the techniques above, along with others, are employed in many ways in caregiver–infant interactions.

One finding from this work is that the early routines taught to Kwara'ae children are closely interrelated. For analytical purposes we can isolate them, give them labels, and describe their structures. And they seem separate and distinct from each other because they are first introduced in versions that seem to stress their individuality. *Lia* and calling out and "Where's *x?*", for example, seem to be "different things to do." Yet caregivers and infants very quickly begin to interweave one routine with another, such that *lia* becomes interwoven with repeating and reporting, and so on. Interactions that began as chains of routines become tapestries instead. And early routines share an underlying form that becomes clearer over time. For as the child's linguistic and social competence grows, the routines become increasingly integrated toward adult expectations and norms in conversation. In this respect they channel the child's developing communicative and behavioral competence towards the adult ideal. Vestiges of the early routines remain – as in adults speaking for each other prefaced by *'uri* – but the routines of childhood finally merge and evolve into the routines of adulthood.

Notes

This research was partially supported by three small grants from the Spencer Foundation, July 1, 1979–June 30, 1982. We are very grateful to the families in West Kwara'ae who participated in this research with us, to members of Gegeo's family who gave us support and research assistance, and to all others who helped us when we were on Malaita. We are also indebted to Stephen T. Boggs, Courtney Cazden, Raymond Firth, John Gleason, Andrew Pawley, Leialoha Apo Perkins, Ann Peters, Bambi Schieffelin, and Linda Simons, who commented on a longer version of the paper (see n. 2).

1 We follow the definition of "routine" offered by Peters & Boggs (this volume; see also Boggs & Watson-Gegeo 1978; Watson 1975, 1977; Watson-Gegeo & Boggs 1977; and Hymes 1971).

2 This paper is an abbreviated version of a longer treatment (105-page typescript, available from the authors), "Calling Out and Repeating: Two Key Routines in Kwara'ae Children's Language Acquisition." The longer paper considers variation across families in how routines are used to organize discourse, and includes much more theoretical and cultural information as well as more analyzed examples.

3 Observations were made in 1979 of an infant 11–13 months old with her caregivers, and detailed notes taken of interactional routines. This family became one of the focal families in the 1981 study.

4 In the following examples, family pseudonyms identify the source of each example. Primary stress is marked by italic type and utterance termination by a slash; brackets enclose overlapping utterances, which are prefaced by double slashes; sustained or held syllables are followd by colons representing comparative length of hold; latching between utterances (no break) is indicated by #; pauses longer than that normal within an utterance or between utterances are marked by the number of seconds in parentheses, or, for pauses just under one second, by a period; sentences given to children to repeat are enclosed in quotes. The orthography is that designed by Gegeo (Gegeo & Watson-Gegeo in prep.), based on the one already used in Kwara'ae. Long vowels are marked by a macron or bar over the vowel, and glottal stops by an apostrophe. The consonant cluster "ng" would be represented phonetically as ŋ.

5 Grammatical abbreviations are as follows: art = article; cl = classifier; compl = completive; df = definite; dl = dual; e = emphatic (suffix, etc.); emph = emphatic expression; ex = exclusive of speaker; f = feminine; fr = far, farther; gen = generic noun marker; h = high rhetoric; in = inclusive of speaker; int = intensifier; loc = locative; m = masculine; miv = middle voice; n = neuter; neg = negative; om = object marker; ovth = over there (demonstrative); p = past; perf = perfective; pl = pluralizer; poss = possessive; rpl = reduplication; sg = singular; sm = subject marker; th = there (demonstrative); upth = up there (demonstrative). Bound constructions are indicated by a +.

6 Boggs (personal communication) notes that "the Hawaiian case equates contradicting with equality and contrasts both with hierarchy. Kwara'ae does neither. An Hawaiian 3-year-old demonstrating adult-like behavior would be regarded as brash. Hawaiians cannot openly endorse expressions of equality by subordinates. But they playfully encourage it via the contradicting routine, laughing at kolōhe (mischievous, naughty) behavior, etc. This has always reminded me of Bateson's meta-message: 'This is play.' "

7 Baebae is a Solomon Islands Pijin word, from the English "byebye." Most West Kwara'ae people speak at least a little Pijin, and Pijin phrases and words, along with English expressions, are part of every speaker's everyday repertoire.

8 This is not to suggest that Kwara'ae speakers exclusively or even usually refer to siblings with Pijin terms, for they do not. Pijin words are common slang expressions, however. In Kwara'ae one refers to one's same-sex sibling as futa'a (born as one in a line) and cross-sex sibling as ngwaingwaina. So the use of "brother" for "sister" here is not strange in Kwara'ae thinking.

9 There are two levels in Kwara'ae discourse. Ala'anga kwalabasa 'speaking/ speech vinelike' refers to ordinary, everyday speaking, including caregiver speech to children; we call it "low rhetoric." Kwalabasa (kwala = vine) suggests a root that goes down for a distance and then suddenly splits into many lesser roots. Of speech, it implies ideas that go every which way. It is contrasted with ala'anga

lalifu 'speaking/speech taproot + public', which we call "high rhetoric." *Lali* suggests a tap or other strong root that goes straight down into the ground, and *fu* means publicly known; hence speech that carries important sociocultural meaning. High rhetoric is characterized by a special vocabulary, a special set of pronouns, heavy use of underlying form words, very abstract phrasing, complex syntactical forms, special intonation contours, and other markers.

References

Boggs, S. T. 1985. *Speaking, relating, and learning: a study of Hawaiian children at home and at school.* Norwood, N.J.: Ablex.

Boggs, S. T. & K. A. Watson-Gegeo. 1978. Interweaving routines: strategies for encompassing a social situation. *Language in Society* 7:375–392.

Bruner, J. S. 1978. The role of dialogue in language acquisition. In A. Sinclair, R. J. Jarvella, & W. J. M. Levelt, eds., *The child's conception of language.* New York: Springer-Verlag, pp. 241–256.

Firth, R. 1957. *We, the Tikopia: kinship in primitive Polynesia.* 2d ed. Boston: Beacon.

Gegeo, D. W. & Watson-Gegeo, K. A. In prep. *A dictionary of the Kwara'ae language.*

Gleason, J. B. & Weintraub, S. 1978. Input language and the acquisition of communicative competence. In K. E. Nelson, ed., *Children's language,* vol. 1. New York: Gardner Press, pp. 171–222.

Hymes, D. 1971. On linguistic theory, communicative competence, and the education of disadvantaged children. In M. L. Wax, S. Diamond, & F. O. Gearing, eds., *Anthropological perspectives on education.* New York: Basic, pp. 51–66.

1974. *Foundations in sociolinguistics: an ethnographic approach.* Philadelphia: University of Pennsylvania Press.

Jefferson, G. 1972. Side sequences. In David Sudnow, ed., *Studies in social interaction.* New York: Free Press, pp. 294–338.

Ochs, E. 1982. Talking to children in Western Samoa. *Language in Society* 11:77–104.

Peters, A. 1983. *The units of language acquisition.* Cambridge Monographs and Texts in Applied Psycholinguistics. Cambridge: Cambridge University Press.

Philips, S. U. 1972. Participant structures and communicative competence: Warm Springs children in community and classroom. In C. B. Cazden, V. P. John, & D. Hymes, eds., *Functions of language in the classroom.* New York: Columbia University Teacher's College Press, pp. 370–394.

Schieffelin, B. B. 1979. How Kaluli children learn what to say, what to do, and how to feel: an ethnographic study of the development of communicative competence. Unpublished Ph.D. thesis, Columbia University.

Watson, K. A. 1975. Transferable communicative routines: strategies and group identity in two speech events. *Language in Society* 4:53–72.

1977. Understanding human interaction: the study of everyday life and ordinary talk. In R. W. Brislin, ed., *Culture learning: concepts, applications, and research.* Honolulu: University Press of Hawaii (East–West Center), pp. 101–110.

Watson-Gegeo, K. A. & Boggs, S. T. 1977. From verbal play to talk story: the role of routines in speech events among Hawaiian children. In S. Ervin-Tripp & C. Mitchell-Kernan, eds., *Child discourse.* New York: Academic Press, pp. 67–90.

Watson-Gegeo, K. A. & Gegeo, D. W. 1983. *Fa'amanata'anga:* family teaching and counselling in West Kwana'ae child socialization. Paper for Conference on Talk and Social Inference, Pitzer College, Claremont, Calif., October.
　　In press. Shaping the mind and straightening out conflicts: the discourse of Kwara'ae family counselling. In Watson-Gegeo and G. M. White, eds., *Disentangling: the discourse of conflict and therapy in Pacific cultures.*

3. Prompting routines in the language socialization of Basotho children

K ATHERINE D EMUTH

The learning of socially appropriate norms of behavior is a complex and multifaceted process. Prompting for the use of appropriate verbal behavior plays an active role in the social development of children in Basotho society. This chapter examines the prominent use of *ere* . . . 'say . . .' and other prompts by Sesotho-speaking caregivers during interaction with children. It identifies the forms these linguistic routines take and the functional contexts in which they occur. Finally, it examines how these prompts are used in the socialization of young children, providing them with a framework from which to recognize social situations and respond accordingly.

Background

Lesotho is a small, dry, mountainous country completely surrounded by the Republic of South Africa. Sesotho, or Southern Sotho, is a southern Bantu language used by approximately three million speakers, half of whom reside in Lesotho, the other half resident in South Africa. The people who live in Lesotho and speak Sesotho call themselves Basotho. Many Basotho men have been employed in the mines in South Africa since the mid 1800s. Fosterage, whereby children are sent to live with grandparents, aunts, or uncles, has long been practiced and is still common in both rural and urban areas. Rural women have traditionally worked in the fields, leaving children to entertain themselves, or, in the case of infants, leaving them with grandmother or neighbors. Women in rural areas are increasingly seeking a means of cash income, usually leaving children in the care of mother-in-law or another responsible relative for weeks or months at a time.

The children who provided the focus of this study included two preverbal infants, seven children between the ages of 25 months and 7 years, and five

51

older children between the ages of 7 and 12 who functioned as occasional caregivers. The four focus children for the study were girls Litlhare (25;2–37;2 months), 'Neuoe (28;0–40;0 months), and Tsebo (3;7–4;7 years) and boy Hlobohang (25;0–37;0 months). Audiotape recordings of children's spontaneous speech were made at five-week intervals over a duration of fourteen months, each session including between three and four hours of taped interaction.

These children and their families live in a large mountain village (approximately 550 persons) on the main road to the district headquarters, an hour's walk away. People generally live in small extended family units, each son and his family having one or two dwellings (one for cooking, the other for sleeping and entertaining visitors) in fairly close proximity to the parents' home. Young children sleep with their parents. As children become older the girls or the boys will sleep at the grandparents' house or in a separate dwelling. With the exception of herdboys who tend the cattle in the fields, most children attend a local primary school until three in the afternoon. At the time of the study a preschool was being initiated, and children between the ages of 2 and five also began attending "school."

As men in many families are rarely at home, they play a very minor role in the upbringing of their children. Mothers, grandmothers, and older siblings, both girls and boys, share the responsibility for the very young child, the grandmother taking over for the mother when the latter must work in the fields, the older brother or especially sister (or in some cases a live-in niece) taking over from mother or grandmother once school is out in the afternoon. Infants are usually secured on the back, are nursed when they cry, and accompany the mother or caregiver everywhere. Children are spaced about two and a half years apart (though children are usually weaned before this time – often by the age of 18 months), and it is at the time of the arrival of a new sibling that the child enters a new social stage. From this time on the mother is preoccupied with the new infant and the older child begins to spend more time with his or her peer group or in helping with household chores and care of the new infant. Verbal interaction between mother and the 2-year-old assumes a more directive and disciplinary, rather than an engaging and entertaining, function. This shift in the type of speech to children will be noted later in a discussion of the data. It is influenced by the fact that the mother's main preoccupation has become the infant and, except for morning, evening, and mealtimes, the loosely structured peer group now dominates the older child's social and linguistic interaction.

Interaction with infants begins while mother and newly born infant are in confinement for the first two to three months of the infant's life. During this time female relatives and older children care for the mother and child, cooking food for them, doing laundry and other household chores. Female visitors come to bring food and to see, hold, talk with, and talk about the infant. The infant's older sibling spends much time in verbal interaction with the mother and infant, often imitating the mother's responses to the infant by telling it to be quiet, to nurse, or to go to sleep. The older child will often play with an "infant" (a rock, shoe, or empty lotion bottle) of his or her own, telling the mother, "My baby has gone to sleep, has yours?" Thus the infant quickly becomes the center of household and visitor attention, and the older child shifts roles from being the cared-for to helping care for the younger child, including occasionally telling the infant what to say.

Speech to infants and young children includes the use of a high-pitched register, the repetition of utterances, questions, and the use of terms of respectful address – *ntate* 'father' and *'me* 'mother', terms of endearment such as *ngoanes'o* 'my sibling', clan names, and nicknames. In contrast, however, infants' and young children's attention is often secured through the use of abrupt physical movement and/or loud vocalizations. Indeed the mother of one of the children in the study used a loud shouting voice equally with adults, her 2-month-old infant and her 30-month-old daughter. Daily speech and threats both were delivered with the same volume. Normal pitch and syntactic constructions are used with infants and young children when they are being talked to seriously or reprimanded. High pitch and modified phonology and syntax appear to be used mostly in contexts where the intent is to amuse or pacify the child. Verbal interaction from infancy is both dyadic (between two people) and triadic (among three people – Schieffelin 1979). The use of assisting prompts by older children during question routines used with younger children and infants is one of the principle cases of child-to-child use of *ere*.

Threats are a common means of social control over children. The phrase *Ke tla u shapa* 'I will lash you' is used from infancy on through older childhood, though it is rarely, if ever, enacted. These threats normally take the first person form in Sesotho, though they are occasionally found in the agentless passive form *U tla shapuoa* 'You will be lashed'.

Basotho view of how children learn to talk

There is no single explanation of how children learn to talk. Some Basotho say that children learn to talk by listening to what adults and those of the household say and then repeating. Others say that children are taught to talk by example (*Ere 'me* 'Say "mother"') or by pointing to an object and asking *Ke eng ntho eo?* 'What is that thing?', and that the child will try to repeat/answer and will gradually learn. Some say speech to children should be slow so the child will understand. Still others maintain that children who are frequently interacted with and encouraged to respond will begin to verbalize at an earlier age than their peers. (The woman who professed this philosophy had children who were extremely verbal at age 2.)

Regardless of the individual theories about how children learn how to talk, there is a general consensus that children are taught how to speak and act appropriately, and that, when they produce a new grammatical construction, someone must have taught it to them. Indeed, teaching one's child how to talk is seen as one of the major responsibilities of mothers, other caregivers, and the community at large. The Sesotho proverb *Ngoana ea sa lleng o shoela tharing* 'The child who doesn't cry will die in bed' or 'A quiet person (one who can't voice his/her feelings) will perish' seems to capture some of the importance placed on learning how to verbalize. Children need to know how to interact with others, and they must be taught the appropriate ways of doing so. As a result, frequent "practice sessions," or verbal routines, take place. These include prompting, question routines, and recitation of songs, numbers, names of family members, clan recitations (*thothokiso*), and church prayers. These routines often appear to be for the caregiver's entertainment as much as for the education of the child, there being frequent accompaniment by laughter, praise, and clapping of hands. The belief that children are taught how to speak is evidenced over and over again by comments of mothers and other caregivers concerning children's acquisition of new verbal behavior. This is illustrated in Ex. 1 (see appendix for transcription notations).

Example 1

[Hlobohang (27; 3 months) and male cousin Mololo (5 years) are playing "cars" indoors. Grandmother MM approaches and tries to engage H in conversation. Female cousin Ntsoaki (8 years) reprimands Mol for prompting H unnecessarily.]

MM > H, Mol: Batla-ng bolo.   E   kae   bolo?
              look-for-pl ball   it's where ball
              Look for the ball. Where's the ball?

[H points under bed]

                                H: tse tseena.
                                   (ke eena)
                                   cop dem
                                   Here it is.

Mol > H: *Ere* e   teng ka mona,
              Say it's here in here,

              ere e teng.
              say it's here.

N > Mol: U   mo ruta ho-bua empa [o nts'a   tseba
              you him teach to-talk but   he cont-he know
              You teach him how to talk, but he already knows

              ho-bua.]
              to talk
              how to talk.

MM > H: [E   kae   bolo?]
           it's where ball?
           Where's the ball?

                    H: E te–, e   teng
                        It's–, it's there

                        ka   mane.
                        over there.

Here Ntsoaki accuses Mololo of "teaching" the younger Hlobohang how to respond to the question. Contrary to some Basotho adult beliefs, children *do* initiate speech on their own without being taught to do so. Prompts, then, are most commonly used when a child does not have a response, is slow in providing a response, or gives one that the prompter feels is inadequate or inappropriate.

The use of prompts

Sesotho prompts are used for various social and linguistic functions. *Ere* is the most frequently used, but others also occur, some of them in functionally restricted ways. *Ere* is used in both direct reported speech ("Say 'I'm going to hit you' ") and indirect reported speech ("Say you're going to hit him"); other prompts are usually used in either direct or indirect constructions, but rarely in both. Prompting also occurs between prompter and child (dyadic interaction) or among prompter, child, and a third party (triadic interaction). The large majority of Sesotho prompts were used in triadic speech contexts and in direct reporting form, as seen in Table 3.1. Dyadic use of *ere* is found in question routines, including the recitation of lineage, numbers, and songs, in some prompts for politeness and pronunciation, and in children's play with each other. These are contexts where the speaker tells the child to respond with a certain verbal form. Triadic prompts are used extensively in question routines, transmission of messages, or in getting a child to talk or perform for others in general conversation and in corrections for politeness. In these situations the speaker tells the child to respond to another person with a particular verbal construction. The individual kinds of prompts found in dyadic and triadic prompting situations with Basotho children will be identified below. Table 3.1 provides the number and percentage of dyadic versus triadic prompting situations, and the amount of direct versus indirect prompting. It should be noted that there is far less prompting used with older children 'Neuoe and Tsebo.

There were only three prompts used between adult and 'Neuoe and nine prompts used between adult and Tsebo. Data on 'Neuoe are much sparser than on the other three children, accounting for the small number of prompts

Table 3.1. *Prompting forms (number and percentage of prompts directed toward each child)*

	Dyadic vs. triadic		Indirect vs. direct		Total
Adult > child					
H	15 (14%)	93 (86%)	34 (31%)	74 (69%)	108
L	31 (32%)	66 (68%)	20 (21%)	77 (79%)	97
N	—	3 (100%)	3 (100%)	—	3
T	4 (44%)	5 (55%)	—	9 (100%)	9
Child > child					
H	4 (8%)	44 (92%)	13 (27%)	35 (73%)	48
L	25 (58%)	18 (42%)	10 (23%)	33 (77%)	43
N	—	16 (100%)	3 (19%)	13 (81%)	16
T	2 (100%)	—	—	2 (100%)	2

directed toward her. Note, however, that while she is still a young child and would be expected to receive several prompts from adults, she has actually received many more from other children. This reflects the fact that her primary orientation is already that of the older siblings and peers to which Tsebo belongs. The small number of prompts directed toward Tsebo by both adults and other children reflects the tendency to use more prompts with younger children and fewer prompts with older children as they exhibit more social and linguistic sophistication and spend more time with peers. Prompts directed toward older Tsebo show a tendency to use fewer question-routine prompts and more politeness or socialization prompts. Prompts to younger children included many triadic prompting routines; and over two-thirds were direct. The higher percentage of dyadic child–child prompts used with Litlhare is due to a large amount of one-to-one interaction with her older brother while looking at pictures from a schoolbook.

Adults and older children (7–12 years) accounted for approximately 70 percent of prompts to Hlobohang and Litlhare; young children (4–6 years) provided about 30 percent, primarily in the areas of prompting assistance in question routines and in correcting for politeness responses, and some in general play situations. In contrast, adults and older children spend much more time and effort in trying to get children to perform verbally, either through question routines and prompts therein or by telling a child to *bina* 'sing', *bala* 'count', *juetsa* 'tell', *botsa* 'ask', or *(tsamaea) u re* '(go) and tell', *echo* 'say so', *bitsa* 'call', *hoelehetsa* 'call out to', and *bolella* 'tell'. Occasionally prompts will also be given without any of these prompting words used, but rather directed toward the child as a response to a question or in correcting speech using a politeness form (see Ex. 8 at 1). *Ere* 'say', *juetsa* 'tell' and *bolella* 'tell' (in the sense of "tell me"), *bina* 'sing', and *bala* 'count' are used during interaction between two people where the prompter is trying to get the child to talk. These are also found in triadic interaction, where the prompter tries to get the child to perform for another person. *Tsamaea u re* 'go and tell', *botsa* 'ask', and the calling-out prompts are all used in triadic contexts. Only *echo* 'say so' is found exclusively in dyadic interactions.

Contexts in which prompts are used

Getting children to talk – ho buisa ngoana

Ho buisa ngoana 'to make a child talk' was one of the activities of caregivers with young children. Getting children to talk was not a problem for the researcher, as all children but one in the study were extremely verbal and usually responded enthusiastically to prompts. However, between a fourth and a third of prompts to 2- to 3-year-olds were specifically initiated in order to make children talk. In the case of Hlobohang, grandmother MM spent much time in getting him to talk, not only to the researcher, but in general. It is obvious that Hlobohang was well versed in various verbal routines, including some of the basic elements of lineage recitation, clan recitation, songs, and games by the age of 24 months, and that much time was spent with him in mastering these routines.[1] Hlobohang's family situation was somewhat different from that of most children. He was still an only child at the age of 3½ years and in many ways was still deferentially treated as the *ngoana* 'child' of the family when most of his peers had a year-old sibling who assumed that role. In addition to an older male and female cousin Hlobohang had a grandmother, mother, and maternal uncle sharing the same small house and providing him with much more one-to-one adult attention, both male and female, than most children received. This would account in part for the high instance of both dyadic and triadic prompts associated with getting Hlobohang to talk. In the following example Hlobohang's mother encourages him to talk to the researcher.

Example 2
[Mother MH tries unsuccessfully to get her son Hlobohang (25;0 months) to talk. She is pointing toward the researcher's tape recorder and telling him to ask the researcher to give it to him.]

MH: (1) *Ere* m-phe   ntho eo.
　　　 say "me-give thing that"
　　　 Say "Give me that thing."

　　 (2) *Ere* ausi Mamello a   u   fe   ntho.
　　　 say sister M   she you give thing
　　　 Say that sister M should give you the thing.

(3) *Ere* a   u   fe   ntho.
    say she you give thing
    Say that she should give (it) to you.

(4) *Ere.*   (5) *Echo.*
    say   say so
    Say (it).   Say so.

(6) *Ere* m-phe   ntho ena,   *echo,   mo juetse.*
    say "me-give thing this," say so, her tell
    Say "Give me this thing," say so, tell her.

(7) *Ere* a   u   lets-etse   kumba-kumba.
    say she you play-ben/prf tape recorder
    Say that she should play the tape recorder for you.

Here *ere* 'say' is used in both direct reporting (turns 1 and 6) as well as indirect reporting (turns 2, 3, and 7). In turns 4 and 5 the child is left to fill in what is to be said. *Echo* 'say so' is used in isolation, while *ere* 'say' is followed by either direct or indirect speech. Notice here the use of repetition, of the imperative message through various nonidentical forms, all relaying the same message. The child is thus presented with a variety of direct and indirect reporting forms from which to construct his or her response.

Ere 'say', *echo* 'say so', and *juetsa* 'tell' are not the only prompts used in getting children to talk. On occasion, several prompts are used in the same speech act, as seen in Ex. 2. *Juetsa* 'tell', *botsa* 'ask', and (*tsamaea*) *u re* are used as prompts of indirect reporting, necessitating a shift of pronoun usage on the part of the child. Almost half of the question-routine prompts to Hlobohang included instances of "tell" or "ask." Some of these were used by themselves, but many were used in full sentences, most in indirect reporting form. Young children do occasionally have problems with the shift from indirect reporting to direct reporting ("Say you want to go" versus "Say 'I want to go' "), but they usually produce the correct transpositions by the age of 30 months.[2] Such indirect triadic prompts are often used in the reporting or asking of information, as will be seen in Exx. 6 and 8.

Bina 'sing' and *bala* 'count', a somewhat different sort of prompt, were also used to get children to respond verbally. They were used especially in prompts to Litlhare, accounting for almost half of adult attempts to get her to talk. Older sibling caregivers (aged 7–12 years) frequently used this kind of prompt to encourage children to talk. In the process, children learned songs and learned how to count. These are skills that they would be called on to demonstrate once they started school.

The use of *ere* 'say' and other prompts for getting children to talk provides adults and other caregivers with ways in which to initiate and maintain verbal and social interaction with children. *Bitsa* 'call' and *hoelehetsa* 'call out to' are triadic prompts used to persons visible in the distance or not visibly present. This kind of prompt is often used to distract a child's attention or to change the course of interaction. Hlobohang's mother, in calming his crying, prompted him at 25;0 months to call out to the neighbor girl: *Ere a tle le tl'o bapala. Mo hoelehetse. Mo juetse. Ere a tle le tl'o bapala* 'Say she should come and you can play. Call out to her. Tell her. Say she should come and you can play.' Calling out in rural Lesotho is a particularly important means of communication, as open expanses of mountain grassland enable persons to see each other and communicate for miles. Village meetings are frequently heralded by an early-morning caller who stands on the hill above the village and informs people when and where to meet. Thus calling out is a very functional means of communication, and children are prompted early on to communicate in this way.

Prompts used in question routines

Question routines are another means of engaging children in conversation (Demuth 1983). They are used for "practice" in talking, to see if the child understands and can respond intelligently or with a sense of humor, to engage the child in social interaction, and occasionally to find out specific information (Where is your mother? When did she leave? Where did she go?). Questions are often game-oriented with children of 2 years, but later in life such question sequences play an important role in a child's social interactions. At early ages prompts in question routines are used to help initiate or direct conversation toward the topic the prompter chooses. Prompts are used to maintain conversation when a child needs assistance with a response, or on the rare occasion when a child refuses to participate in the interaction. Prompts in question routines are used frequently by adults speaking to children and occasionally by older children speaking to younger children (Ex. 1). Topics include everything from name and lineage routines to clan recitations, questions concerning travel, the whereabouts of a family member, food, and the acquisition of a new article of clothing. In Ex. 3 mother S constructs a question routine by prompting Litlhare, who is interacting with her brother.

Example 3

[Brother Namane (5;5 years) is conversing indoors with sister Litlhare (30;2 months). Mother S is attending to her newborn infant and prompts L to ask N questions in a question-routine format.]

N > L: Ke tla re Elisha a tle.
      I will say E   he come
      I'll say that E should come.

S > L: *Ere* ke ngoan'a mang?
      say cop child-pos who
      Say "Whose child is he?"

                    L > N: ana mang?
                          (ke ngoana (oa) mang?)
                          cop child pos who
                          Whose child is he?

N > L: Ke ngoan'a bo-Linpoetseng.
cop child-pos pl-Lpts
He's Lpts's family's child.

S > L: *Ere* o   kae?
say he's where?
Say "Where is he?"

                L > N: o   kae?
                          he's where
                          Where is he?

N > L: Ke ngoana holima tsela– oa lisa.
cop child on-top road he herd
He's the child above road– he herds.

S > L: *Ere* o   lisa-ng?
say he herds-what?
Say "What does he herd?"

                L > N: isa-ng?
                          (o lisa-ng)
                          he herd-what
                          What does he herd?

N > L: O lisa   likhomo.
He herds cattle.

S > L: *Ere* o   moholo?
say he's big
Say "Is he big?"

                L > N: o holo?
                          (o moholo)
                          he's big
                          Is he big?

N > L: E-ea.
Yes.

S > L: *Ere* oo.
say oh
Say "Oh."

                L > N: Oo.
                          Oh.

S > L: *Ere* kea utloa 'nake.
say I   hear brother.
Say "I hear (you), brother."

                L > N Ke ukoe 'nake.
                        (kea utloa)
                        I hear (you), brother.

           [L laughs.]

Litlhare laughs at the end of this prompting/question period, realizing it is a game or routine. Mother S has provided Litlhare with a framework for constructing her own question sequences, a skill that begins to develop during the third year of life.

It is not only adults who prompt in question routines, but also older siblings. Ex. 4 illustrates a prompting assist by an older child to a younger child in a question routine initiated by an adult. The older child imposes her bias on how the question should be answered.

Example 4

[It is raining outside. 'Neuoe (30;1 months) and cousin Tsebo (46;1 months) are indoors with grandmother J and various other neighbor women. The girls are playing house together on the floor. Grandmother J asks N what she is doing and T prompts her.]

J > N: 'Neuoe uena le   etsa joang?
　　　　N   you you-pl do   what
　　　　N what are you doing?

　　　　　　　　　　　　N > J: Re i-sa–
　　　　　　　　　　　　　　　(rea i-tlhatsoa)
　　　　　　　　　　　　　　　we rfl-wash
　　　　　　　　　　　　　　　We're washing.

J > N: E?
　　　　What?

　　　　　　　　　　　　N > J: rea i-satsoa.
　　　　　　　　　　　　　　　　(i-tlhatsoa)
　　　　　　　　　　　　　　　we   rfl-wash
　　　　　　　　　　　　　　　We're washing.

J > N: Lea   i-tlhatsoa?
　　　　you-pl rfl-wash
　　　　You're washing yourselves?

　　　　　　　　　　　　N > J: E.
　　　　　　　　　　　　　　　Yes.

J > N: Le   i-tlhatsoa ho-kae?
　　　　you-pl rfl-wash where
　　　　Where are you washing?

T > N: *Ere* nokan-eng.
　　　　say creek-loc
　　　　Say "At the creek."

J > N: Le   i-tlhatsoa ho-kae?
　　　　you-pl rfl-wash where
　　　　Where are you washing?

　　　　　　　　　　　　N > J: Linokan-eng–eng.
　　　　　　　　　　　　　　　creeks-loc–loc
　　　　　　　　　　　　　　　At–at the creeks.

J > N: Linokan-eng?
　　　　creeks-loc
　　　　At the creeks?

　　　　　　　　　　　　N > J: E,   lukan-eng.
　　　　　　　　　　　　　　　　(linokan-eng)
　　　　　　　　　　　　　　　yes,   creek(s)-loc
　　　　　　　　　　　　　　　Yes, at the creek(s).

[J pauses, giving N a chance to
　　correct her pronunciation.]

J > N: Au, u   i-tlhatsoa kae?
　　　　oh, you rfl-wash where
　　　　Oh, where are you washing?

T > N: *Ere* ke i–   i-tlhatsoa linokan-eng.
　　　 say "I rfl– rfl-wash creeks-loc"
　　　 Say "I w–wash at the creeks."

Children's use of prompting for question routines is usually of the isolated, one-turn type used by Tsebo above. Adults also use one-liner prompts, but during question routines they often use multiple prompts as in Ex. 3.

Prompts for politeness

Ere is the main prompt used for eliciting appropriate and/or politeness responses. These forms are always used in direct reporting form and are often triadic, though occasionally dyadic. In Sesotho, politeness routines take the form of thank you's, greetings, acknowledgements of being spoken to, acknowledgements of receipt of gifts, respect to elders, and proper terms of address. Appropriate responses to these social situations are taught from an early age, though lapses in the children's performance still occur at 5 and 6 years of age, as seen in Ex. 5.

Example 5
[Mother S gives son Namane (5;3 years) and daughter Litlhare (28;0 months) part of an apple. S prompts L to say "thank you," then reprimands N for not having said "thank you" on his own, without being told to do so.]
[S finishes cutting apple and N grabs for his share.]

S > N: Hei– motho oa   khala enoa. Ache!
　　　 hey– person pos greedy that Hey!
　　　 Hey–that greedy person.
　　　　　　　　　　　　　　　 L:　　 Apole (4×)
　　　　　　　　　　　　　　　　　　 Apple
[S gives L her share of apple.]

S > L: E nke ke ena, ua e batla?
　　　 it take cop dem you it want
　　　 Take it, here it is, do you want it?
　　　　　　　　　　　　　　　 [L starts to take apple with one hand.]
　　　　　　　　　　　　　　　 L > S: Ena empe.
　　　　　　　　　　　　　　　　　　 dem bad
　　　　　　　　　　　　　　　　　　 This one is dirty.

S > L: E-e, nka ka   matsoho amabeli.
　　　 no, take with hands   two.
　　　 No, take with both hands.
　　　　　　　　　　　　　　　 [L takes apple with two hands]

S > L: *Ere* danki[3] 'me.
　　　 Say "Thank you, mother."
　　　　　　　　　　　　　　　 L > S: Danki 'me.
　　　　　　　　　　　　　　　　　　 Thank you, mother.

[N quietly munching apple]

S > N: Helang, motho ena o   fapane   hloho ena.
hey,   person this he's mixed-up head   this
Hey, this person is crazy.

Ere danki 'me.   Pateriki, na ha   u
Say "Thank you, mother." N,   ?   neg you
                          N, don't you know how

nts'o   sa   tsebe ho re   danki   'me?!
cont you still know to   say   thank-you mother
to say "Thank you, mother" yet?!

N > S: Danki   'me.
Thank-you mother.

S > N: He! Mehlolo he!
Hey! Miracles, really!

S > N: Haeba monna ea makalo ka uena o   ntsa sa   tseba
if   man   of size   of you SC still neg know
If a man the size of you still doesn't know

ho-tankisa. Mm!
to thank   exlc
how to thank. Really!

Learning proper forms of politeness is an important kind of socialization for young children, accounting for 27 percent and 22 percent of adult prompts to Hlobohang and Litlhare respectively. Though Basotho society is not highly stratified, there is a definite organization toward the respect of elders, and children are taught to indicate this deference verbally. When Litlhare is 28;0 months her mother, after prompting her to use a term of address with an older person's proper name, asks her, *U motho a joang ea sa hlompeng batho ba baholo?* 'What kind of person are you who doesn't respect elders?'

Prompting for social instruction

Prompts also function in the general instruction of various socially important issues (giving and receiving of gifts and food, assertion, talking to infants) and the teaching of certain values that are not explicitly discussed but rather implicitly suggested or demonstrated. This kind of prompt is used more and more frequently as children mature. With Litlhare it was used hardly at all, whereas with Hlobohang it accounted for 8 percent of the prompts used by adults and was used once by an older child. Occasionally it is introduced into the creation of stories and indicates what the child should do in a hypothetical situation, as seen in the following example.

Example 6

[Father Rm is home from the mines, engaged in fabrication of a story with his son Hlobohang (34;3 months) and cousin Mololo (5;6 years). Rm is helping H to express what he is going to buy for whom when he goes to the city of the mines.]

Rm > H: U   il'o   etsa-ng Khaute-ng?
        you going-to do-what mines-loc
        What are you going to do in Johannesburg?

                                        H > Rm: Ke il'o   thonaka lieta.
                                                I going-to pick-up shoes
                                                I'm going to get some shoes.

Rm > H: U   il'o   thonaka lieta?
        you going-to pick-up shoes
        You're going to get some shoes?

Rm > H: [Le eng hape?]   H > Rm: E-ea, [tse] nyanyane.
        And what else?   Yes, little ones.

                                        H > Rm: Ha   keta,   ke li
                                                (ke qeta)
                                                when I   finish, I   them
                                                When I finish, I'll kick

                                                raha ka   bolo encha:.
                                                kick with ball new
                                                them with a *new* ball.

                                        H > Rm: Le   ea Bololo, k'il'o
                                                                (ke il'o)
                                                and of Mol,   I going-to
                                                And for Mol, I'm going to

                                                mo rek-ela   eona.
                                                him buy-ben it
                                                buy some for him too.

Rm > H: Ausi Mamello u   na   u   tla mo rek-ela eng?
        sister M   you   you will her buy-ben what
        Sister M, what would you you buy for her?
                                :
Rm > H: *Mo juetse* hore u   tla mo rek-ela eng?
        her tell   that you will her buy-ben what
        Tell her what you will buy for her.

Mol > H, Rm: 'Na ke tla mo rek-ela   kompa-kompa.
             me I will her buy-ben tape recorder
             As for me, I'll buy her a tape recorder.

                                        H > Mol, Rm: 'Na ke tla mo rek-ela
                                                     me I will her buy-ben
                                                     As for me, I'll buy her

                                                     retuoe!
                                                     radio
                                                     a radio!

Here the prompt *juetsa* is used to have Hlobohang include the researcher (sister Mamello) in the hypothetical buying spree that would take place. Mololo has picked up on what kind of response the situation calls for and furthermore selects an appropriate item for the researcher to receive. Hlobohang then too responds, modifying his response, but staying within the general semantic domain of items that he knows the researcher would be happy to receive. The sharing of goods and giving of gifts after a trip are essential to appropriate Basotho values and are often "taught" in question routines and with the aid of prompts, as illustrated here. Children must learn how to interpret situational contexts such as these so that they can respond in the appropriate manner. The learning of such skills requires of the child a certain ability to interpret social values, norms, and beliefs.

With household possessions, and food in particular, there are certain socially acceptable means of sharing and distribution. The learning of appropriate behavior in these socially delicate and potentially embarrassing situations involves careful observation on the part of the child as well as direct instruction by caregivers. The following example illustrates the subtle use of a prompt to an older child in a potentially face-threatening situation.

Example 7

[Tsebo (4;3 years) is putting the tea kettle on the stove when hard-of-hearing neighbor man Tbs wanders in. There is only enough tea for researcher Mamello. Mother M prompts her daughter Tsebo.]

Tbs > T: U   pheh-etse   Mamello tee?
         you cook-ben/prf M   tea
         Are you cooking tea for Mamello?
                                    (1) T > Tbs: Aa.
                                          No.

Tbs > T: E?
         What?

(2) M > T: *Ere* tsoekere ha e-e'o.
            say sugar   neg any
            Say "There isn't any sugar."
                             T > Tbs: Ah– tsoekere ha e-e'o
                                        no– sugar   neg any
                                        No– there isn't any sugar.

Tbs > T: Ketlele ee   u   nts'o
         kettle   this you cont you
         This kettle, what are you

         [etsa-ng   ka   eona?]   T > Tbs: [Tsoekere ha e-e'o.]
         doing-what with it?   sugar   neg any
         doing with it?   There isn't any sugar.
Tbs > T: E?
         What?

                             T > Tbs:Tsoekere ha   e-e'o
                                        sugar   neg any
                                        There isn't any sugar.

Tbs > T: Tsoekere ha   e-e'o?
         sugar   neg any?
         There isn't any sugar?
                          T > Tbs: E.
                                     Yes.

Tbs > T: Oo.
         Oh.

[Tbs takes the hint and exits.]

Food is a precious commodity, and, while it is to be shared with family, family visitors, and friends, it is a limited good and cannot always be shared with everyone. Here Tsebo realizes that there is not enough tea and responds negatively to the old man's question in (1). Her mother then prompts her in (2) with the socially appropriate response for saying that there is not enough tea to go around.

The example given above is an instance of adults talking through a child. Note that the old man does not ask the mother for tea, nor does the mother tell him there is none. Rather the entire transaction takes place with the child as the intermediary. This serves not only to socialize the child, but also to avoid possible embarrassment between the actual negotiating parties. As this example illustrates, prompts begin to assume a more serious and "real life" role as children become older. Less of an emphasis is placed on play or getting older children to talk, and prompting takes on a more instructional function.

Children are also prompted to talk to infants, as well as infants being "prompted" to talk to others. In Ex. 8 mother S prompts Litlhare in how to tell her infant sister to be quiet.

Example 8

[Mother S and daughter Litlhare (36;0 months) are talking about the fact that infant Kp (1;0 month) has woken on the bed and is crying. Notice in the fifth turn (1) the use of a direct prompt with no prompting word used.]

[Kp crying]

S > L: Ach, 'na ke utloa hore oa lla.
    Oh, me, I hear that she's crying.

                      L > S: a   hlo[l]iea!
                            (oa hlolia)
                            She's making-noise!

S > L > Kp: E,   a   s'ka re hlolia,
            yes, she/sb neg us make-noise
            Yes, she shouldn't make noise for us,

            mo juetse, mo juetse.
            her tell,   her tell
            tell her, tell her.

                      L > Kp: A   nhlolia   uena!
                            (s'ka n-hlolia   uena)
                            neg   me-make-noise, you!
                            Don't make noise for me, you!

(1) S > L > Kp: *S'ka n-hlolia uena!*
              neg me-make-noise you
              "Don't make noise for me, you!"

                      L > Kp: A   nhlo[l]ia.
                            (sk'a n-hlolia)
                            neg   me-make-noise
                            Don't make noise for me.

S > L > Kp: E,   *ere* s'ka n-hlolia moholoane.
            yes, say neg me-make-noise
            Yes, say "Don't make noise for me big sister."

```
                              L > Kp: oshian
                                      (moholoane)
                                      big sister.
S > L > Kp: Mo juetse.
            her tell
            Tell her.
                              L > Kp: A     nhloea           oholoane.
                                      (s'ka n-hlolia         moholoane)
                                      neg  me-make-noise big sister
                                      Don't make noise for me big
                                              sister.
S > L > Kp: Ere s'ka hlolia      moholoane oa-hau.
            say neg make-noise big-sister   your
            Say "Don't make noise (for) your big sister."
                              L > Kp: A     kolia          oholo
                                      (s'ka hlolia         moholoane
                                      neg   make-noise big-sister
                                      Don't make noise (for) your big

                                      a-hau.
                                      oa-hau)
                                      your
                                      sister.
```

Here Litlhare is provided with a model for the kind of behavior that is appropriate for interaction with infants. Social instruction also takes place in telling children how to act and react to interaction with one another. Some of this interaction takes the form of prompting for assertive behavior. In the following example, it is another member of the peer group who prompts the younger child.

Example 9

[Two boys are fighting. Hlobohang (31;0 months) hits Kh (6 years) with a stick. Lk (6 years) prompts H in how to defend himself verbally.]

[Kh threatening H with hand]

```
Kh > H: (Ka     u     mula.
         (ke tla)
         I will  you beat
         I'll beat you.
                              [H trying to avoid a blow]
                              H > Kh: Hei, hei uena, hei uena.
                                      Hey, hey you, hey you.

Kh > H: Ka      u     shapa.
         (ke tla)
         I will  you lash
         I'll lash you.
Lk > H: Ere ua hana Hloboang.
         Say you refuse H.
                              H > Kh: Kea hana.
                                      I refuse.

[Kh shows fist]
```

Kh > H: Ke tla   ore.
         I   will like-this
         I'll do like this.

                          [H shows fist back]
                          H > Kh: Ke tla   ore.
                                   I   will like-this
                                   I'll do like this.

Assertion is an important part of the socialization of Basotho children, and it is not infrequent to find children having multiple-turn threatening, insulting, and challenging sessions, as seen in Ex. 9. Adults too participate in such sessions with children in a play type of routine, as well as in serious everyday interaction, thus helping children establish the kinds of verbal behavior that they will need to hold their own among their peers. The actual percentage of assertion prompts, however, is small in comparison with those used for getting children to talk, for politeness, and for question routines.

Again, *ere* 'say' features prominently, though not exclusively, in socialization prompts. The majority of the interaction is triadic, where the child is being directed in how to act with or react to others. The form of these prompts therefore almost always involves direct reporting. Adults provide the bulk of the socialization prompts to children, though older children will also occasionally direct younger children in assertive behavior, as was seen in Ex. 9.

Word games

Prompts such as *ere* and *echo* are usually employed with word games. Word games are primarily dyadic and always involve direct reporting, with emphasis being placed on the direct repetition or imitation of what the speaker has said. Prompts used in word games occured in 7 percent of Hlobohang's and 8 percent of Litlhare's corpus. Examples of word-game prompts include prompting for tongue twisters, story introductions, counting (in English and Sesotho), learning songs, mothers' grade-school approximations of English (Ex. 10), and the "test" word for determining when a child should be weaned, as in Ex. 11. These routines serve to amuse, distract, or entertain the child (and/or the adults), as seen in the following examples.

Example 10

[Litlhare (30;2 months) is jumping up and down and calling to mother S. S prompts with a bit of her grade-school English.]

                          L: ko   vona.
                             (tloo bona)
                             Come see.

                          [L jumping up and down]

S: a:yam jəmping.
   I am   jumping.

S: *Choo* joalo–jəmping.
   Say likewise–jumping.

S: a:yam jəmping. (×3)

S: E,   bua   joale.
   Right, talk then.

                                          L: E?
                                          What?

S: *Ere* a:yam jəmping.
   Say "I am jumping."

Example 11

[Neighbor woman N and son Jobo (5 years) are visiting Hlobohang (25;0 months), cousin Mololo (4;8 years), mother MH and grandmother MM. The women are trying to get the boys to say difficult words, among them the "test" word for weaning, *Ha Makunyapane* 'at M's place'.[4]]

[MH trying to get H's attention]

MH > H: Hloboang.

                                 H > MH: M?
                                        What?

MH > H: *Ere* Ha Makunyapane.
   Say "Ha Makunyapane."

[Mol and MM talking]

MM > H: Ntate?
   Father?

                                 H > MM: M?
                                        What?

MM > H: Ha Makunyapane.

                                 H > MM: a–ne.

MM > H: M? [Ha Makunyapane.]   H > MM: [a–nyu–ne.]
   What? Ha Makunyapane.

N > MM, MH: [Lea   mo khuisa ka poso]   ha a e'so
               you-pl him wean by mistake neg he yet
               You wean him by mistake if he doesn't

               tsebe ho re   Ha Makunyapane.
               know to say Ha Makunyapane
               yet know how to say Ha Makunyapane.

(1) MM > N: O   re   a-nyane.
   He says –.

[Women laugh.]

N > J: Jobo ak'o u   re Ha Makunyapane.
   Jobo please you say Ha Makunyapane
   Jobo, please say "Ha Makunyapane."

                                 J > N: M?
                                        What?

N > J: *Ere* Ha Makunyapane. (×2)
   Say "Ha Makunyapane."

                                   J > N: a-kuenya-ane.

N > J: Ha mang?
    At whose place?

                                            J > N: Ha makuenyatane.
(2) N > MM: Ha makuenyatane!

[All laugh.]

[Women proceed to ask Mololo to repeat, then go on to other
words that are equally difficult for the boys to pronounce.]

Such word games seem to be directed most commonly to children under 5
years of age such as those above, rather than to children above the age of 6.

Corrections and prompts

The correction of pronunciation and grammar is another area where the use of
prompts is occasionally found. Most corrections are dyadic and direct. Again,
as in the use of prompts with word games and politeness prompts, the direct
prompt from the speaker is what the child should repeat exactly. *Ere* again
features prominently in this kind of construction. Correction prompts accounted for only 2 percent and 5 percent of Hlobohang's and Litlhare's corpus
respectively, but were found slightly more frequently in prompts directed to
older Tsebo.

Example 12

[Mother M and daughter Tsebo (46;1 months) are picking pebbles out of wheat so that
it can be sifted and then ground into flour. As usual, T uses a young child's version of
the future marker, *ta,* instead of the adult form *tla.* (The lateral affricate /tl/ is difficult
for young children to pronounce, but a child of Tsebo's age should have no problem.)
M tries unsuccessfully to correct T's pronunciation.]

M: Ha ke re rea li   sefa ka   sefa.
    neg I   say we them sift with sieve
    Is is not so that we'll sift them (pebbles) out with the sieve?

                                    T: E-ea 'me?
                                       What, mother?

M: Re tla sefa!
    We will sift!

                                    T: Re ta sefa?
                                       (tla)
                                       We'll sift?

M: M.
    Yes.

                                    T: Ke 'na: ta   sefa 'me?
                                       ('na ea   tla)
                                       cop me   who will sift mother
                                       Is it me who will sift mother?

M: M.
    Yes.

                                    T: M.
                                       Oh.

M: *Ere* ke 'na ea   tla–
   say cop me who will
   Say "It's me who will"–

                                           T: sefa.
                                           Sift.

M: a tla sefa.
   "who will sift".

                                           T: Ke 'na a   ta–
                                                (ea   tla)
                                           cop me who will
                                         It's me who'll–

M: *Ere* a tla.
   Say "who *will*".

                                           T: –sefa.
                                             sift.

M: –a tla sefa.
   "who will sift".

                                           T: E.
                                           Yes.

M: *Ere* a tla.
   Say "who will".

                                           T: a   tla.
                                           who will.

M: M,   a   tla   sefa.
   Yes, "who will sift".

                                           T: M.
                                           Yes.

[M and T finish picking pebbles out of wheat and T goes on using *ta* instead of *tla*.]

Basotho children below the age of about 30 months are not usually corrected for phonology, but their deviant phonological forms are often echoed, or commented on, as in (1) and (2) in Ex. 11.

Prompts are also used in general conversation, primarily with children under 3 years of age. Such prompts include asking people for things, accomplishing a task, or asking for assistance. These prompts differ from the above in that they are less "routine" and more spontaneous than those discussed above. The following section discusses the use of general prompts.

Prompts used in daily discourse

Many of the prompts discussed above have largely been used in play or routine situations, where interaction had an entertaining function. Prompts are also used in everyday conversational situations where young children are told how to request, how to give instructions to others, and how to participate in daily interactions that are not necessarily culturally defined, as were the prompts for social instruction. These prompts are found in indirect form.

Thus, when Hlobohang (26.6 months) was having trouble tying his shoes, his grandmother finally told him to ask his older cousin for help: *Ere abuti Mololo a u roese* 'Say (that) brother Mololo should put (them) on for you.' And, when Litlhare (28.0 months) was hungry and her mother was occupied, she was told to ask her older sister for food: *Ere Sebina o tl'o u ngoatela* 'Say (that) Sebina should come to dish out (food) for you.' In this way, children continue to learn how to interact with others in everyday situations. General prompts such as these accounted for 27 percent of Litlhare's adult prompts and 8 percent of Hlobohang's, Hlobohang having a much higher percentage of prompts of a play and fantasy nature than Litlhare.

Speaker, addressee, and developmental prompting trends

These, then, are the contexts in which prompts are used with young Basotho children. Table 3.2 provides a summary of these findings for each of the children in this study. Notice again here the very few prompts directed toward older Tsebo. In addition, the function of these prompts is quite different from that used with younger children. For Tsebo, prompts were mostly for politeness, or were corrections, while adults prompted the younger children for politeness, but also to get them to talk and in general daily interaction. The major focus of prompting by siblings and peers was that of assisting in adult-initiated question routines. Brother Namane used many prompts to Litlhare in general conversation (as did Litlhare's mother), whereas there was comparatively less general conversational prompting found in other sibling/peer-to-child interacting. Older siblings and peers (upwards of 8 years) tended to prompt much more like adults than did younger children.

Basotho adult modes of prompting to children change as the social and linguistic sophistication of the child increases. It has been noted that Hlobohang was in many ways still treated as a *ngoana* and that verbal interaction with his grandmother still included extensive prompting solely for the purpose of getting him to talk to her or to others. By this time his peers had younger siblings, and mothers and grandmothers were preoccupied with the younger child as well as several other children in the household. Interaction with these other 3-, 4-, and 5-year-olds is less social and more directive, and the peer group becomes the primary source of verbal interaction for the child. At this later stage adults still serve an important function in the teaching of appropriate social values and verbal usage. A large portion of her mother's speech to Tsebo (3;7–4;7 years) was of a specific socializing nature, as was seen in Ex. 8. Even at this age, she still had lapses of socially appropriate verbal responses, and had to be prompted occasionally for politeness, though in a different way from that in which a younger child would have been prompted.

Table 3.2. *Functions of prompts (number and percentage of different prompting functions)*

	Talk	Politeness	Question routines	General	Social instruction	Games	Correction	Total
Adult > children								
H	32 (30%)	29 (27%)	19 (18%)	9 (8%)	9 (8%)	8 (7%)	2 (2%)	108
L	23 (24%)	21 (22%)	14 (14%)	26 (27%)	—	8 (8%)	5 (5%)	97
N	1 (33%)	—	—	1 (33%)	1 (33%)	—	—	3
T	—	4 (44%)	—	—	1 (11%)	—	4 (44%)	9

	Talk	Politeness	Question routines	General	Assertion	Games	Correction	Total
Sibling/peer > children								
H	12 (27%)	—	34 (71%)	6 (12%)	1 (2%)	7 (15%)	—	48
L	—	5 (12%)	7 (16%)	13 (30%)	—	—	6 (14%)	43
N	—	—	13 (81%)	1 (6%)	2 (13%)	—	—	16
T	—	1 (50%)	—	—	—	1 (50%)	—	2

The different use of prompts with younger, as opposed to older, children was illustrated clearly in the politeness prompt in Ex. 5, where the older child was shamed into responding appropriately.

Prompting to children decreases as a child matures and is better able to converse without adult use of these interactional tools. It appears that the skills learned through routines then provide the groundwork for the kind of verbal and social interaction a child will face throughout life. An encounter with a stranger in Lesotho always includes a barrage of questioning, and one must be well versed in what to say and how to say it. Prompting serves an important function in socializing children toward the use of linguistically appropriate responses to these various types of social interaction.

Adults seem concerned with a child's social (and therefore verbal) performance and interaction with others. In contrast, the peer group is more preoccupied with a playmate's contribution to the maintenance of ongoing interactive situations. Adults use a larger number of the prompts, in a large variety of contexts. Older children begin to demonstrate this wider usage of prompts to younger children, while younger children rarely, though occasionally, use prompts to those older than themselves. When older children do use prompts to younger children (Exx. 1, 4, and 9), they tend to prompt primarily in question routines initiated by others, and occasionally for politeness, assertion, and in general play situations. *Ere* and other prompts are occasionally used between adults, especially when one is at a loss to know how to communicate with another. Such cases include that of a mother telling a visitor what to say to attract a child's attention, or a woman providing a friend with a witty line to avoid a potentially embarrassing situation. A similar use of prompts between adults is found with Kaluli, Kwara'ae, and Mexican-American adults. Foreigners too are occasionally told what to say, in terms of both actual linguistic form and social or humorous appropriateness. Further research is needed to determine the extent to which these and similar adult–adult uses of prompting will be found in other groups and societies.

Prompting across cultural/linguistic groups

Other ethnographically based studies of child language acquisition and socialization have considered the role of the "Say . . ." prompt in various cultural and linguistic groups. As has been illustrated in the foregoing discussion, there are several contexts in which children are told what to say. The case of *ere* 'say' and parallel constructions in Sesotho in some way resemble the use of *ɛlɛma* among the Kaluli (Schieffelin 1979), *dile* among Mexican-American families (Eisenberg 1982), *wax* among the Wolof of Senegal (Wills 1977), *uri* reporting in Kwara'ae (Watson-Gegeo & Gegeo this volume), and "say" among various English-speaking children (Iwamura 1980; Miller

1982). Many of these studies note the instructional function of such prompts. The use of prompts varies from one linguistic and cultural group to the next, as well as between families within one social group, as noted in various Kwara'ae households and among Baltimore English-speaking children studied. The findings reported above for Sesotho-speaking children seem most closely to resemble the use of prompts described for Mexican-American and Kwara'ae families. Some of these cross-cultural similarities and differences are briefly considered below. It was noted above that Sesotho prompts are used in both direct and indirect reporting form, though direct reporting is most common. Findings from other societies (Kaluli) indicate that only direct prompts are used. It was also found that both triadic and dyadic prompting forms are used in Sesotho, though triadic is most common. It is triadic prompts that are used most often with the Kaluli, Mexican-American, and Kwara'ae cases studied. Only among the three Baltimore children were interaction and prompting primarily dyadic. Thus, except for the South Baltimore children, where interaction was largely mother–child, cultural groups use prompts most frequently in situations of three or more persons, where the child is told to say something directly to a third party. It was only in cases of indirect reporting that Sesotho-speaking children had to change person (i.e. "Tell him you will . . ." versus "Tell him 'I will . . .' "), and they usually did so correctly by about 30 months.

Basotho prompt children not only to say certain things but also to sing, to count, and to call out to others. Various prompts are also found among the Kwara'ae (counting and calling out), Baltimore children (singing, rhymes, and verbal games), and Mexican-American children (calling out). It is suggested that the functions of prompting will differ from culture to culture.

Politeness prompts appear to be a type of socialization activity important to many cultures. As one might imagine, the kinds of behavior that are emphasized as being polite differ from one society to the next. Among Baltimore children "thank you," "excuse me," "please," and "I'm sorry" feature most prominently. Mexican-American children are told how to make polite requests, and to say "thank you" and "please." Kaluli children are taught to use appropriate terms of address, and Kwara'ae children are prompted for the polite use and answering of questions, greetings, and leave-takings, making requests, accepting food, and carrying on polite conversation.

Basotho adults use prompting as a means to talk "through" children in potentially embarrassing situations. This type of prompting is also noted with Kwara'ae in talking through children. Eisenberg (1982) too notes that the information conveyed in triadic prompts is often directed toward the third person as much as it is used for the instructional benefit of the child.

It was noted that prompting in Sesotho is used to provide children with models for how to interact with infants as well as how to assert themselves in play situations with peers. Socialization for appropriate speech to dolls, or potential infants, made up a large proportion of the prompts used in the study of English-speaking children in Miller (1982) and are also found directed toward infants with Mexican-American children. In contrast, prompting for assertion is one of the major functions of prompting among the Kaluli (Schieffelin 1979b).

Very few of the Sesotho prompts are used for corrections. Again, we find that with the Baltimore, Kwara'ae, Kaluli, and Mexican-American children studied, correction prompts play a minor if existent role in relation to prompting for appropriate social response.

The present study indicates that the nature of prompting changes as children mature socially and linguistically, and that old routines evolve into actual speech patterns. Watson-Gegeo & Gegeo (this volume) note similarly that calling-out routines used by Kwara'ae adults have been replaced by real calling out by the time children reach the age of 3 years and that other instructional routines have also tapered off by the time the child is 5 years old. Prompts are occasionally used between Basotho adults to each other in embarrassing situations or to provide a witty response. A similar use of prompts between adults is found with Kaluli, Kwara'ae, and Mexican-American adults.

From this brief overview of prompting in other cultures, we find that many of the aspects of prompting found in Basotho culture are also found elsewhere. What is most interesting is that prompting in other languages and cultures appears to be more limited in both form and application than the use of prompts by Basotho. Further research with larger sample populations and from a larger variety of cultures will someday provide us with a better understanding of the social and linguistic roles that prompting can play.

Discussion

Basotho adults say that the use of prompts is one of the ways in which they teach their children how to speak. As Brown (1971) notes, many cultures place emphasis on the social appropriateness of speech rather than on its correct grammatical representation. The teaching of appropriate social speech is one of the goals of prompting in Sesotho. It also serves to initiate, maintain, direct, and control behavior (Exx. 1, 2, 4, and 5). Prompting is used to bring a child into social interaction with others (Exx. 6–9), to learn the use of verbal routines (Ex. 3), for play and amusement (Exx. 10–11), and only occasionally for the correction of phonological or grammatical errors (Ex. 12). But perhaps the major, and increasingly important, function of prompts as a child matures is the imparting of social norms and values, providing the child with a framework for recognizing social cues and for responding accordingly.

The importance and predominance of these same prompting functions in other societies has been mentioned above. It is suggested here that the frequency of one function over another will necessarily depend on the importance placed on the values of a given society (i.e. Kaluli emphasis on assertion rather than appeal and the lack of naming objects; South Baltimore English-speakers' emphasis on naming and caregiving). It is also suggested that, just as interactional styles differ from one society to the next, some interacting physically and verbally much more with young children (Basotho) than others (Maya Quiche – Pye 1980), each society will also reflect some family variation in what is most important for their children to learn. Such family diversity is amply illustrated by Watson-Gegeo & Gegeo (this volume) in discussion of the Kwara'ae.

Ashton (1967) in his description of the Basotho makes the observation that caregivers do not educate their children until early adolescence, when they are finally taught rules, behaviors, virtues, self-respect, and respect for others. Ashton's concept of "educate" must have been limited to formal means of instruction, for he notes that language and other training does take place in the form of "unobtrusive help and encouragement, rather than direct instruction" (1967:43). It is true that children are not specifically told, "When you are given something you are supposed to say 'Thank you'." Rather, from repeated prompting of the kind demonstrated in Ex. 5, the child learns that it is in these contexts of receiving that the response "Thank you" is appropriate and, in fact, required. Other deductions, such as when and how to give or refuse food, require a greater awareness of cultural norms and integration of contextual cues. Prompting does play a "formal" role in that it provides a model for the child to imitate (in the case of direct reporting prompts), and gives practice with linguistic forms when they occur repeatedly in the same kind of context. But a behaviorist explanation for how children learn to respond appropriately in some contexts will hardly account for the learning of more subtle and complex situations such as when and how to share food. Though Basotho adults say that they use prompts in teaching their children to talk, prompting is also simply part of how one interacts with young children, and the two activities cannot necessarily be specified as distinct. Prompting helps to identify the contexts for which certain verbal responses are appropriate. In this way linguistic forms gradually acquire specific meanings appropriate to given contexts.

Prompts are only one of the many means used in the socialization of Basotho children. Question routines also play a large part in this process, as do games, naming, and peer-group interaction. Prompting has been discussed here in isolation, but it is the integration of all of these forms of social and linguistic interaction that enables a child to become a competent social being.

Prompting thus functions in two ways. It provides a child with a model of appropriate responses to different social situations. In addition, it supplies practice with the linguistic forms by which these appropriate responses should

be realized. Prompting promotes the learning of social competence, and part
of this social competence is realized as verbal competence.

Appendix: Transcription conventions

In general, adult and other child speech is found on the left side of the page,
while the younger and/or focus child's speech is on the right. The following
transcription conventions are used in the examples:

Ages of the children are given at the head of each example in months and
weeks (30;2 months) or in years and months (4;5 years).

X > Y or X > Y, Z indicates that X is speaking to person Y or persons Y
and Z respectively.

In contrast, X > Y > Z indicates that X is prompting Y to say something to
Z.

Sesotho words contained in parentheses () indicate the adult form of the
child's utterance.

English words contained in brackets [], but separate from other speech,
provide contextual information.

Sesotho utterances which are enclosed by brackets indicate overlapping
speech.

(×4) indicates that an utterance was exactly repeated four times.

A colon (a:) indicates nonphonemic vowel lengthening.

Vertical dots .

.

. indicate the passage of time or a pause or break in the
discourse.

Brackets around the letter *l* indicate that the sound was rendered as an /l/
rather than its expected allophone /d/ before high vowels.

Glosses include (1) a morpheme-by-morpheme translation and (2) a running translation.

Notes

Research for this paper was carried out with support from Fulbright–Hays and Social
Science Research Council doctoral dissertation research grants, a Graduate School
Fellowship from Indiana University, and funds from the Indiana University African
Studies Program. Revision for publication was undertaken while I was on NICHD
Developmental Training Grant no. 5T32 HD07181 administered by the University of
California at Berkeley. I thank Bambi Schieffelin for comments on earlier drafts of this
paper.
1 Miller (1982), Eisenberg (1982), and Wills (1977) have similarly noted that,
although children might have been prompted to perform for the researcher, in fact

prompting was frequently engaged in both with visitors and with other family members.

2 Eisenberg (1982) also notes that Mexican-American children did not change person marking on indirect verb forms until 26 months and 33 months, though they did change pronouns before that age. Such indirect triadic prompts are often used in the reporting or asking of information, as will be seen in Exx. 6 and 8.

3 *Danki* is a loan word from Dutch/Afrikaans meaning ''thank you.'' The equivalent Sesotho word is *kea leboha*.

4 In the past, when men spent years at the mines before returning home, children were nursed till the age of 5 or so, being finally weaned when they were old enough to say something difficult like *Ha Makunyapane,* the choice of word varying with the region (personal communication, 'Mamolete Mohapi). Here, the women prompt the boys to say difficult words, and the neighbor woman protests when Hlobohang, who was weaned at 18 months, has problems saying *Ha Makunyapane.*

References

Ashton, E. H. 1967. *The Basotho: a social study of traditional and modern Lesotho.* 2d ed. Oxford: Oxford University Press.

Brown, H. D. 1971. Children's comprehension of relativized English sentences. *Child Development* 42:1923–1936.

Demuth, K. A. 1983. The role of question routines in the socialization of Basotho children. In K. Demuth, *Aspects of Sesotho language acquisition.* Bloomington: Indiana University Linguistics Club, pp. 57–88.

Eisenberg, A. 1982. Learning language in cultural perspective: a study of three Mexicano families. Unpublished Ph.D. dissertation, University of California, Berkeley.

Iwamura, S. G. 1980. *The verbal games of pre-school children.* New York: St. Martin's.

Miller, P. J. 1982. *Amy, Wendy, and Beth: learning language in South Baltimore.* Austin: University of Texas Press.

Pye, C. 1980. The acquisition of grammatical morphemes in Quiche-Mayan. Unpublished Ph.D. dissertation, University of Pittsburgh.

Schieffelin, B. B. 1979. Getting it together: an ethnographic approach to the study of communicative competence. In E. Ochs & B. B. Schieffelin, eds., *Developmental pragmatics.* New York: Academic Press, pp. 73–108.

Wills, D. D. 1977. Culture's cradle: social structural and interactional aspects of Senegalese socialization. Unpublished Ph.D. dissertation, University of Texas, Austin.

4. Interactional routines as cultural influences upon language acquisition

ANN M. PETERS AND STEPHEN T. BOGGS

Introduction

We wrote this paper as an introduction to the symposium in which a number of the papers herein were presented. In it we intended to propose three hypotheses. The first is that children learn language in the process of interacting with others in patterned ways. We believe that the papers in this volume provide abundant evidence for the plausibility of this hypothesis. Secondly, we wanted to go further by suggesting that interactional routines facilitate the child's perception, analysis, and practice of utterances. Here we have offered examples in order to illustrate how such linkage may occur. Finally, we suggest that culturally formulated ways of communicating motivate both linguistic and social development: that in learning how to speak appropriately a child learns both language and social rules.

This paper is motivated by the belief that we need an account of language acquisition that does not avoid the question of learning. In particular, we want to be able to portray the *processes* of language learning so as to show how the learner's systems evolve rather than just to describe static stages. We also want to account, if possible, for the motivation that produces language development. We believe that cross-disciplinary research is needed in order to provide such an account. This is because socialization and language learning are closely intertwined. Socializing situations occur fairly predictably as to time, place, participants, and desired outcomes, all of which greatly facilitate language learning. Moreover, teaching children to participate in speech events in certain ways helps to inculcate cultural values. Interactional routines tend to structure these situations. The child learns how to participate by first learning one part of a routine and then the entire routine, with subsequent new and more complex performances being expected. Routines simultaneously provide a framework for input to the child's developing linguistic systems.

80

We propose that once such routines have been identified ethnographically they must be analyzed linguistically if we are to understand how the child's language system evolves. Thus ethnographic description provides the context for understanding the socialization process within which linguistic evolution occurs.

We will first discuss the concept of interactional routine, and then exemplify the kinds of analysis that linguists can make of the linguistic information that is made available to the child by such routines. We conclude by suggesting a view of linguistic and social development that makes use of the concept of interactional routine, and the related concepts of participation structure and mode of speaking, both of which express cultural values.

Interactional routines

An *interactional routine* is a *sequence of exchanges* in which one speaker's utterance, accompanied by appropriate nonverbal behavior, calls forth one of a limited set of responses by one or more other participants (Boggs & Peters 1980; Hymes 1962, 1971, 1982; Sacks, Schegloff & Jefferson 1974). Embodied in interactional routines are *participation structures* (cf. Philips 1972). Whereas routines specify generally the content and kinds of utterances to be expected in sequences, participation structures specify who can say what to whom. In learning an interactional routine a child thus develops an understanding of social role appropriate to age and sex.

For example, in the culture of contemporary part-Hawaiians, when a child of any age is being scolded the caregiver first shows signs of genuine anger, then specifies the circumstances in which punishment will be meted out and waits for signs of compliance. During the period following the caregiver's first utterance the child is expected to give verbal assurances of compliance, or remain silent, but not to complain or argue ("Don't talk back"). The child may or may not comply. If not, a final confrontation is likely to ensue, which has its own subroutines. A different structure of participation is seen in playful contradicting with young children. In this case a caregiver will make a patently false statement, threat, or insult directed at the child. The child is expected to contradict the statement and return the threat or insult, each party responding alternately (Boggs 1985). The young child is thus allowed to compete for equality when playing (although only caregivers can initiate these play routines) but not to do anything interpretable as a challenge when being scolded.

Certain general features transcend the participation structures accompanying given routines. These general features are referred to as *modes of speaking*. Since these modes of speaking reflect key cultural values that guide the socialization process, they are discussed in the section "Further Development." Here we note only that participation structures together with their associated routines provide the opportunity for a child to hear linguistic input and respond to it verbally or in other ways that are immediately reinforced.

Routines vary from those with nearly fixed content to those calling forth a series of speech acts whose content and form may be quite varied. In other words, they can be conceived as varying along a continuum of fixedness. At one extreme the response called for is prescribed exactly (e.g., "How are you?" → "Fine"; "Knock-knock" → "Who's there?"). Further along the continuum are formulaic responses that have empty slots to be filled in (e.g., "What's that?" → "That's a _____"). Even less fixed, but still predictable enough to be called routines, are situations in which the kind of response is prescribed but not its exact form or content (e.g., "What do you say, dear?" → "Please / Thank you / Excuse me / I'm sorry / . . ."; or the game of "sounding" among black Americans, which follows a rule in which a formal insult must be followed by a counterinsult, but not by a denial or an evidential argument – Labov et al. 1968). That is to say, routines are structured even when they are not formulaic (cf. Hymes 1982).

This continuum of fixedness can cause problems for the researcher who is trying to identify routines. How fixed does a sequence of exchanges have to be in order to count as a routine? One useful rule of thumb is a predictability test: to what extent and how reliably can either investigators or members of the culture being studied predict the next line in an exchange?[1] If even the *kind* of language can be reliably predicted, we judge this to be a sufficient criterion for a routine. The more exactly the response can be predicted the more formulaic the routine.

Children's consistent responses to particular cues can also constitute evidence for the existence of routines, because the child appears to recognize what kind of response should come next. This is highlighted when the child responds to the right cue but in the wrong context. More generally, the kind of response made by a speaker provides evidence as to how the prior utterance was perceived, whatever may have been the intent of the prior speaker.[2] For instance, among the Kwara'ae of the Solomon Islands (see Watson-Gegeo & Gegeo this volume) children are taught from babyhood to respond to a certain adult intonation contour (the "invitational" contour) by imitating the utterance accompanying that contour. This particular intonation pattern is not, however, restricted to eliciting imitations from children – it can also occur in adult conversations. The interesting point is that Kwara'ae 3-year-olds, playing nearby during an adult conversation and seemingly paying little attention to its content, will spontaneously start to imitate an adult who happens to use this particular contour, without realizing that imitation is not being invited (Watson-Gegeo & Gegeo this volume). In such a situation, even though the language involved is not formulaically fixed, the kind of response is, leading us to identify it as being associated with a routine, albeit mistakenly so in this case.

A third possible test for routines is an awareness test: To what extent are the participants aware of fixed structure within an exchange? To what extent are they able to verbalize what is going on? Such questions can be investigated by discussing tapes containing hypothesized routines with caregivers and/or other members of the culture, much as Schieffelin (1979) did in her work with the Kaluli. This sort of evidence about the participants' awareness of the invoking of a routine may also sometimes be found in the original data. For instance when, as described above, a Kwara'ae child spontaneously begins to imitate an adult's utterances and the circumstances are informal enough, caregivers acknowledge (and reward) this activity by immediately turning to the child and giving him or her more sentences to repeat (Watson-Gegeo & Gegeo this volume). Thus what starts out as the accidental invoking of a routine by the child is deliberately metamorphosed into the routine, owing to the caregiver's awareness of the routine as a unique kind of speech event. This case also illustrates the participation structure implicit in imitation routines: They can be initiated by either party.

Other evidence of awareness is provided by caregivers' glosses. Thus Hawaiian mothers of young children would often write "teasing sister" when transcribing a tape, instead of writing the actual sounds as they were instructed to do (Boggs field notes). Further formal analysis can then be made of the tokens glossed in this way in order to determine whether more than a single set of forms is reacted to as "teasing." These same kinds of procedures can also be used to determine the extent to which an observer's analysis corresponds to a participant's set of categories, even though it is often the case that speakers participate in routines without being consciously aware of them.

Another way to look at identification of routines is to consider what is *not* a routine. Certainly the heart of any conversation is relatively unpredictable, although its framing (opening and closing) may be governed by routines. Thus an 18-month-old may have discovered that telephone conversations have a fixed (predictable) skeleton: "Hi fine bye" (Ervin-Tripp 1982), but for older speakers the core of the conversation is not at all fixed in this way.

Since we propose that routines may be particularly fruitful places to investigate the process of language *development*, it is crucial to be able to identify them as they exist at a given point in time. This is because in the course of development a particular routine may gradually undergo change to the point where it is no longer immediately recognizable. In such a developmental study it is the sequence of changes from a (relatively) fixed base that will constitute the evidence for development. We will further discuss the developmental aspects of routines in the section "Further Development."

Linguistic analysis of routines

As suggested at the outset of this paper, our approach to routines is motivated by the assumption that a great deal of language development is not due to some sort of unknowable innate process, but that evidence of learning and how it takes place can be demonstrated under the proper circumstances. We also have begun to notice that caregiver support, such as is present in socialization routines, may in fact be helpful for learning such purely linguistic matters as morphology and syntax, even though it may not be absolutely necessary in order for the latter to develop. Furthermore, we believe that comparison of situations in which morphology and syntax develop with varying degrees of support may help us to learn what aspects of such development are dependent upon support. In other words, our hypothesis is that, once identified, routines will provide particularly revealing kinds of data for investigating linguistic development.

As stated earlier, interactional routines may serve to promote language learning because they are so predictable: Specific configurations of time, place, participants, and goals tend to recur, leading the child to expect particular verbal and nonverbal behaviors.

Predictability can help the language learner in several ways. The simplest is a consequence of repetition: Passive listening to regularly repeated utterances can lead to improved perception of the utterances as previously missed or poorly perceived pieces are filled in. In order to convey a more concrete idea of how such filling-in can occur in a predictable situation, we will cite a personal experience. Last summer one of us was traveling through Germany on a train that made many stops. She noticed that at the end of each stop, as the train was getting ready to leave, a gong would sound and a male voice would make an announcement. Because her comprehension of loudspeaker German was not very good, she was unable to make much of this announcement at first, but as the train proceeded from stop to stop she found that she was progressively able to fill in more and more details, especially with the sound of the gong serving as a signal to pay attention.

Once a learner has begun to participate in a routine, its predictable structure affords an arena for practice and reinforcement. Good examples are early repetition routines, such as those found among the Kwara'ae, in which the child is encouraged to imitate and is then reinforced for his efforts (Watson-Gegeo & Gegeo this volume). One of these routines is designed to distract fussy babies (from approximately 6 to 18 months of age) and direct their attention away from themselves, thus calming them. Here the "child is taken to a door or window in a caregiver's arms. The caregiver points to a butterfly, bird, flower, or other object while chanting *lia* 'look' in a low to middle pitch, and then describes the object, encouraging the infant to repeat its name or label" (Watson-Gegeo & Gegeo this volume). This routine provides vocabulary information and practice.

In addition, if there are small variations in the repetitions, that is, if the language used is not *identical* from one time to the next, data are provided with which the child can do internal analysis on any memorized chunks. In

Example 1. English, from Peters (1983). Mother's speech to son (1;2)

You go *show* mommy.	stress on "show"
Show mommy.	reduction
Show mommy whatcha talking about.	expansion/variation
Birdie birdie.	repetition
Where's birdie?	expansion
Birdie's we::t.	expansion/lengthening
Birdie's all *wet* 'cause it's raining.	stress on "wet"
Chopstick.	theme 1
That's Chopstick.	expansion
An' you pick up *food* with that.	theme 2
Can you say again chopstick?	expansion of 1
Chopstick.	repetition/reduction
Chopstick, to pick up *food*.	reduction/variation
	stress on "food"
[18 turns later]	
Pick up food.	reduction
Ooh you pick up food like *that*.	expansion
I don't see birdie.	
Do you see birdie?	variation
Do you see any doggie too?	substitution

this way morphological and syntactic information may be made available. Among middle-class Americans it has been repeatedly noted that caregivers "simplify" their language to babies, repeating, expanding, and otherwise varying their utterances in order to enhance comprehension by their charges. Ex. 1 presents four sets of consecutive utterances to a middle-class 14-month-old from an English-speaking family living in Hawaii (Peters 1983). We have formatted the sentences in such a way that it is easy to see the range of types of modifications, including stress on key words ("show," "wet," "chop-stick," "food") and substitutions within slots ("birdie," "any-," "dog-gie"). These partially repeated sentences make available information regarding the segmentation of utterances into smaller linguistic units, as well as information about simple syntactic frames and where the substitution points occur.

Within the format of particular routines, specific aspects of the language may be made salient for the child, for example by the use of exaggerated stress (as in Ex. 2, from Kwara'ae) and/or breaking into "digestible" chunks (Exx. 3 and 4, also from Kwara'ae). In all three of these examples a child is being encouraged to repeat sentences, some of which are quite complex. The caregivers have broken these sentences into chunks that they feel are manage-able by the child but that also honor constituent boundaries in the Kwara'ae language, thus providing syntactic information as well. For ease of com-parison the repetitions by the child have been written directly underneath the adult models.

Having identified routines of potential linguistic significance, the next step

Example 2. Kwara'ae, from Watson-Gegeo & Gegeo this volume, Ex. 4

[Here, the child F (1;9) is most successful at picking up the stressed syllables uttered by his father's sister (fasi).][3]

fasi: No'o ne'e *ki--/*	bird+here+pl [high rise on *ki*]
F: [mumbles] *ki--/*	[same contour as fasi]
fasi: -'ain kataoh *ki/*	-eat+papaya+pl [same contour as above]
F: [mumbles] *ki/*	

is to see what kind of linguistic information they make available to the learner, whether lexical (Ex. 1), morphological (Ex. 2), and/or syntactic (Exx. 1, 3, 4). Once the kinds of linguistic information available in specific routines have been identified, linguists then need to look for ways in which children are able to make use of such information. Ex. 5 (from Snow 1981), although schematic, indicates how such a developmental sequence can be traced. Snow recorded book-reading sessions between herself and her son Nathaniel when he was 2½ years old. These sessions followed a routine format that the two of them had negotiated between themselves by the time Nathaniel was this age. The data on which Ex. 5 is based are taken from eight tapes in which mother and son were looking at the same book from one session to the next. They show how, within the by then well-known format of the routine, Nathaniel is able to make progressive use of information he receives from his mother.

Note that the data needed to show that a routine does indeed provide usable information for language learning must be collected in a (nearly) consecutive sequence of "same" situations. In most cases, especially when the child-rearing practices of the culture being studied are not well known, the acquisition of such data will involve at least two distinctly different types of data collection: a first ethnographically oriented project in which routines of potential significance to linguistic development are identified, and a second project in which a closely spaced sequence of such routines is recorded for linguistic and developmental analysis. To our knowledge, except for Snow's work on English, such data are not available in any language.

Further development

Interactional routines are a focus of development in a number of ways. First, they can provide "building blocks" for social and linguistic interactions at a time when a child has few linguistic resources at her disposal. Routines are like miniscripts where both caregiver and baby know all the "lines" so that in order to initiate a satisfying, though largely predictable, interaction all that is needed is enough of a cue as to which routine is being invoked. Ex. 6 (A and B) presents two such miniroutines for a 14-month-old child learning English: four instances of a summons–response routine ("Mommy!" + "What?/

Example 3. Kwara'ae, from Watson-Gegeo & Gegeo this volume, part of Ex. 10

[The father (fa) is teaching Susuli (3;3) about her future role as an adult woman by asking her to repeat a long sentence which he breaks up for her into chunks of length deemed appropriate for her linguistic development. This interchange consists of five turns each by father and child. The repetitions by the child have been written underneath the father's models so the reader can see just how well the child was able to imitate. Thus, the example must be read by alternating lines at the utterance breaks (/). Approximate glosses are included for the reader's benefit.]

fa: 'Uri: Ngeal kami   teo 'amu/   (Thus: Our child rest yourself.)
S: Ngeal kami   teo 'amu ne'e/
     Thus: child   our   rest you   here
                            (excl.)

...

fa: 'Uri: *Barat   nai/ . . . Ngwae huat nau/   Rorod   ni   *doe:-/-kero'*   ka   leak *kwai'   soi'/*
S: *Balat   nai/   Ngwae *huat* nau/   Ni   *doe-/*   *Kwai'   soi'/*
     Thus: Brother my/   person born with me tomorrow she big/   —we two sm go   chop   firewood
                                                                                          (excl.)

(Thus: My brother, person born in my line, when she grows up, we two will go chop firewood.)

Example 4. Kwara'ae, from Watson-Gegeo & Gegeo this volume, Ex. 5

[Here the layout is intended to help the reader see how the pieces of a fairly complex sentence are gradually being provided, but not in direct linear order. In this example a 15-year-old sister (si) is trying to put her brother (F, 2;3) to sleep by invoking the repeating routine. The child's utterances have been omitted (except for indications of where they occur) so the reader can see what kind of linguistic information the child is getting here as the sister builds up the construction for him. A gloss for the whole construction is provided at the bottom with "optional" elements in parentheses.]

```
si: Go' 'aok
    go' 'aok hat na'                 abus              na'  nai''
F:                      "Nauk 'aial                    na'  nai''

si: Go' 'aok              'uri
F:  "Aul- m/''

si: Go' 'aok                         "Nauk 'aial    si hang  na'  nai''
F:

si: Go' 'aok hat 'unair# 'uri        "Nauk 'aial            na'  nai''
F:

si:                          "Nauk a:bus na'''
F:
si:         "Nauk–  nauk abus                          si hang: na'''
F:          "Nauk abus na'''
si:

    Go' 'aok hat na' 'uri–
    Go' 'aok hat na' 'uri            "Aul na'''
    Go' hat na' 'uri                 "Aul na'  Nauk 'aial#  si hang  na'''
just you speak (perf.) thus: "Put now  susuh ki  Nauk abus na'  Nauk 'aial#  si hang  na'''
sm                           away      (stew) pl  I+sm full (now) I+sm don't want (not eat) now (that)''
```

Example 5. English, reformatted from Snow 1981, Table 7

[X, Y, and Z represent generalized slots in which specific lexical items actually occur.]
In an early session a new topic (and label) may be jointly introduced:

N:	Who's that?	
Mo:	*X*.	
N:	*X*.	
Mo:	*X*, right.	

At a subsequent session N may reintroduce the topic, using the recently acquired label, which his mother confirms before she offers more information about this topic:

N:	Who's that	*X*.
Mo:	*X*, right. What's *X*	doing?
N:	*X*	doing?
Mo:	*X* is *Y*-ing.	
N:	*X* *Y*-ing.	

The expression and development of topic *X* may get carried yet a step further in a still later session, with N again introducing the topic at the level of his expanded ability:

N:		*X*	*Y*ing.
Mo:	That's	right.	
N:		*X* have?	
Mo:		*X* has	a *Z*.
N:			a *Z*.
Mo:	Right,		a *Z*.

Example 6. English, from Peters (unpublished data). C = child (1;2), M = Mother

A. The "Mommy!" routine – a summons–response sequence:

	Summons	Response	Guess at topic
285 C:	xxxx mommy, mommy–		
M:		What– Hm.	
			Want me t'chew it up for you. [6-sec. silence]
293 C:	wã wã. xxxxxx! ã–		
M:		What.	
C:	manI–		
M:		What.	
C:	mI– manI.		[6-sec. silence]
319 C:	nanEh.		
M:		Huh?	
C:	mamI. xxxxxxx.		[4-sec. silence]
373 C:	mami:.		
M:		Yes?	[7-sec. silence]

Example 6 (*cont.*)

B. The "Ooh!" routine, which is characterized by some form of "Ooh" uttered in a low, intense, and somewhat breathy voice. Judging from the mother's response it seems to signal "Notice that" and functions as a topic initiator (if the mother can guess the topic):

	Summons	Response	Attention	Guess at topic
230 C:			dI:w– 'u:w [low, intense] ĵuI'?	
M:		What.		
312 C:			evUk. 'Owh (breathy)	
M:				Tha's chopstick.

C. Concatenation of two routines: summons–response and topic–notice:

	Summons	Response	Attention	Guess at topic
396 C:	ma::nih.			
M:		Wha' do you want?		
C:			'ew:– (breathy) uwu:. (breathy) xxx	
M:				That machine scare you? Hm?
C:			'o:h (breathy)	
M:				Duzzat scare you? Hm? Izzat why you say "oh"?

Huh?") and two instances of a topic-nominating routine ("Ooh!" + guess at topic).

Such interactive building blocks can lay a foundation for further development. One way this can happen is through linking two such routines, either by simple linear concatenation or, once more control has been gained, by invoking two at once and interweaving them. A simple juxtaposition has taken place in part C of Ex. 6 (from the same tape as parts A and B). Here the child first manages to get his mother's attention with "Mommy!" and then to indicate a topic with "Ooh!" Examples of the interweaving of routines by young speakers can be found in the Kwara'ae and Hawaiian data (Watson-Gegeo & Gegeo this volume; Boggs & Watson-Gegeo 1978).

Development also takes place when children learn the scripts well enough to take on roles other than those they were originally assigned (Bruner 1978;

Cazden 1979). They may initiate the routines themselves (rather than waiting for the caregiver to do so) or they may say some of the caregiver's lines instead of or as well as their own, as at the end of Ex. 7. As in Exx. 3 and 4, the father (fa) builds up a sentence for the child Fita (2;4) by chunking it into small enough bits for him to repeat.[4] The format is as in Ex. 4 above: The interchange actually consists of four turns each by father and child. Here Fita dutifully imitates his father three times, but the sentence (and precept) being modeled for him is so familiar (a routine) that he is able to supply the ending on his own: After the fourth chunk is presented he skips ahead and produces the concluding line on his own. Note that this conclusion embeds the *lia* routine.

As learning takes place within a given routine, its once-fixed structure may slowly disintegrate. Not only may the participation structure change, in the sense that the child is ready and allowed to take on roles other than the one originally assigned to him or her, but the language itself may become less fixed as the child no longer needs to rely on formulaic phrases to make participation possible. Consider, for example, an American child learning about telephone conversations. The formulaic skeleton of a conversation perceived by the 18-month-old described in "Interactional Routines" will slowly be expanded as the child's mother models the kinds of language appropriate to the core of such a conversation. One of us had the experience of speaking with a 2½-year-old who, after the opening "Hello" volunteered, "I ate pancake for breakfast." His mother reported that this was the first time her son had known what to say – up to that day she had had to help him satisfy his desire to talk on the telephone by prompting him with appropriate lines to imitate. From this day on, his conversations could be that much freer and less bound by a routine format. Foster suggests that as routines develop they "don't disappear, they become progressively more actively controlled and manipulated by the child until it is hard to recognize them as routines at all" (1982:68).

As particular routines are learned in this way, others succeed them. Advancement from one routine to another is systematically encouraged, usually unconsciously, and backsliding discouraged, except in moments of justifiable emotional distress, where earlier, abandoned routines may be used as expressions of solidarity, as in the case of the *lia* routine among Kwara'ae. In this way linguistic development is motivated, after basic rules of morphology and syntax have been learned, as a part of social development.

Modes of speaking provide continuity as certain routines succeed others during development. By *mode of speaking* we refer to general features that transcend particular routines. For instance, speech in situations that are culturally defined as hierarchical may be marked by particular lexical items, grammatical features, and/or style, such as high rhetoric (cf. Hymes 1974). In the Hawaiian case, speech in the hierarchical mode is marked by the adult's

Example 7. Kwara'ae, from Watson-Gegeo & Gegeo this volume, part of Ex. 6

[An approximate gloss is included underneath.]

fa: 'Uri: Gwata ne'-/ -ādmia   nam/   Sirai'   ngwae ke-/ -'aok'aok *liu*:#
F: Kwata ne'-/ -ādmia   na'/   e   ka   ke'# # lia   ni *sil*   na'/
Thus: pork   that/   eat it together   rather/   stomach of person /#   -hot   very/ look he diarrhea now
        with other food

(This pork has to be eaten together with other food or else a person's stomach will become very hot. Look, he has diarrhea now.)

possessing the sole right to initiate or frame the situation, to escalate or terminate the interaction, and to evaluate the child's responses unilaterally. This mode of speaking extends over several routines. It is reflected in the adult's requests for information, commands, and scolding and the child's initiations of requests in a subdued fashion, patiently awaiting a response and not escalating requests (Boggs 1985; Howard 1974).

Modes of speaking reflect or express key cultural values. In the Hawaiian case, families were traditionally organized upon the basis of seniority and age with the leader being accorded respect in the form of implicit obedience in routine matters. Complementing this emphasis upon obedience was status rivalry, particularly among chiefs, which was marked by a distinct mode of speaking. Competitions for status were frequently carried out by means of verbal contests that involved riddles and plays upon words, which often led to armed combat. Ordinary people also enjoyed the practice of similar verbal arts in friendly contests on the occasion of feasts. It is probably not coincidental, therefore, that adults today use playful contradicting and verbal play when they wish to express a mood of egalitarianism with their children. It is to be noted, however, that adults reserve the right to initiate and terminate these routines.[5]

The entire process of socialization needs to be described ethnographically. While successive, more complex routines often continue a given, already established mode of speaking, occasionally a contrast is introduced. When this happens we can be certain that a significant cultural lesson is occurring. Both these points can be illustrated in the Kwara'ae data. Among the Kwara'ae the *lia* routine is used primarily to entertain, but also to distract a crying infant. When used in the latter way, however, it also has the effect of encouraging the infant to downplay emotion in favor of social conversation. After 18 months of age, the function of entertaining and promoting social conversation is carried out by means of repetition routines (cf. Watson-Gegeo & Gegeo this volume). Simultaneously, *lia* is no longer used when young children are distressed by some accident over which they are expected to have some control. Instead "serious talk" is used. Such talk entails a mode of speaking that is likewise used in family counseling sessions. It begins a child's exposure to high rhetoric, which is a marked, highly developed feature of the Kwara'ae language. High rhetoric is used primarily by men in the serious matters of marriage negotiation, conflict resolution, and other community problems. This case illustrates the way in which central values and modes of speaking are systematically related and the fact that both guide the development of interactional routines (Gegeo & Watson-Gegeo 1981; Watson-Gegeo personal communications).

A most useful concept for analyzing the entire process of linguistic and social development is that of *speech economy,* introduced by Hymes (1974). The distribution of specific routines and modes of speaking over the various relationships and situations in a society constitutes its speech economy. We can see this reflected in the development just described. First, social sensitivity is inculcated via entertainment in the *lia* routine with infants. The inculcation of social sensitivity is continued via conversation in repetition routines. Third, "serious talk" introduces a contrast, while continuing to emphasize social sensitivity. It comes as no surprise that the contrasting modes of speaking among adults are marked by high rhetoric versus a "lightly serious, bantering tone" used in polite conversation. The intonation pattern of the latter closely resembles the repetition routines used with young children.[6] The full meaning and value of any mode of speaking depends upon its relationship to others and its place in the speech economy of a culture.

All of this is reflected in the process of linguistic and social development. As a child learns new and more flexible routines over time, certain generalized participation structures emerge. These modes of speaking embody values that are appropriate for relationships between persons of particular age and sex. With further development, alternative, and in some cases contrasting, modes of speaking are introduced into comparable situations and relationships. Once various modes of speaking are established in the speech economy, culturally and individually, the choice of one of several modes of speaking in a given situation can serve as one of several means of negotiating status in that situation (for an example, see Irvine 1974). Moreover, because of their association with early experience, modes of speaking may be particularly effective in helping to frame relationships.

Conclusion

In this paper we have tried to construct a preliminary and partial account of the processes of language learning that may provide insights into how the child's linguistic systems evolve, and what motivates this evolution. We view the acquisition of language not as an unknowable process in which inherent stages unfold, but as fundamentally embedded in the process of socialization. We have proposed that *interactional routines* tend to structure the situations through which socialization occurs. On the one hand, such routines provide a considerable amount of linguistic input to the child's developing linguistic systems, enabling her to perceive and analyze speech in a predictable and recurring context and to practice utterances with immediate reinforcement. On the other hand, through specific interactional routines the child is learning ways of communicating that are considered appropriate for her age and sex. Values embedded in the culture and social structure are expressed in these ways of communicating, which we have termed here *modes of speaking*. The systematic encouragement given to the child to learn modes of speaking appropriate to age and sex motivates both linguistic and social development long after basic rules of morphology and syntax have been learned. In this way adults are trained not simply to utter grammatical sentences, but to utter and convey the full range of meanings carried by the various modes of speaking that are available in the speech economy of any society and culture.

Notes

We would like to thank the following people for their helpful comments on this and earlier versions of this paper: Elizabeth Barber, Courtney Cazden, Susan Ervin-Tripp, Robert Hsu, Clifton Pye, Karen Watson-Gegeo.
1 This idea has been developing in the air around us for some time. In particular we recollect conversations with Karen Watson-Gegeo and Susan Ervin-Tripp.
2 This rule of procedure introduces a certain indeterminacy in identifying a routine. Thus it is common experience that a request for information may be interpreted as an accusation, directive, etc. Such indeterminacy cannot be eliminated because speakers may choose to respond in such a way as to transform one type of exchange into another. This is one aspect of the negotiation of meaning through dialogue (Bilmes & Boggs 1979). It is usually possible to distinguish this kind of indeterminacy from one in which no limited set of alternative responses is predictable.
3 Grammatical abbreviations are as in Watson-Gegeo & Gegeo this volume: pl = plural, sm = subject marker.
4 Watson-Gegeo & Gegeo point out that the father's chunking of this long sentence follows Kwara'ae intonation and phrasing. It also serves to indicate to Fita the boundary between noun phrase and verb phrase.
5 For detailed supporting evidence, see Boggs 1985.
6 These data are from Watson-Gegeo personal communications. We are also much indebted to her and to David Gegeo for their interpretation.

References

Bilmes, J. & Boggs, S. T. 1979. Language and communication: the foundations of culture. In A. Marsella, T. Ciborowski, & R. Tharp, eds., *Perspectives on cross-cultural psychology*. New York: Academic Press, pp. 47–76.
Boggs, S. T. 1985. *Speaking, relating, and learning: a study of Hawaiian children at home and at school*. Norwood, N.J.: Ablex.
Boggs, S. T. & Peters, A. M. 1980. An ethnographic–linguistic study of child language. Proposal to Linguistics Program, National Science Foundation. Honolulu: University of Hawaii at Manoa.
Boggs, S. T. & Watson-Gegeo, K. A. 1978. Interweaving routines: strategies for encompassing a social situation. *Language in Society* 7:375–392.
Bruner, J. S. 1978. The role of dialogue in language acquisition. In A. Sinclair, R. J. Jarvella, & W. J. M. Levelt, eds., *The child's conception of language*. New York: Springer-Verlag, pp. 241–256.
Cazden, C. B. 1979. Peekaboo as an instructional model: discourse development at home and at school. *Stanford Papers and Reports in Child Language Development* 17:1–29.

Ervin-Tripp, S. 1982. Activity structure as scaffolding for children's second language learning. Paper presented at International Sociology Meetings, Mexico City.

Foster, S. 1982. Learning to develop a topic. *Stanford Papers and Reports in Child Language Development* 21:63–70.

Gegeo, D. W. & Watson-Gegeo, K. A. 1981. Courtship among the Kuarafi of Malaita: an ethnography of communication approach. *Kroeber Anthropological Society Papers* 56–58:95–121.

Howard, A. 1974. *Ain't no big thing: coping strategies in a Hawaiian-American community.* Honolulu: University Press of Hawaii.

Hymes, D. H. 1962. The ethnography of speaking. In Anthropological Society of Washington, ed., *Anthropology and human behavior.* Washington, D.C.: Anthropological Society of Washington, pp. 13–53.

1971. On linguistic theory, communicative competence, and the education of disadvantaged children. In M. L. Wax, S. Diamond, & F. O. Gearing, eds., *Anthropological perspectives on education.* New York: Basic.

1974. Ways of speaking. In R. Bauman & J. Sherzer, eds., *Explorations in the ethnography of speaking.* Cambridge: Cambridge University Press, pp. 433–451.

1982. Ethnolinguistic study of classroom discourse. Final report to the National Institute of Education. Washington, D.C.

Irvine, J. T. 1974. Strategies of status and manipulation in the Wolof greeting. In R. Bauman & J. Sherzer, eds., *Explorations in the ethnography of speaking.* Cambridge: Cambridge University Press, pp. 167–191.

Labov, W., Cohen, P., Robins, C., & Lewis, J. 1968. *A study of the non-standard English of Negro and Puerto Rican speakers in New York City,* vol. 2. C.R.P. Report no. 3288. New York: Columbia University.

Peters, A. M. 1983. *The units of language acquisition.* Cambridge: Cambridge University Press.

Philips, S. U. 1972. Participant structures and communicative competence: Warm Springs children in community and classroom. In C. B. Cazden, V. P. John, & D. Hymes, eds., *Functions of language in the classroom.* New York: Columbia University Teacher's College Press, pp. 370–394.

Sacks, H., Schegloff, E., & Jefferson, G. 1974. A simplest systematics for the organization of turn-taking for conversation. *Language* 50:696–735.

Schieffelin, B. B. 1979. Getting it together: an ethnographic approach to the study of the development of communicative competence. In E. Ochs & B. B. Schieffelin, eds., *Developmental pragmatics.* New York: Academic Press, pp. 73–108.

Snow, C. E. 1981. Saying it again: the role of expanded and deferred imitations in language acquisition. Unpublished manuscript, Harvard University.

5. What no bedtime story means: narrative skills at home and school*

SHIRLEY BRICE HEATH

In the preface to *Introduction to S/Z*, Roland Barthes's work on ways in which readers read, Richard Howard writes: "We require an education in literature . . . in order to discover that *what we have assumed* – with the complicity of our teachers – *was nature is in fact culture, that what was given is no more than a way of taking*" (emphasis not in the original; Howard 1974:ix).[1] This statement reminds us that the *culture* children learn as they grow up is, in fact, "ways of taking" meaning from the environment around them. The means of making sense from books and relating their contents to knowledge about the real world is but one "way of taking" that is often interpreted as "natural" rather than learned. The quote also reminds us that teachers (and researchers alike) have not recognized that ways of taking from books are as much a part of learned behavior as are ways of eating, sitting, playing games, and building houses.

As school-oriented parents and their children interact in the preschool years, adults give their children, through modeling and specific instruction, ways of taking from books that seem natural in school and in numerous institutional settings such as banks, post offices, businesses, and government offices. These *mainstream* ways exist in societies around the world that rely on formal educational systems to prepare children for participation in settings involving literacy. In some communities these ways of schools and institutions are very similar to the ways learned at home; in other communities the ways of school are merely an overlay on the home-taught ways and may be in conflict with them.[2]

Yet little is actually known about what goes on in story-reading and other literacy-related interactions between adults and preschoolers in communities around the world. Specifically, though there are numerous diary accounts and

*Originally published in *Language in Society* 11:49–76, 1982, Cambridge University Press.

experimental studies of the preschool reading experiences of mainstream middle-class children, we know little about the specific literacy features of the environment upon which the school expects to draw. Just how does what is frequently termed "the literate tradition" envelop the child in knowledge about interrelationships between oral and written language, between knowing something and knowing ways of labeling and displaying it? We have even less information about the variety of ways children from *nonmainstream* homes learn about reading, writing, and using oral language to display knowledge in their preschool environment. The general view has been that whatever it is that mainstream school-oriented homes have, these other homes do not have it; thus these children are not from the literate tradition and are not likely to succeed in school.

A key concept for the empirical study of ways of taking meaning from written sources across communities is that of *literacy events:* occasions in which written language is integral to the nature of participants' interactions and their interpretive processes and strategies. Familiar literacy events for mainstream preschoolers are bedtime stories; reading cereal boxes, stop signs, and television ads; and interpreting instructions for commercial games and toys. In such literacy events, participants follow socially established rules for verbalizing what they know from and about the written material. Each community has rules for socially interacting and sharing knowledge in literacy events.

This paper briefly summarizes the ways of taking from printed stories families teach their preschoolers in a cluster of mainstream school-oriented neighborhoods of a city in the southeastern region of the United States. I then describe two quite different ways of taking used in the homes of two English-speaking communities in the same region that do not follow the school-expected patterns of bookreading and reinforcement of these patterns in oral storytelling. Two assumptions underlie this paper and are treated in detail in the ethnography of these communities (Heath 1983): (1) Each community's ways of taking from the printed word and using this knowledge are interdependent with the ways children learn to talk in their social interactions with caregivers; (2) there is little or no validity to the time-honored dichotomy of "the literate tradition" and "the oral tradition." This paper suggests a frame of reference for both the community patterns and the paths of development children in different communities follow in their literacy orientations.

Mainstream school-oriented bookreading

Children growing up in mainstream communities are expected to develop habits and values that attest to their membership in a "literate society." Children learn certain customs, beliefs, and skills in early enculturation experiences with written materials: The bedtime story is a major literacy event that helps set patterns of behavior that reoccur repeatedly through the life of mainstream children and adults.

In both popular and scholarly literature, the bedtime story is widely accepted as a given – a natural way for parents to interact with their child at bedtime. Commercial publishing houses, television advertising, and children's magazines make much of this familiar ritual, and many of their sales pitches are based on the assumption that in spite of the intrusion of television into many patterns of interaction between parents and children, this ritual remains. Few parents are fully conscious of what bedtime storyreading means as preparation for the kinds of learning and displays of knowledge expected in school. Ninio & Bruner (1978), in their longitudinal study of one mainstream middle-class mother–infant dyad in joint picturebook reading, strongly suggest a universal role of bookreading in the achievement of labeling by children.

In a series of "reading cycles," mother and child alternate turns in a dialogue: The mother directs the child's attention to the book and/or asks what-questions and/or labels items on the page. The items to which the what-questions are directed and labels given are two-dimensional representations of three-dimensional objects, so that the child has to resolve the conflict between perceiving these as two-dimensional objects and as representations of a three-dimensional visual setting. The child does so "by assigning a privileged, autonomous status to pictures as visual objects" (1978:5). The arbitrariness of the picture, its decontextualization, and its existence as something that cannot be grasped and manipulated like its "real" counterparts are learned through the routines of structured interactional dialogue in which mother and child take turns playing a labeling game. In a "scaffolding" dialogue (cf. Cazden 1979), the mother points and asks "What is *x?*" and the child vocalizes and/or gives a nonverbal signal of attention. The mother then provides verbal feedback and a label. Before the age of 2, the child is socialized into the initiation–reply–evaluation sequences repeatedly described as the central structural feature of classroom lessons (e.g., Sinclair & Coulthard 1975; Griffin & Humphry 1978; Mehan 1979). Teachers ask their students questions to which the answers are prespecified in the mind of the teacher. Students respond, and teachers provide feedback, usually in the form of an evaluation. Training in ways of responding to this pattern begins very early in the labeling activities of mainstream parents and children.

Maintown ways

This patterning of "incipient literacy" (Scollon & Scollon 1979) is similar in many ways to that of the families of fifteen primary-level schoolteachers in

Maintown, a cluster of middle-class neighborhoods in a city of the piedmont Carolinas. These families (all of whom identify themselves as "typical," "middle-class," or "mainstream") had preschool children, and the mother in each family was either teaching in local public schools at the time of the study (early 1970s) or had taught in the academic year preceding participation in the study. Through a research dyad approach, using teacher-mothers as researchers with the ethnographer, the teacher-mothers audiorecorded their children's interactions in their primary network – mothers, fathers, grandparents, maids, siblings, and frequent visitors to the home. Children were expected to learn the following rules in literacy events in these nuclear households:

(1) As early as 6 months of age, children *give attention to books and information derived from books*. Their rooms contain bookcases and are decorated with murals, bedspreads, mobiles, and stuffed animals that represent characters found in books. Even when these characters have their origin in television programs, adults also provide books that either repeat or extend the characters' activities on television.

(2) Children, from the age of 6 months, *acknowledge questions about books*. Adults expand nonverbal responses and vocalizations from infants into fully formed grammatical sentences. When children begin to verbalize about the contents of books, adults extend their questions from simple requests for labels ("What's that?" "Who's that?") to ask about the attributes of these items ("What does the doggie say?" "What color is the ball?")

(3) From the time they start to talk, children *respond to conversational allusions to the content of books; they act as question-answerers who have a knowledge of books*. For example, a fuzzy black dog on the street is likened by an adult to Blackie in a child's book: "Look, there's a Blackie. Do you think *he's* looking for a boy?" Adults strive to maintain with children a running commentary on any event or object that can be book-related, thus modeling for them the extension of familiar items and events from books to new situational contexts.

(4) Beyond 2 years of age, children *use their knowledge of what books do to legitimate their departures from "truth."* Adults encourage and reward "book talk," even when it is not directly relevant to an ongoing conversation. Children are allowed to suspend reality, to tell stories that are not true, to ascribe fictionlike features to everyday objects.

(5) Preschool children *accept book and book-related activities as entertainment*. When preschoolers are "captive audiences" (e.g., waiting in a doctor's office, putting a toy together, or preparing for bed), adults reach for books. If there are no books present, they talk about other objects as

though they were pictures in books. For example, adults point to items and ask children to name, describe, and compare them to familiar objects in their environment. Adults often ask children to state their likes or dislikes, their view of events, etc. at the end of the captive-audience period. These affective questions often take place while the next activity is already under way (e.g., moving toward the doctor's office, putting the new toy away, or being tucked into bed), and adults do not insist on answers.

(6) Preschoolers *announce their own factual and fictive narratives* unless they are given in response to direct adult elicitation. Adults judge as most acceptable those narratives that open by orienting the listener to setting and main character. Narratives that are fictional are usually marked by formulaic openings, a particular prosody, or the borrowing of episodes in storybooks.

(7) When children are about 3 years old, adults discourage the highly interactive participative role in bookreading children have hitherto played and children *listen and wait as an audience.* No longer does either adult or child repeatedly break into the story with questions and comments. Instead, children must listen, store what they hear, and, on cue from the adult, answer a question. Thus children begin to formulate "practice" questions as they wait for the break and the expected formulaic questions from the adult. It is at this stage that children often choose to "read" to adults rather than be read to.

A pervasive pattern of all these features is the authority that books and book-related activities have in the lives of both the preschoolers and members of their primary network. Any initiation of a literacy event by a preschooler makes an interruption, an untruth, a diverting of attention from the matter at hand (whether it be an uneaten plate of food, a messy room, or an avoidance of going to bed) acceptable. Adults jump at openings their children give them for pursuing talk about books and reading.

In this study, writing was found to be somewhat less acceptable as an "anytime activity," since adults have rigid rules about times, places, and materials for writing. The only restrictions on bookreading concern taking good care of books: They should not be wet, torn, drawn on, or lost. In their talk to children about books and in their explanations of why they buy children's books, adults link school success to "learning to love books," "learning what books can do for you," and "learning to entertain yourself and to work independently." Many of the adults also openly expressed a fascination with children's books "nowadays." They generally judged them as more diverse, wide-ranging, challenging, and exciting than books they had as children.

The mainstream pattern

A close look at the way bedtime-story routines in Maintown taught children how to take meaning from books raises a heavy sense of the familiar in all of us who have acquired mainstream habits and values. Throughout a lifetime, any school-successful individual moves through the same processes described above thousands of times. Reading for comprehension involves an internal replaying of the same types of questions adults ask children about bedtime stories. We seek *what-explanations,* asking what the topic is, establishing it as predictable and recognizing it in new situational contexts by classifying and categorizing it in our minds with other phenomena. The what-explanation is replayed in learning to pick out topic sentences, write outlines, and answer standardized tests that ask for the correct titles to stories, and so on. In learning to read in school, children move through a sequence of skills designed to teach what-explanations. There is a tight linear order of instruction that recapitulates the bedtime-story pattern of breaking down the story into small bits of information and teaching children to handle sets of related skills in isolated sequential hierarchies.

In each individual reading episode in the primary years of schooling, children must move through what-explanations before they can provide *reason-explanations* or *affective commentaries.* Questions about why a particular event occurred or why a specific action was right or wrong come at the end of primary-level reading lessons, just as they come at the end of bedtime stories. Throughout the primary-grade levels, what-explanations predominate, reason-explanations come with increasing frequency in the upper grades, and affective comments most often come in the extra-credit portions of the reading workbook or at the end of the list of suggested activities in textbooks across grade levels. This sequence characterizes the total school career. Highschool freshmen who are judged poor in compositional and reading skills spend most of their time on what-explanations and practice in advanced versions of bedtime-story questions and answers. They are given little or no chance to use reason-giving explanations or assessments of the actions of stories. Reason-explanations result in configurational rather than hierarchical skills, are not predictable, and thus do not present content with a high degree of redundancy. Reason-giving explanations tend to rely on detailed knowledge of a specific domain. This detail is often unpredictable to teachers, and is not as highly valued as is knowledge that covers a particular area of knowledge with less detail but offers opportunity for extending the knowledge to larger and related concerns. For example, a primary-level student whose father owns a turkey farm may respond with reason-explanations to a story about a turkey. His knowledge is intensive and covers details perhaps not known to the teacher and not judged as relevant to the story. The knowledge is unpredictable and questions about it do not continue to repeat the common core of content knowledge of the story. Thus such configured knowledge is encouraged only for the "extras" of reading – an extra-credit oral report or a creative picture and story about turkeys. This kind of knowledge is allowed to be used once the hierarchical what-explanations have been mastered and displayed in a particular situation and, in the course of one's academic career, only when one has shown full mastery of the hierarchical skills and subsets of related skills that underlie what-explanations. Thus reliable and successful participation in the ways of taking from books that teachers view as natural must, in the usual school way of doing things, precede other ways of taking from books.

These various ways of taking are sometimes referred to as "cognitive styles" or "learning styles." It is generally accepted in the research literature that they are influenced by early socialization experiences and correlated with such features of the society in which the child is reared as social organization, reliance on authority, male–female roles, and so on. These styles are often seen as two contrasting types, most frequently termed "field independent–field dependent" (Witkin et al. 1966) or "analytic–relational" (Kagan, Sigel & Moss 1963; Cohen 1968, 1969, 1971). The analytic/field-independent style is generally presented as that which correlates positively with high achievement and general academic and social success in school. Several studies discuss ways in which this style is played out in school – in preferred ways of responding to pictures and written text and selecting from among a choice of answers to test items.

Yet we know little about how behaviors associated with either of the dichotomized cognitive styles (field-dependent/relational and field-independent/analytic) were learned in early patterns of socialization. To be sure, there are vast individual differences that may cause an individual to behave so as to be categorized as having one or the other of these learning styles. But much of the literature on learning styles suggests that a preference for one or the other is learned in the social group in which the child is reared and in connection with other ways of behaving found in that culture. But how is a child socialized into an analytic/field-independent style? What kinds of interactions does he enter into with his parents and the stimuli of his environment that contribute to the development of such a style of learning? How do these interactions mold selective attention practices such as "sensitivity to parts of objects," "awareness of obscure, abstract, nonobvious features," and identification of "abstractions based on the features of items" (Cohen 1969:844–5)? Since the predominant stimuli used in school to judge the presence and extent of these selective attention practices are written materials, it is clear that the literacy orientation of preschool children is central to these questions.

The foregoing descriptions of how Maintown parents socialize their children into a literacy orientation fit closely those provided by Scollon & Scollon for their own child, Rachel. Through similar practices, Rachel was "literate before she learned to read'' (1979:6). She knew, before the age of 2, how to focus on a book and not on herself. Even when she told a story about herself, she moved herself out of the text and saw herself as author, as someone different from the central character of her story. She learned to pay close attention to the parts of objects. to name them, and to provide a running commentary on features of her environment. She learned to manipulate the contexts of items, her own activities, and language to achieve booklike, decontextualized, repeatable effects (such as puns). Many references in her talk were from written sources; others were modeled on stories and questions about these stories. The substance of her knowledge, as well as her ways of framing knowledge orally, derived from her familiarity with books and book-reading. No doubt this development began by labeling in the dialogue cycles of reading (Ninio & Bruner 1978), and it will continue for Rachel in her preschool years along many of the same patterns described by Cochran Smith (1984) for a mainstream nursery school. There teacher and students negotiated storyreading through the scaffolding of teachers' questions and running commentaries that replayed the structure and sequence of storyreading learned in their mainstream homes.

Close analyses of how mainstream school-oriented children come to learn to take from books at home suggest that such children learn not only how to take meaning from books, but also how to talk about it. In doing the latter, they repeatedly practice routines that parallel those of classroom interaction. By the time they enter school, they have had continuous experience as information givers; they have learned how to perform in those interactions that surround literate sources throughout school. They have had years of practice in interaction situations that are the heart of reading – both learning to read and reading to learn in school. They have developed habits of performing that enable them to run through the hierarchy of preferred knowledge about a literate source and the appropriate sequence of skills to be displayed in showing knowledge of a subject. They have developed ways of decontextualizing and surrounding with explanatory prose the knowledge gained from selective attention to objects.

They have learned to listen, waiting for the appropriate cue that signals it is their turn to show off this knowledge. They have learned the rules for getting certain services from parents (or teachers) in the reading interaction (Merritt 1979). In nursery school, they continue to practice these interaction patterns in a group rather than in a dyadic situation. There they learn additional signals and behaviors necessary for getting a turn in a group and for responding to a central reader and to a set of centrally defined reading tasks. In short, most of their waking hours during the preschool years have enculturated them into: (1) all those habits associated with what-explanations, (2) selective attention to items of the written text, *and* (3) appropriate interactional styles for orally displaying all the know-how of their literate orientation to the environment.

This learning has been finely tuned and its habits are highly interdependent. Patterns of behaviors learned in one setting or at one stage reappear again and again as these children learn to use oral and written language in literacy events and to bring their knowledge to bear in school-acceptable ways.

Alternative patterns of literacy events

But what corresponds to the mainstream pattern of learning in communities that do not have this finely tuned, consistent, repetitive, and continuous pattern of training? Are there ways of behaving that achieve other social and cognitive aims in other sociocultural groups?

The data below are summarized from an ethnography of two communities – Roadville and Trackton – located only a few miles from Maintown's neighborhoods in the piedmont Carolinas. Roadville is a white working-class community of families steeped for four generations in the life of the textile mill. Trackton is a working-class black community whose older generations have been brought up on the land, either farming their own land or working for other landowners. However, in the past decade, they have found work in the textile mills. Children of both communities are unsuccessful in school; yet both communities place a high value on success in school, believing earnestly in the personal and vocational rewards school can bring and urging their children "to get ahead" by doing well in school. Both Roadville and Trackton are literate communities in the sense that the residents of each are able to read printed and written materials in their daily lives, and on occasion they produce written messages as part of the total pattern of communication in the community. In both communities, children go to school with certain expectancies of print and, in Trackton especially, children have a keen sense that reading is something one does to learn something one needs to know (Heath 1980). In both groups, residents turn from spoken to written uses of language and vice versa as the occasion demands, and the two modes of expression seem to supplement and reinforce each other. Nonetheless there are radical differences between the two communities in the ways in which children and adults interact in the preschool years; each of the two communities also differs from Maintown. Roadville and Trackton view children's learning of language from two radically different perspectives: In Trackton, children "learn to talk"; in Roadville, adults "teach them how to talk."

Roadville

In Roadville, babies are brought home from the hospital to rooms decorated with colorful, mechanical, musical, and literacy-based stimuli. The walls are decorated with pictures based on nursery rhymes, and from an early age children are held and prompted to "see" the wall decorations. Adults recite nursery rhymes as they twirl the mobile made of nursery-rhyme characters. The items of the child's environment promote exploration of colors, shapes, and textures: A stuffed ball with sections of fabrics of different colors and textures is in the crib; stuffed animals vary in texture, size, and shape. Neighbors, friends from church, and relatives come to visit and talk to the baby and about him to those who will listen. The baby is fictionalized in the talk to him: "But this baby wants to go to sleep, doesn't he? Yes, see those little eyes gettin' heavy." As the child grows older, adults pounce on wordlike sounds and turn them into "words," repeating the "words," and expanding them into well-formed sentences. Before they can talk, children are introduced to visitors and prompted to provide all the expected politeness formulas, such as "Bye, bye," "Thank you," and so forth. As soon as they can talk, children are reminded about these formulas, and book or television characters known to be "polite" are involved as reinforcement.

In each Roadville home, preschoolers first have cloth books, featuring a single object on each page. They later acquire books that provide sounds, smells, and different textures or opportunities for practicing small motor skills (closing zippers, buttoning buttons, etc.). A typical collection for a 2-year-old consisted of a dozen or so books – eight featured either the alphabet or numbers; others were books of nursery rhymes, simplified Bible stories, or "real-life" stories about boys and girls (usually taking care of their pets or exploring a particular feature of their environment). Books based on Sesame Street characters were favorite gifts for 3- and 4-year-olds.

Reading and reading-related activities occur most frequently before naps or at bedtime in the evening. Occasionally an adult or older child will read to a fussy child while the mother prepares dinner or changes a bed. On weekends, fathers sometimes read with their children for brief periods of time, but they generally prefer to play games or play with the children's toys in their interactions. The following episode illustrates the language and social interactional aspects of these bedtime events; the episode takes place between Wendy (2;3 at the time of this episode) and Aunt Sue, who is putting her to bed.

[Aunt Sue (AS) picks up book, while Wendy crawls about the floor, ostensibly looking for something]

W: Uh uh

AS: Wendy, we're gonna read, uh, read this story, come on, hop up here on this bed.
    [Wendy climbs up on the bed, sits on top of the pillow, and picks up her teddy bear. Aunt Sue opens book, points to puppy]

AS: Do you remember what this book is about? See the puppy? What does the puppy do?
    [Wendy plays with the bear, glancing occasionally at pages of the book, as Aunt Sue turns. Wendy seems to be waiting for something in the book]

AS: See the puppy?
[Aunt Sue points to the puppy in the book and looks at Wendy to see if she is watching]
W: Uh huh, yea, yes ma'am
AS: Puppy sees the ant, he's a li'l [Wendy drops the bear and turns to book] fellow. Can you see that ant? Puppy has a little ball.
W: Ant bite puppy [Wendy points to ant, pushing hard on the book]
AS: No, the ant won't bite the puppy, the [turns page] puppy wants to play with the ant, see? [Wendy tries to turn the page back; AS won't let her, and Wendy starts to squirm and fuss]
AS: Look here, here's someone else, the puppy [Wendy climbs down off the bed and gets another book]
W: Read this one
AS: Okay, you get back up here now. [Wendy gets back on bed]
AS: This book is your ABC book. See the A, look, here, on your spread, there's an A. You find the A. [The second book is a cloth book, old and tattered, and long a favorite of Wendy's. It features an apple on the cover, and its front page has an ABC block and ball. Through the book, there is a single item on each page, with a large representation of the first letter of the word commonly used to name the item. As AS turns the page, Wendy begins to crawl about on her quilt, which shows ABC blocks interspersed with balls and apples. Wendy points to each of the A's on the blanket and begins talking to herself. AS reads the book, looks up, and sees Wendy pointing to the A's in her quilt]
AS: That's an A, can you find the A on your blanket?
W: There it is, this one, there's the hole too. [Pokes her finger through a place where the threads have broken in the quilting]
AS: [Points to ball in book] Stop that, find the ball, see, here's another ball.

This episode characterizes the early orientation of Roadville children to the written word. Bookreading time focuses on letters of the alphabet, numbers, names of basic items pictured in books, and simplified retellings of stories in the words of the adult. If the content or story plot seems too complicated for the child, the adult tells the story in short, simple sentences, frequently laced with requests that the child give what-explanations.

Wendy's favorite books are those with which she can participate; that is, those to which she can answer, provide labels, point to items, give animal sounds, and "read" the material back to anyone who will listen to her. She memorizes the passages and often knows when to turn the pages to show that she is "reading." She holds the book in her lap, starts at the beginning, and often reads the title – "Puppy."

Adults and children use either the title of the book (or phrases such as "the book about a puppy") to refer to reading material. When Wendy acquires a new book, adults introduce the book with phrases such as "This is a book about a duck, a little yellow duck. See the duck. Duck goes quack quack." On introducing a book, adults sometimes ask the child to recall when they have seen a real specimen of the one treated in the book: "Remember the duck on the College lake?" The child often shows no sign of linking the yellow fluffy duck in the book with the large brown and gray mallards on the lake, and the adult makes no effort to explain that two such disparate-looking objects go by the same name.

As Wendy grows older, she wants to "talk" during the stories and Bible stories, and carry out the participation she so enjoyed with the alphabet books. However, by the time she reaches 3½, Wendy is restrained from such wide-ranging participation. When she interrupts, she is told: "Wendy, stop that, you be quiet when someone is reading to you" or "You listen; now sit still and be quiet." Often Wendy will immediately get down and run away into the next room, saying "No, no." When this happens, her father goes to get her, pats her bottom, and puts her down hard on the sofa beside him. "Now you're gonna learn to listen." During the third and fourth years, this pattern occurs more and more frequently; only when Wendy can capture an aunt who does not visit often does she bring out the old books and participate with them. Otherwise, parents, Aunt Sue, and other adults insist that she be read a story and that she "listen" quietly.

When Wendy and her parents watch television, eat cereal, visit the grocery store, or go to church, adults point out and talk about many types of written material. On the way to the grocery, Wendy (3;8) sits in the back seat, and when her mother stops at a corner, Wendy says, "Stop." Her mother says, "Yes, that's a stop sign." Wendy has, however, misread a yield sign as a stop. Her mother offers no explanation of what the actual message on the sign is, yet when she comes to the sign she stops to yield to an oncoming car. Her mother, when asked why she had not given Wendy the word "yield," said it was too hard, Wendy would not understand, and "It's not a word we use like *stop*."

Wendy recognized animal-cracker boxes as early as 10 months, and later, as her mother began buying other varieties, Wendy would see the box in the grocery store and yell, "Cook cook." Her mother would say, "Yes, those are cookies. Does Wendy want a cookie?" One day Wendy saw a new type of cracker box, and screeched, "Cook cook." Her father opened the box and gave Wendy a cracker and waited for her reaction. She started the "cookie," then took it to her mother, saying, "You eat." The mother joined in the game and said, "Don't you want your *cookie?*" Wendy said, "No cookie. You eat." "But Wendy, it's a cookie box, see?" and her mother pointed to the C of "crackers" on the box. Wendy paid no attention and ran off into another room.

In Roadville's literacy events, the rules for cooperative discourse around print are repeatedly practiced, coached, and rewarded in the preschool years. Adults in Roadville believe that instilling in children the proper use of words and understanding of the meaning of the written word are important for both their educational and religious success. Adults repeat aspects of the learning of literacy events they have known as children. In the words of one Roadville parent, "It was then that I began to learn . . . when my daddy kept insisting I *read* it, *say* it right. It was then that I *did* right, in his view."

The path of development for such performance can be described in three overlapping stages. In the first, children are introduced to discrete bits and pieces of books – separate items, letters of the alphabet, shapes, colors, and commonly represented items in books for children (apple, baby, ball, etc.). The latter are usually decontextualized, and they are represented in two-dimensional, flat line drawings. During this stage, children must participate as predictable information givers and respond to questions that ask for specific and discrete bits of information about the written matter. In these literacy events, specific features of the two-dimensional items in books that are different from their real counterparts are not pointed out. A ball in a book is flat; a duck in a book is yellow and fluffy; trucks, cars, dogs, and trees talk in books. No mention is made of the fact that such features do not fit these objects in reality. Children are not encouraged to move their understanding of books into other situational contexts or to apply it in their general knowledge of the world about them.

In the second stage, adults demand an acceptance of the power of print to entertain, inform, and instruct. When Wendy could no longer participate by contributing her knowledge at any point in the literacy event, she learned to recognize bookreading as a performance. The adult exhibited the book to Wendy: She was to be entertained, to learn from the information conveyed in the material, and to remember the book's content for the sequential follow-up questioning, as opposed to ongoing cooperative, participatory questions.

In the third stage, Wendy was introduced to preschool workbooks that provided story information and was asked questions or provided exercises and games based on the content of the stories or pictures. Follow-the-number coloring books and preschool push-out-and-paste workbooks on shapes, colors, and letters of the alphabet reinforced repeatedly that the written word could be taken apart into small pieces and one item linked to another by following rules. She had practice in the linear, sequential nature of books: Begin at the beginning, stay in the lines for coloring, draw straight lines to link one item to another, write your answers on lines, keep your letters straight, match the cutout letter to diagrams of letter shapes.

The differences between Roadville and Maintown are substantial. Roadville adults do not extend either the content or the habits of literacy events beyond bookreading. They do not, upon seeing an item or event in the real world, remind children of a similar event in a book and launch a running commentary on similarities and differences. When a game is played or a chore done, adults do not use literate sources. Mothers cook without written recipes most of the time; if they use a recipe from a written source, they do so usually only after confirmation and alteration by friends who have tried the recipe. Directions to games are read, but not carefully followed, and they are not talked about in a series of questions and answers that try to establish their meaning. Instead, in the putting together of toys or the playing of games, the abilities or preferences of one party prevail. For example, if an adult knows how to put a toy together, he does so; he does not talk about the process, refer to the written material and "translate" for the child, or try to sequence steps so the child can do it.[3] Adults do not talk about the steps and procedures of how to do things; if a father wants his preschooler to learn to hold a miniature bat or throw a ball, he says, "Do it this way." He does not break up "this way" into such steps as "Put your fingers around here," "Keep your thumb in this position," "Never hold it above this line." Over and over again, adults do a task and children observe and try it, being reinforced only by commands such as "Do it like this" and "Watch that thumb."

Adults at tasks do not provide a running verbal commentary on what they are doing. They do not draw the attention of the child to specific features of the sequences of skills or the attributes of items. They do not ask questions of the child, except questions which are directive or scolding in nature ("Did you bring the ball?" "Didn't you hear what I said?"). Many of their commands contain idioms that are not explained: "Put it up" or "Put that away now" (meaning "Put it in the place where it usually belongs") or "Loosen up," said to a 4-year-old boy trying to learn to bat a ball. Explanations that move beyond the listing of names of items and their features are rarely offered by adults. Children do not ask questions of the type "But I don't understand? What is that?" They appear willing to keep trying, and if there is ambiguity in a set of commands, they ask a question such as "You want me to do this?" (demonstrating their current efforts), or they try to find a way of diverting attention from the task at hand.

Both boys and girls during their preschool years are included in many adult activities, ranging from going to church to fishing and camping. They spend a lot of time observing and asking for turns to try specific tasks, such as putting a worm on the hook or cutting cookies. Sometimes adults say, "No, you're not old enough." But if they agree to the child's attempt at the task, they watch and give directives and evaluations: "That's right, don't twist the cutter." "Turn like this." "Don't try to scrape it up now, let me do that." Talk about the task does not segment its skills and identify them, nor does it link the particular task or item at hand to other tasks. Reason-explanations such as "If you twist the cutter, the cookies will be rough on the edge" are rarely given – or asked for.

Neither Roadville adults nor children shift the context of items in their talk. They do not tell stories that fictionalize themselves or familiar events. They reject Sunday school materials that attempt to translate Biblical events into a modern-day setting. In Roadville, a story must be invited or announced by someone other than the storyteller, and only certain community members are designated good storytellers. A story is recognized by the group as a story about one and all. It is a true story, an actual event that happened to either the storyteller or someone else present. The marked behavior of the storyteller and audience alike is seen as exemplifying the weaknesses of all and the need for persistence in overcoming such weaknesses. The sources of stories are personal experience. They are tales of transgressions that make the point of reiterating the expected norms of behavior of man, woman, fisherman, worker, and Christian. They are true to the facts of the event.

Roadville parents provide their children with books; they read to them and ask questions about the books' contents. They choose books that emphasize nursery rhymes, alphabet learning, animals, and simplified Bible stories, and they require their children to repeat from these books and to answer formulaic questions about their contents. Roadville adults also ask questions about oral stories that have a point relevant to some marked behavior of a child. They use proverbs and summary statements to remind their children of stories and to call on them for simple comparisons of the stories' contents to their own situations. Roadville parents coach children in their telling of a story, forcing them to tell about an incident as it has been precomposed or pre-scripted in the head of the adult. Thus in Roadville children come to know a story as either an accounting from a book or a factual account of a real event in which some type of marked behavior occurred and there is a lesson to be learned. Any fictionalized account of a real event is viewed as a *lie;* reality is better than fiction. Roadville's church and community life admit no story other than that which meets the definition internal to the group. Thus children cannot decontextualize their knowledge or fictionalize events known to them and shift them about into other frames.

When these children go to school they perform well in the initial stages of each of the three early grades. They often know portions of the alphabet, some colors and numbers, and can recognize their names and tell someone their address and their parents' names. They will sit still and listen to a story, and they know how to answer questions asking for what-explanations. They do well in reading workbook exercises that ask for identification of specific portions of words, items from the story, or the linking of two items, letters, or parts of words on the same page. When the teacher reaches the end of storyreading or the reading circle and asks questions such as ''What did you like about the story?'' relatively few Roadville children answer. If asked questions such as ''What would you have done if you had been Billy [a story's main character]?'' Roadville children most frequently say, ''I don't know'' or shrug their shoulders.

Near the end of each year, and increasingly as they move through the early primary grades, Roadville children can handle successfully the initial stages of lessons. But when they move ahead to extra-credit items or to activities considered more advanced and requiring more independence, they are stumped. They turn frequently to teachers, asking, ''Do you want me to do this? What do I do here?'' If asked to write a creative story or tell it into a tape recorder, they retell stories from books; they do not create their own. They rarely provide emotional or personal commentary on their accounting of real events or book stories. They are rarely able to take knowledge learned in one context and shift it to another; they do not compare two items or events and point out similarities and differences. They find it difficult either to hold one feature of an event constant and shift all others or to hold all features constant but one. For example, they are puzzled by questions such as ''What would have happened if Billy had not told the policemen what happened?'' They do not know how to move events or items out of a given frame. To a question such as ''What habits of the Hopi Indians might they be able to take with them when they move to a city?'' they provide lists of features of life of the Hopi on the reservation. They do not take these items, consider their appropriateness in an urban setting, and evaluate the hypothesized outcome. In general, they find this type of question impossible to answer, and they do not know how to ask teachers to help them take apart the questions to figure out the answers. Thus their initial successes in reading, being good students, following orders, and adhering to school norms of participating in lessons begin to fall away rapidly about the time they enter the fourth grade. As the importance and frequency of questions and reading habits with which they are familiar decline in the higher grades, they have no way of keeping up or of seeking help in learning what it is they do not even know they don't know.

Trackton

Babies in Trackton come home from the hospital to an environment that is almost entirely human. There are no cribs, car beds, or carseats, and only an occasional highchair or infant seat. Infants are held during their waking hours, occasionally while they sleep, and they usually sleep in the bed with parents until they are about 2 years of age. They are held, their faces fondled, their cheeks pinched, and they eat and sleep in the midst of human talk and noise from the television, stereo, and radio. Encapsulated in an almost totally human world, they are in the midst of constant human communication, verbal and nonverbal. They literally feel the body signals of shifts in emotion of those who hold them almost continuously; they are talked about and kept in the midst of talk about topics that range over any subject. As children make cooing or babbling sounds, adults refer to this as ''noise,'' and no attempt is made to interpret these sounds as words or communicative attempts on the part of the baby. Adults believe they should not have to depend on their babies to tell them what they need or when they are uncomfortable; adults know, children only ''come to know.''

When a child can crawl and move about on his or her own, he or she plays with the household objects deemed safe for him or her – pot lids, spoons, plastic food containers. Only at Christmastime are there special toys for very young children; these are usually trucks, balls, doll babies, or plastic cars, but rarely blocks, puzzles, or books. As children become completely mobile, they demand ride toys or electronic and mechanical toys they see on television. They never request nor do they receive manipulative toys, such as puzzles, blocks, take-apart toys or literacy-based items, such as books or letter games.

Adults read newspapers, mail, calendars, circulars (political and civic-events-related), school materials sent home to parents, brochures advertising new cars, television sets, or other products, and the Bible and other church-related materials. There are no reading materials especially for children (with the exception of children's Sunday school materials), and adults do not sit and read to children. Since children are usually left to sleep whenever and wherever they fall asleep, there is no bedtime or naptime as such. At night, they are put to bed when adults go to bed or whenever the person holding them gets tired. Thus going to bed is not framed in any special routine. Sometimes in a play activity during the day an older sibling will read to a younger child, but the latter soon loses interest and squirms away to play. Older children often try to "play school" with younger children, reading to them from books and trying to ask questions about what they have read. Adults look on these efforts with amusement and do not try to persuade the small child to sit still and listen.

Signs from very young children of attention to the nonverbal behaviors of others are rewarded by extra fondling, laughter, and cuddling from adults. For example, when an infant shows signs of recognizing a family member's voice on the phone by bouncing up and down in the arms of the adult who is talking on the phone, adults comment on this to others present and kiss and nudge the child. Yet when children utter sounds or combinations of sounds that could be interpreted as words, adults pay no attention. Often by the time they are 12 months old, children approximate words or phrases of adults' speech; adults respond by laughing or giving special attention to the child and crediting him with "sounding like" the person being imitated. When children learn to walk and imitate the walk of members of the community, they are rewarded by comments on their activities: "He walks just like Toby when he's tuckered out."

Children between the ages of 12 and 24 months often imitate the tune or "general Gestalt" (Peters 1977) of complete utterances they hear around them. They pick up and repeat chunks (usually the ends) or phrasal and clausal utterances of speakers around them. They seem to remember fragments of speech and repeat these without active production. In this first stage of language learning, the *repetition* stage, they imitate the intonation contours and general shaping of the utterances they repeat. Lem (1;2) in the following example illustrates this pattern.

Mother [talking to neighbor on porch while Lem plays with a truck on the porch
nearby]: But they won't call back, won't happen=
Lem: =call back
Neighbor: Sam's going over there Saturday, he'll pick up a form=
Lem: =pick up on, pick up on [Lem here appears to have heard "form" as "on"]

The adults pay no attention to Lem's "talk," and their talk, in fact, often
overlaps his repetitions.

In the second stage, *repetition with variation,* Trackton children manipulate
pieces of conversation they pick up. They incorporate chunks of language
from others into their own ongoing dialogue, applying productive rules, inserting new nouns and verbs for those used in the adults' chunks. They also
play with rhyming patterns and varying intonation contours.

Mother: She went to the doctor again.
Lem (2;2): Went to de doctor, doctor, tractor, dis my tractor, [in a singsong fashion]
doctor on a tractor, went to de doctor.

Lem creates a monologue, incorporating the conversation about him into his
own talk as he plays. Adults pay no attention to his chatter unless it gets so
noisy as to interfere with their talk.

In the third stage, *participation,* children begin to enter the ongoing conversations about them. They do so by attracting the adult's attention with a tug on
the arm or pant leg, and they help make themselves understood by providing
nonverbal reinforcements to help recreate a scene they want the listener to
remember. For example, if adults are talking, and a child interrupts with
seemingly unintelligible utterances, the child will make gestures or extra
sounds, or act out some outstanding features of the scene he is trying to get the
adult to remember. Children try to create a context, a scene, for the understanding of their utterance.

This third stage illustrates a pattern in the children's response to their
environment and their ways of letting others know their knowledge of the
environment. Once they are in the third stage, their communicative efforts are
accepted by community members, and adults respond directly to the child
instead of talking to others about the child's activities as they have done in the
past. Children continue to practice for conversational participation by playing, when alone, both parts of dialogues, imitating gestures as well as intonation patterns of adults. By 2;6 all children in the community can imitate the
walk and talk of others in the community or of frequent visitors such as the
man who comes around to read the gas meters. They can feign anger, sadness,
fussing, remorse, silliness, or any of a wide range of expressive behaviors.
They often use the same chunks of language for varying effects, depending on
nonverbal support to give the language different meanings or cast it in a
different key (Hymes 1974b). Girls between 3 and 4 years of age take part in
extraordinarily complex stepping and clapping patterns and simple repetitions
of handclap games played by older girls. From the time they are old enough to

stand alone, they are encouraged in their participation by siblings and older children in the community. These games require anticipation and recognition of cues for upcoming behaviors, and the young girls learn to watch for these cues and to come in with the appropriate words and movements at the right time.

Preschool children are not asked for what-explanations of their environment. Instead, they are asked a preponderance of analogical questions that call for nonspecific comparisons of one item, event, or person with another: "What's that like?" Other types of questions ask for specific information known to the child but not the adults: "Where'd you get that from?" "What do you want?" "How come you did that?" (Heath 1982b). Adults explain their use of these types of questions by expressing their sense of children: They are "comers," coming into their learning by experiencing what knowing about things means. As one parent of a 2-year-old boy put it: "Ain't no use me tellin' 'im, 'Learn this, learn that, what's this, what's that?' He just gotta learn, gotta know; he see one thing one place one time, he know how it go, see sump'n like it again, maybe it be the same, maybe it won't." Children are expected to learn how to know when the form belies the meaning, and to know contexts of items and to use their understanding of these contexts to draw parallels between items and events. Parents do not believe they have a tutoring role in this learning; they provide the experiences on which the child draws and reward signs of their successfully coming to know.

Trackton children's early stories illustrate how they respond to adult views of them as "comers." The children learn to tell stories by drawing heavily on their abilities to render a context, to set a stage, and to call on the audience's power to join in the imaginative creation of story. Between the ages of 2 and 4 years, the children, in a monologue-like fashion, tell stories about things in their lives, events they see and hear, and situations in which they have been involved. They produce these spontaneously during play with other children or in the presence of adults. Sometimes they make an effort to attract the attention of listeners before they begin the story, but often they do not. Lem, playing off the edge of the porch, when he was about 2½ years of age, heard a bell in the distance. He stopped, looked at Nellie and Benjy, his older siblings, who were nearby, and said:

Way
Far
Now
It a churchbell
Ringin'
Dey singin'
Ringin'
You hear it?
I hear it
Far
Now.

Lem had been taken to church the previous Sunday and had been much impressed by the churchbell. He had sat on his mother's lap and joined in the singing, rocking to and fro on her lap, and clapping his hands. His story, which is like a poem in its imagery and linelike prosody, is in response to the current stimulus of a distant bell. As he tells the story, he sways back and forth.

This story, somewhat longer than those usually reported from other social groups for children as young as Lem,[4] has some features that have come to characterize fully developed narratives or stories. It recapitulates in its verbal outline the sequence of events being recalled by the storyteller. At church, the bell rang while the people sang. In the line "It a churchbell," Lem provides his story's topic and a brief summary of what is to come. This line serves a function similar to the formulas often used by older children to open a story: "This is a story about (a church bell)." Lem gives only the slightest hint of story setting or orientation to the listener; where and when the story took place are capsuled in "Way / Far." Preschoolers in Trackton almost never hear "Once upon a time there was a _____" stories, and they rarely provide definitive orientations for their stories. They seem to assume listeners "know" the situation in which the narrative takes place. Similarly, preschoolers in Trackton do not close off their stories with formulaic endings. Lem poetically balances his opening and closing in an *inclusio,* beginning "Way / Far / Now" and ending "Far / Now." The effect is one of closure, but there is no clearcut announcement of closure. Throughout the presentation of action and result of action in their stories, Trackton preschoolers invite the audience to respond or evaluate the story's actions. Lem asks, "You hear it?" which may refer either to the current stimulus or to yesterday's bell, since Lem does not productively use past tense endings for any verbs at this stage in his language development.

Preschool storytellers have several ways of inviting audience evaluation and interest. They may themselves express an emotional response to the story's actions; they may have another character or narrator in the story do so, often using alliterative language play; or they may detail actions and results through direct discourse or sound effects and gestures. All these methods of calling attention to the story and its telling distinguish the speech event as a story, an occasion for audience and story teller to interact pleasantly and not simply to hear an ordinary recounting of events or actions.

Trackton children must be aggressive in inserting their stories into an ongoing stream of discourse. Storytelling is highly competitive. Everyone in a conversation may want to tell a story, so only the most aggressive wins out. The content ranges widely, and there is "truth" only in the universals of human experience. Fact is often hard to find, though it is usually the seed of the story. Trackton stories often have no point – no obvious beginning or ending; they go on as long as the audience enjoys and tolerates the storyteller's entertainment.

Trackton adults do not separate out the elements of the environment around their children to tune their attentions selectively. They do not simplify their language, focus on single-word utterances by young children, label items or features of objects in either books or the environment at large. Instead, children are continuously contextualized, presented with almost continuous communication. From this ongoing, multiple-channeled stream of stimuli, they must themselves select, practice, and determine rules of production and structuring. For language, they do so by first repeating, catching chunks of sounds and intonation contours, and practicing these without specific reinforcement or evaluation. But practice material and models are continuously available. Next, the children seem to begin to sort out the productive rules for the speech and practice what they hear about them with variation. Finally, they work their way into conversations, hooking their meanings for listeners into a familiar context by recreating scenes through gestures, special sound effects, and so on. These characteristics continue in their story-poems and their participation in jump-rope rhymes. Because adults do not select out, name, and describe features of the environment for the young, children must perceive situations, determine how units of the situations are related to each other, recognize these relations in other situations, and reason through what it will take to show their correlation of one situation with another. The children can answer questions such as ''What's that like?'' (''It's like Doug's car''), but they can rarely name the specific feature or features that make two items or events alike. For example, in saying a car seen on the street is ''like Doug's car,'' a child may be basing the analogy on the fact that this car has a flat tire and Doug's also had one last week. But the child does not name (and is not asked to name) what is alike between the two cars.

Children seem to develop connections between situations or items not by specification of labels and features in the situations but by configuration links. Recognition of similar general shapes or patterns of links seen in one situation and connected to another seems to be the means by which children set scenes in their nonverbal representations of individuals, and later of their verbal chunking, and then their segmentation and production of rules for putting together isolated units. They do not decontextualize; instead they heavily contextualize nonverbal and verbal language. They fictionalize their ''true stories,'' but they do so by asking the audience to identify with the story through making parallels from their own experiences. When adults read, they often do so in a group. One person, reading aloud, for example, from a brochure on a new car decodes the text and displays illustrations and photographs, and listeners relate the text's meaning to their experiences, asking questions and expressing opinions. Finally, the group as a whole synthesizes the written text and the negotiated oral discourse to construct a meaning for the brochure (Heath 1982a).

When Trackton children go to school, they face unfamiliar types of questions that ask for what-explanations. They are asked as individuals to identify items by name and to label features such as shape, color, size, number. The stimuli to which they are to give these responses are two-dimensional flat representations that are often highly stylized and bear little resemblance to the real items. Trackton children generally score in the lowest percentile range on the Metropolitan Reading Readiness tests. They do not sit at their desks and complete reading workbook pages; neither do they tolerate questions about reading materials that are structured in the usual lesson format. Their contributions are in the form of "I had a duck at my house one time"; "Why'd he do that?" or they imitate the sound effects teachers may produce in stories they read to the children. By the end of the first three primary grades, their general language-arts scores have been consistently low, except for those few who have begun to adapt to and adopt some of the behaviors they have had to learn in school. But the majority not only fail to learn the content of lessons, but also do not adopt the social-interactional rules for school literacy events. Print in isolation bears little authority in their world. The kinds of questions asked about reading books are unfamiliar. The children's abilities to link metaphorically two events or situations and to recreate scenes are not tapped in the school; in fact, *these abilities often cause difficulties,* because they enable children to see parallels teachers did not intend and, indeed, may not recognize until the children point them out (Heath 1978).

By the end of the lessons or by the time in their total school career when reason-explanations and affective statements call for the creative comparison of two or more situations, it is too late for many Trackton children. They have not picked up along the way the composition and comprehension skills they need to translate their analogical skills into a channel teachers can accept. They seem not to know how to take meaning from reading; they do not observe the rules of linearity in writing, and their expression of themselves on paper is very limited. Taped oral stories are often much better, but these rarely count as much as written compositions. Thus Trackton children continue to collect very low or failing grades, and many decide by the end of the sixth grade to stop trying and turn their attention to the heavy peer socialization that usually begins in these years.

From community to classroom

A recent review of trends in research on learning pointed out that "learning to read through using and learning from language has been less systematically studied than the decoding process" (Glaser 1979:7). Put another way, how children learn to use language to read to learn has been less systematically studied than decoding skills. Learning how to take meaning from writing before one learns to read involves repeated practice in using and learning from language through appropriate participation in literacy events such as exhibitor/questioner and spectator/respondent dyads (Scollon & Scollon 1979) or group negotiation of the meaning of a written text. Children have to learn to select, hold, and retrieve content from books and other written or printed texts in accordance with their community's rules or "ways of taking," and the children's learning follows community paths of language socialization. In each society, certain kinds of childhood participation in literacy events may precede others, as the developmental sequence builds toward the whole complex of home and community behaviors characteristic of the society. The ways of taking employed in the school may in turn build directly on the preschool development, may require substantial adaptation on the part of the children, or may even run directly counter to aspects of the community's pattern.

At home. In *Maintown* homes, the construction of knowledge in the earliest preschool years depends in large part on labeling procedures and what-explanations. Maintown families, like other mainstream families, continue this kind of classification and knowledge construction throughout the child's environment and into the school years, calling it into play in response to new items in the environment and in running commentaries on old items as they compare to new ones. This pattern of linking old and new knowledge is reinforced in narrative tales that fictionalize the teller's events or recapitulate a story from a book. Thus for these children the bedtime story is simply an early link in a long chain of interrelated patterns of taking meaning from the environment. Moreover, along this chain the focus is on the individual as respondent and cooperative negotiator of meaning from books. In particular, children learn that written language may represent not only descriptions of real events, but decontextualized logical propositions, and the occurrence of this kind of information in print or in writing legitimates a response in which one brings to the interpretation of written text selected knowledge from the real world. Moreover, readers must recognize how certain types of questions assert the priority of meanings in the written word over reality. The "real" comes into play only after prescribed decontextualized meanings; affective responses and reason-explanations follow conventional presuppositions that stand behind what-explanations.

Roadville also provides labels, features, and what-explanations, and prescribes listening and performing behaviors for preschoolers. However, Roadville adults do not carry on or sustain in continually overlapping and interdependent fashion the linking of ways of taking meaning from books to ways of relating that knowledge to other aspects of the environment. They do not encourage decontextualization; in fact, they proscribe it in their own stories about themselves and their requirements of stories from children. They do not themselves make analytic statements or assert universal truths, except those related to their religious faith. They lace their stories with synthetic (nonanalytic) statements that express, describe, and synthesize real-life materials. Things do not have to follow logically so long as they fit the past experience of individuals in the community. Thus children learn to look for a specific moral in stories and to expect that story to fit their facts of reality explicitly. When they themselves recount an event, they do the same, constructing the story of a real event according to coaching by adults who want to construct the story as they saw it.

Trackton is like neither Maintown nor Roadville. There are no bedtime stories; in fact, there are few occasions for reading to or with children specifically. Instead, during the time these activities would take place in mainstream and Roadville homes, Trackton children are enveloped in different kinds of social interactions. They are held, fed, talked about, and rewarded for nonverbal, and later verbal, renderings of events they witness. Trackton adults value and respond favorably when children show they have come to know how to use language to show correspondence in function, style, configuration, and positioning between two different things or situations. Analogical questions are asked of Trackton children, although the implicit questions of structure and function these embody are never made explicit. Children do not have labels or names of attributes of items and events pointed out for them, and they are asked for reason-explanations, not what-explanations. Individuals express their personal responses and recreate corresponding situations with often only a minimal adherence to the germ of truth of a story. Children come to recognize similarities of patterning, though they do not name lines, points, or items that are similar between two items or situations. They are familiar with group literacy events in which several community members orally negotiate the meaning of a written text.

At school. In the early reading stages, and in later requirements for reading to learn at more advanced stages, children from the three communities respond differently, because they have learned different methods and degrees of taking from books. In contrast to Maintown children, Roadville children's habits learned in bookreading and toy-related episodes have not continued for them through other activities and types of reinforcement in their environment. They have had less exposure to both the content of books and ways of learning from books than have mainstream children. Thus their need in schools is not necessarily for an intensification of presentation of labels, a slowing down of the sequence of introducing what-explanations in connection with bookreading. Instead they need *extension of these habits to other domains* and to opportunities for practicing habits such as producing running commentaries, creating exhibitor/questioner and spectator/respondent roles, etc. Perhaps, most important, Roadville children need to have articulated for them *distinctions in discourse strategies and structures*. Narratives of real events have certain strategies and structures; imaginary tales, flights of fancy, and affective expressions have others. Their community's view of narrative discourse style is very narrow and demands a passive role in both creation of and response to the account of events. Moreover, these children have *to be reintroduced to a participant frame of reference to a book.* Though initially they were participants in bookreading, they have been trained into passive roles since the age of 3 years, and they must learn once again to be active information givers, taking from books and linking that knowledge to other aspects of their environment.

Trackton students present an additional set of alternatives for procedures in the early primary grades. Since they usually have few of the expected ''natural'' skills of taking meaning from books, they must not only learn these but also *retain their analogical reasoning practices* for use in some of the later stages of learning to read. They must *learn to adapt the creativity in language, metaphor, fictionalization, recreation of scenes, and exploration of functions and settings of items they bring to school.* These children already use narrative skills highly rewarded in the upper primary grades. They distinguish a fictionalized story from a real-life narrative. They know that telling a story can be in many ways related to play; it suspends reality and frames an old event in a new context; it calls on audience participation to recognize the setting and participants. They must now *learn as individuals to recount factual events in a straightforward way* and *recognize appropriate occasions for reason-explanations and affective expressions.* Trackton children seem to have skipped learning to label, list features, and give what-explanations. Thus they need to *have the mainstream or school habits presented in familiar activities with explanations related to their own habits of taking meaning* from the environment. Such ''simple,'' ''natural'' things as distinctions between two-dimensional and three-dimensional objects may need to be explained to help Trackton children learn the stylization and decontextualization that characterize books.

To lay out in more specific detail how Roadville's and Trackton's ways of knowing can be used along with those of mainstreamers goes beyond the scope of this paper. However, it must be admitted that a range of alternatives to ways of learning and displaying knowledge characterizes all highly school-successful adults in the advanced stages of their careers. Knowing more about how these alternatives are learned at early ages in different sociocultural conditions can help the schools to provide opportunities for all students to avail themselves of these alternatives early in their school careers. For example, mainstream children can benefit from early exposure to Trackton's creative, highly analogical styles of telling stories and giving explanations, and they can add the Roadville true story with strict chronicity and explicit moral to their repertoire of narrative types.

In conclusion, if we want to understand the place of literacy in human societies and ways children acquire the literacy orientations of their communities, we must recognize two postulates of literacy and language development:

(1) Strict dichotomization between oral and literate traditions is a construct of researchers, not an accurate portrayal of reality across cultures.
(2) A unilinear model of development in the acquisition of language structures and uses cannot adequately account for culturally diverse ways of acquiring knowledge or developing cognitive styles.

Roadville and Trackton tell us that the mainstream type of literacy orientation is not the only type even among Western societies. They also tell us that the mainstream ways of acquiring communicative competence do not offer a universally applicable model of development. They offer proof of Hymes's assertion a decade ago that "it is impossible to generalize validly about 'oral' vs. 'literate' cultures as uniform types" (1974a:54).

Yet in spite of such warnings and analyses of the uses and functions of writing in the specific proposals for comparative development and organization of cultural systems (cf. Basso 1974:432), the majority of research on literacy has focused on differences in class, amount of education, and level of civilization among groups having different literacy characteristics.

"We need, in short, a great deal of ethnography" (Hymes 1973:57) to provide descriptions of the ways different social groups "take" knowledge from the environment. For written sources, these ways of taking may be analyzed in terms of *types of literacy events,* such as group negotiation of meaning from written texts, individual "looking things up" in reference books, writing family records in Bibles, and the dozens of other types of occasions when books or other written materials are integral to interpretation in an interaction. These must in turn be analyzed in terms of the specific *features of literacy events,* such as labeling, what-explanation, affective comments, reason-explanations, and many other possibilities. Literacy events must also be interpreted in relation to the *larger sociocultural patterns* that they may exemplify or reflect. For example, ethnography must describe literacy events in their sociocultural contexts, so we may come to understand how such patterns as time and space usage, caregiving roles, and age and sex segregation are interdependent with the types and features of literacy events a community develops. It is only on the basis of such thoroughgoing ethnography that further progress is possible toward understanding cross-cultural patterns of oral and written language uses and paths of development of communicative competence.

Notes

1   First presented at the Terman Conference on Teaching at Stanford University, 1980, this paper has benefited from cooperation with M. Cochran Smith of the

University of Pennsylvania. She shares an appreciation of the relevance of Roland Barthes's work for studies of the socialization of young children into literacy; her research (1984) on the storyreading practices of a mainstream school-oriented nursery school provides a much-needed detailed account of early school orientation to literacy.

2 Terms such as *mainstream* and *middle-class* are frequently used in both popular and scholarly writings without careful definition. Moreover, numerous studies of behavioral phenomena (for example, mother–child interactions in language learning) either do not specify that the subjects being described are drawn from mainstream groups or do not recognize the importance of this limitation. As a result, findings from this group are often regarded as universal. For a discussion of this problem, see Chanan & Gilchrist 1974; Payne & Bennett 1977. In general, the literature characterizes this group as school-oriented, aspiring toward upward mobility through formal institutions, and providing enculturation that positively values routines of promptness, linearity (in habits ranging from furniture arrangement to entrance into a movie theatre), and evaluative and judgmental responses to behaviors that deviate from their norms. In the United States, mainstream families tend to locate in neighborhoods and suburbs around cities. Their social interactions center not in their immediate neighborhoods but in voluntary associations across the city. Thus a cluster of mainstream families (and not a community – which usually implies a specific geographic territory as the locus of a majority of social interactions) is the unit of comparison used here with the Trackton and Roadville communities.

3 Behind this discussion are findings from cross-cultural psychologists who have studied the links between verbalization of task and demonstration of skills in a hierarchical sequence, e.g., Childs & Greenfield 1980. See Goody 1979 on the use of questions in learning tasks unrelated to a familiarity with books.

4 Cf. Umiker-Sebeok's (1979) descriptions of stories of mainstream middle-class children, ages 3–5, and Sutton-Smith 1981.

References

Basso, K. 1974. The ethnography of writing. In R. Bauman & J. Sherzer, eds., *Explorations in the ethnography of speaking*. Cambridge: Cambridge University Press, pp. 425–432.

Cazden, C. B. 1979. Peekaboo as an instructional model: discourse development at home and at school. *Stanford Papers and Reports in Child Language Development* 17:1–29.

Chanan, G. & Gilchrist, L. 1974. *What school is for*. New York: Praeger.

Childs, C. P. & Greenfield, P. M. 1980. Informal modes of learning and teaching. In N. Warren, ed., *Advances in cross-cultural psychology*, vol. 2. London: Academic Press, pp. 269–316.

Cochran Smith, M. 1984. *The making of a reader*. Norwood, N.J.: Ablex.

Cohen, R. 1968. The relation between socio-conceptual styles and orientation to school requirements. *Sociology of Education* 41:201–220.

1969. Conceptual styles, culture conflict, and nonverbal tests of intelligence. *American Anthropologist* 71, 5:828–856.

1971. The influence of conceptual rule-sets on measures of learning ability. In C. L. Brace, G. Gamble, & J. Bond, eds., *Race and intelligence*. Anthropological Studies, no. 8. Washington, D.C.: American Anthropological Association, pp. 41–57.

Glaser, R. 1979. Trends and research questions in psychological research on learning and schooling. *Educational Researcher* 8, 10:6–13.

Goody, E. 1979. Towards a theory of questions. In E. N. Goody, ed., *Questions and politeness: strategies in social interaction.* Cambridge: Cambridge University Press, pp. 17–43.

Griffin, P. & Humphry, F. 1978. Task and talk. In *The study of children's functional language and education in the early years.* Final report to the Carnegie Corporation of New York. Arlington, Va.: Center for Applied Linguistics.

Heath, S. 1978. *Teacher talk: language in the classroom.* Language in Education 9. Arlington, Va.: Center for Applied Linguistics.

1980. The functions and uses of literacy. *Journal of Communication* 30, 1:123–33.

1982a. Protean shapes: ever-shifting oral and literate traditions. In Deborah Tannen, ed., *Spoken and written language: exploring orality and literacy.* Norwood, N.J.: Ablex, pp. 91–118.

1982b. Questioning at home and at school: a comparative study. In George Spindler (ed.), *Doing ethnography: educational anthropology in action.* New York: Holt, Rinehart & Winston, pp. 102–131.

1983. *Ways with words: language, life and work in communities and classrooms.* Cambridge: Cambridge University Press.

Howard, R. 1974. A note on S/Z. In R. Barthes, *Introduction to S/Z,* trans. Richard Miller. New York: Hill & Wang, pp. ix–xi.

Hymes, D. H. 1974a. Speech and language: on the origins and foundations of inequality among speakers. In E. Haugen & M. Bloomfield, eds., *Language as a human problem.* New York: Norton, pp. 45–71.

1974b. Models of the interaction of language and social life. In J. J. Gumperz & D. Hymes, eds., *Directions in sociolinguistics.* New York: Holt, Rinehart & Winston, pp. 35–71.

Kagan, J., Sigel, I., & Moss, H. 1963. Psychological significance of styles of conceptualization. In J. Wright & J. Kagan, eds., *Basic cognitive processes in children.* Monographs of the Society for Research in Child Development 28, 2:73–112.

Mehan, H. 1979. *Learning lessons.* Cambridge: Harvard University Press.

Merritt, M. 1979. Service-like events during individual work time and their contribution to the nature of the rules for communication. NIE Report EP 78-0436.

Ninio, A. & Bruner. J. 1978. The achievement and antecedents of labelling. *Journal of Child Language* 5:1–15.

Payne, C. & Bennett, C. 1977. "Middle class aura" in public schools. *Teacher Educator* 13, 1:16–26.

Peters, A. 1977. Language learning strategies. *Language* 53:560–573.

Scollon, R. & Scollon, S. 1979. *The literate two-year-old: the fictionalization of self.* Working Papers in Sociolinguistics. Austin: Southwest Regional Laboratory.

Sinclair, J. M. & Coulthard, R. M. 1975. *Toward an analysis of discourse.* New York: Oxford University Press.

Sutton-Smith, B. 1981. *The folkstories of children.* Philadelphia: University of Pennsylvania Press.

Umiker-Sebeok, J. D. 1979. Preschool children's intraconversational narratives. *Journal of Child Language* 6, 1:91–110.

Witkin, H., Faterson, F., Goodenough, R., & Birnbaum, J. 1966. Cognitive patterning in mildly retarded boys. *Child Development* 37, 2:301–316.

Part II

Acquiring knowledge of status and role through language use

6. Social norms and lexical acquisition: a study of deictic verbs in Samoan child language

MARTHA PLATT

Introduction

This study documents the spontaneous[1] use of two deictic verbs, *sau* 'to come' and *'aumai* 'to bring/give', in the speech of young Samoan children. A major goal of this account is to demonstrate that patterns in young children's language production must be assessed not only in terms of grammatical properties, but also in terms of pragmatic properties as evidenced in spontaneous speech. Deictic verbs are viewed here from two perspectives: as forms that refer to or indicate certain semantic relationships between persons and objects in the speech context and as forms that, when used in a particular context, constitute (wholly or partially) social acts interpreted in particular ways by the speech community.

Previous developmental studies of deictic verbs (e.g., E. V. Clark 1978; Gathercole 1978; Keller-Cohen 1973; Macrae 1976; Richards 1976; Tanz 1980) have discussed the function of deictic verbs in English (specifically, "come," "go," "bring," and "take") in indicating movement relative to persons and objects in the situation of utterance. These analyses view speaker and addressee as having certain semantic roles specified by the utterance, e.g., actor, agent, goal, recipient. The present account focuses not only on the spatial relationships between participants, but also on the social relationships between participants in the situation of utterance and on how these relationships might affect the use of deictic verbs. Speaker and addressee are considered not only in terms of semantic roles, but also in terms of social identities, e.g., young child, sibling caregiver, mother, and the status associated with them in traditional Western Samoan society.

A central question in this analysis is how the young child's rank with respect to other participants in a given context affects how and how much the child uses particular deictic verbs. This issue is discussed in terms of the fact

127

that, for Samoan adults as well as children, the use of imperatives to summon others (using *sau* 'to come') is socially restricted, whereas the use of imperatives to demand or request goods (using *'aumai* 'to bring/give') is not. In particular, imperatives used to summon others are normally directed from high- to low-status persons or between peers. On the other hand, imperatives used to demand or request goods may be directed from low- to high-status persons as well as from high- to low-status individuals and between peers.

Methodology

Data collection on which this study is based was carried out from July 1978 to July 1979 as part of a larger project on Samoan child language (Ochs, in press). The research site was the village of Falefā, a traditional community located on Upolu Island in Western Samoa.

The present account draws on a longitudinal study of the language development of four children: Iakopo (boy, aged 2;1 at onset of study), Matu'u (girl, aged 2;1), Naomi (girl, aged 2;10), and Niulala (boy, aged 2;11). Language data were collected using audio- and videotaping procedures. Three of the children (Matu'u, Naomi, and Niulala) were recorded over a ten-month period and one child (Iakopo) was recorded over nine months. Recordings were made every four to five weeks for a total of three to four hours. For each recording session, a half-hour to one-hour video recording was made in addition to approximately two and one-half hours of audio recordings. The data for the present study are drawn primarily from the first, third, fifth, and seventh recording sessions.

All recordings were made within household compounds,[2] capturing each child interacting with familiar household members. Recordings took place during meals, play activities, and household tasks. Each child was visited in the family compound several times before taping began.

The transcription procedure used for this study involved the production of annotated transcripts of verbal interaction. This procedure followed closely that outlined in Schieffelin (1979:80–1). Transcriptions were made by family members or by neighbors acquainted with the families in the study. Transcribers were trained by one of the researchers to make an initial transcription. The utterances were later translated into English. The transcription and English glosses were then checked by the researcher who had made the recording. Sometimes transcriptions and the meaning of particular utterances were checked again with caregivers who participated in the interactions recorded. Transcriptions include not only a record of utterances and their translations, but also background information pertinent to a particular interaction where appropriate.

Examples drawn from the transcripts for use in documenting child and adult speech are identified in the following way: name of child with age at recording time in years and months in parentheses, session, cassette and side, and tape counter number. The session number is identified with a roman numeral (I, III, V, VII). The cassette number is 1, 2, 3, or 4, and the side number is either 1 or 2. The tape counter number is a three-digit number staring at 000. This number locates the initial utterance in the example on the tape itself and on the transcript. A sample of this identification system is: MATU'U (2;1) I-3(2)-057.

Two Samoan speech registers

Samoan-speakers generally make use of two distinct speaking styles. *Tautala lelei* 'good speech' is used in contexts closely associated with the Western cultural tradition (Shore 1982). It is used in the pastor's school, in the village school, in church hymns and sermons, in talking to foreigners, and in reading and writing. The phonological inventory of *tautala lelei* includes /t, k, n, ŋ/. *Tautala leaga* 'bad speech' is generally used in all other contexts. For example, it is used in casual speech between Samoans and in ceremonial gatherings of chiefs.[3] In *Tautala leaga* /t, k, n, ŋ/ are realized as [k, k, ŋ, ŋ], respectively. Thus, words that are phonetically distinct in *tautala lelei* are homophonous in *tautala leaga*. For example, /tia/ 'grave' and /kia/ 'gear' are both pronounced [kia] in *tautala leaga*. Similarly, /fana/ 'gun, to shoot' and /faŋa/ 'bay' are both pronounced [faŋa]. (These examples are from Duranti 1981:166.) The spontaneous data reproduced for this study primarily involve *tautala leaga,* since recordings were made of casual speech between household members. Following Samoan orthographic conventions, *g* is used in the examples to represent the velar nsala /ŋ/ (and ' is used to represent the glottal stop /ʔ/).

Ethnographic summary

This section is intended to provide a general ethnographic description of traditional Western Samoan communities, particularly as the socialization of children is concerned. For more details in this and other areas, the reader is referred to Duranti (1981), Kernan (1969), Mead (1930), Ochs (1982), and Shore (1982). Three topics are focused on in this section: (1) social status, (2) the organization of caregiving, and (3) exchange and redistribution of goods.

Social status

In traditional Western Samoan society, social status is based on a number of factors. Age, sex, generation, position in the church (e.g., pastor, deacon), whether or not one holds a chiefly title, and whether or not one is a government employee are the primary attributes on which status is based. Depending upon the context and the participants involved, a particular individual may at certain times have higher rank and at other times lower rank with respect to other participants (Shore 1982). For example, in non-church-related contexts, an untitled (male) adult typically has higher rank than a younger untitled man but lower rank than a titled man. In a church-related context (e.g., a meeting of the pastor and church deacons), the pastor, even though he has no chiefly title, has a higher rank than the deacons, who normally do have titles.

Within this hierarchical organization, particular types of behaviors are associated with particular social statuses. Samoan adults as well as children are expected to adopt the behavior appropriate to their rank in a particular situation. These behaviors vary along (primarily) two dimensions: (1) activity, and (2) awareness/involvement (Ochs 1982; Shore 1982).

The behavior of high-status individuals is characterized by relatively little physical activity and minimal awareness of or involvement in the activities of others in the immediate vicinity. Conversely, the behavior of low-status individuals is characterized by relatively greater physical activity and greater awareness of and involvement in the activities of others in the immediate vicinity. For example, untitled men (*taulele'a*) usually carry out the heavy work on the plantations, which entails a great deal of walking between the family compound and the plantation site. Chiefs and orators, on the other hand, are often found among other men of comparable rank performing a variety of relatively stationary activities (e.g., village meetings, drinking *kava*,[4] making rope from coconut fiber – Duranti 1981). Furthermore, untitled men tend to intervene directly in, for example, disputes, often on behalf of a titled member of their extended family (*'āiga*). Although the dispute itself may be between two titled persons, the public display of enmity or disagreement is usually evidenced by lower-ranking family members. In general, high-status individuals tend not to become involved in situations requiring intervention of some kind unless the urgency of the situation demands it.

During village meetings (*fono*), differences in the behavior of titled and untitled persons are also in evidence. Titled persons tend to remain seated while the untitled men carry out the active tasks such as making *kava*, serving food to the titled men, and running errands for them if requested to do so (Duranti 1981). The following excerpt from conversation preceding a *kava* ceremony illustrates this difference in activity between titled and untitled persons. This conversation was recorded by A. Duranti in April 1981.[5]

Example 1

[Three titled men (F, SA, and SM) have been talking about the previous week's church service. F calls his teenaged son, Malakai (M), to run an errand.]

   F: *Ma(la)kai!*
     Malakai
     (Malakai!)

F: *savali a'e   i   le– iā Kavai ma–*
   walk emph to art   to Kavai and
   (Walk over to the– to Kavai's house and–)
M: *'a ga   'ua savalivali mai?*
   foc that tns   walk   dx
   (There he is walking toward us.)
SM: *'a   Kavai gale*
   foc Kavai there
   (There's Kavai.)
F: *'oi!*
   oh
   (Oh!)
[Pause, 7.5 seconds]
   F: [To M] *sau!*
          come
          (Come!)
[Pause, 5.0 seconds]
   SA: [To M] *alu fai iā Iuli po'o iai   soga 'ava*
          go   say to Iuli interr there his   kava
          (Go ask Iuli whether he's got any kava.)

Differences in the behavior of high-status persons relative to low-status persons is evidenced in caregiving as well. This is discussed below.

The organization of caregiving

The distribution of caregiving responsibilities across several generations in traditional Samoan families has been documented by researchers such as Kernan (1969), Korbin (1978), and Mead (1928). One of the salient aspects of caregiving in this society is a heavy reliance on sibling caregivers (Weisner & Gallimore 1977). Observations of interaction in these types of situations indicate that high-status caregivers (e.g., mothers) tend to perform more stationary caregiving tasks and they tend not to become directly involved in the activities of young children. Low-status caregivers, on the other hand (e.g., the mother's younger siblings, the child's older siblings), tend to perform the more active caregiving tasks and they tend to be the ones to intervene directly in the activities of younger children when necessary (Ochs 1982). It is often the mother who summons sibling caregivers or young children, rather than vice versa. This is shown in Ex. 2.

Example 2
NIULALA (3;6) VII-1(2)-237
[Niulala is inside the house with his mother, Akenese (Ak), his mother's sister, Saufo'i (Sau), his older sister, Moana (Mo), his younger brother, Fineaso (F), and his younger sister, Sose (So), who has just begun to crawl. So is crawling away from Ak and toward the edge of the house.]

Ak: *Moana!* (3×) *sau   alu fai Saufo'i mai* [= 'aumai] *kama lāua*
Moana   come go say Saufo'i bring   child tns
alak [= alu aku]
go
(Moana, Moana, Moana come! Go tell Saufo'i to bring the baby, she's
crawling away from me.)
Ak: [To So; rapid, high]
Sose Sos Sos ( ) Sosa, sau   (5×)
Sose Sose Sose   Sose come
(Sose, Sose, Sose, Sose, come, come, come, come, come.)
Ak: [To F]
'aua fai kege [= keige], *'aua, ( ) ōmai 'ī,   ka'ika'i mai le lima*
don't do girl   don't   come here lead   dx   art hand
sou [= si 'ou]*kei*
your+affect little sister
(Don't bother the baby, don't! Come here [you two], take your sister's hand
and lead her over here.)
Ak: [To Mo]
kamo'e fai iā Saufo'i sau   amai kama lea Moana
run   say to Saufo'i come bring child this Moana
(Moana, hurry up, go tell Saufo'i to come and bring the baby over here.)

This example shows clearly the difference between the mother's stationary
role and the more active roles of her younger sister and children. The striking
aspect of this interaction is the fact that in terms of actual distance from the
baby and freedom of movement (that is, the mother is not engaged in some
other activity which prevents her from going after the baby), it is just as easy
for the mother to get the baby as it is for any of the others to do so.

Another example of verbal interaction between high-status (stationary) and
low-status (active) persons is one between the young child Matu'u and her
teenaged sister Mauga.

Example 3
MATU'U (2;2) II-1(2)-077
[Matu'u's older sister, Mauga (Mau), is sitting at the front edge of the house. Matu'u
is at the back of the house.]

Matu'u	*Others*
	Mau: *Matu'u sau*
	Matu'u come
	(Matu'u come here.)
	Maku'u sau
	Matu'u come
	(Matu'u come here.)
[Goes to Mau]	
	alu mai [= 'aumai] *sou 'ie*
	go bring your cloth
	(Go get a piece of cloth [for
	you].)
	alu amai le mea solo ai
	go bring art thing wipe copy pro

> *lou   isu*
> your nose
> (Go get it to wipe your nose.)
> Mau: *kamo'e, alu e   amai le*
>   hurry   go comp bring art
>
> *solosolo   'ua e   loa   'ua*
> handkerchief tns   tns know tns
>
> *e   loa* [= 'ua e iloa][6]
> tns know
> (Hurry, go get the handkerchief.)

[Gets piece of cloth from bed at back of
house]

These examples illustrate that tasks are not distributed simply on the basis of availability or ability to perform a particular task, but rather are carried out largely on the basis of what is viewed as appropriate behavior for persons of higher versus lower rank. (For further discussion, see Ochs 1982.)

Exchange and redistribution of goods

Reciprocity is a highly valued facet of social organization in traditional Samoan communities (Mead 1930; Shore 1982). Exchange and redistribution of goods is a crucial procedure for establishing and maintaining social relationships. On the village level, goods received are redistributed on the basis of a network of social obligations between individuals and between extended families. An equilibrium in the distribution of goods is viewed as essential for maintaining harmony in the village.

Redistribution of goods takes place in a variety of social contexts, ranging from very informal to very formal. For example, when a large number of ripe mangoes from a particular tree fell to the ground in a strong wind, I observed children from neighboring households gather to collect some for distribution to their families. This type of informal redistribution of surplus or unexpected goods is quite common. In fact, there is a great deal of social pressure to distribute surplus or unexpected goods. Samoans use the expression *'ai'ū* 'unwilling, selfish' (*'ai* 'eat' + *ū* 'hold fast, grip') to refer to someone's unwillingness to share food with others.

Goods are often exchanged and redistributed in more formal situations as well. For example, after a funeral service, when titled persons are gathered at the house of relatives of the deceased, goods such as fine mats (*'ie toga*) may be exchanged. In other situations, such as when a fine (often in the form of canned fish or boxes of crackers) is paid at a meeting of village chiefs, these goods are redistributed to the various chiefs to be consumed by their extended families at a later time.[7] This type of formal redistribution may also take place at church functions and other official gatherings.

A central feature of this distribution process across many types of situations is that every individual is entitled to a share, including the young child. On several occasions, I was able to observe food redistribution in a situation that involved young children. This was a weekly or bimonthly meeting of the women's committee of the Samoan Congregational Church (London Missionary Society), on whose land we were living. These women are responsible for maintaining the land surrounding the church and the pastor's house. After working several hours in the morning, the women gather to eat, rest, and discuss church business. This is a time when young children from different families and different parts of the village are together for several hours during which their mothers, aunts, grandmothers, and cousins carry out various tasks. One of these tasks is the distribution of food, either for immediate consumption or for later use. It is quite common for young children to be included in this process and even encouraged to make demands for food themselves. A child may also be instructed to carry out the active task of delivering shares of food to the various women present or to deliver a portion to someone who is not present. The child may also be directed to give part of his or her share to a younger sibling. Ex. 4 shows how one young child engages in this redistribution procedure.

Example 4

NAOMI (3;1) III-3(2)-350

[Naomi's aunt, Fiava'e (F), has called Naomi to come and slice a loaf of bread. Naomi cuts off a large chunk.]

Naomi		Others
[Slicing bread]		F: *tipi 'uma mea ma*
		cut all thing for
		*Taveta**
		Mareta
		(Cut it all for Mareta.)
		[*Naomi's name for researcher]
[Taps chunk of bread with knife, ⇒ F]	*tā'ua lea/*	
	we dual incl this	
	(This is for you and me.)	
		F: *'ioe*
		yes
		(Yes.)
[Slicing off another piece of bread]	*ia temeti* [= tamaiti] *lea/*	
	ok children this	
	(And this is for the children.)	

This seems to be an example of fantasy play by Naomi, in which she pretends to give pieces of bread to other children (none are present).

Redistribution or sharing of goods is also important between individuals, such as immediate family members within the household. This feature of social life is particularly important for the present study, since young children spend most of their time with extended family members in the household compound. One very common interaction observed in these settings is that of demanding or begging for a share of another's food item. Unlike summoning others (as in Exx. 1, 2, and 3), appeals for food can be directed from low- to high-status persons as well as from high- to low-status persons.

In interaction of this type, certain linguistic items that refer to the speaker often occur in utterances used to beg for objects. Milner (1978:220) characterizes these items as denoting "self-abasement together with an appeal for sympathy, love or help." I will focus here on three types, which are virtually always spoken in *tautala leaga* 'bad speech'. They are: (1) *se ka* (also *ska* and *ka*), (2) *ka'ika*, and (3) possessive modifiers having the form *loka/soka* and *laka/saka* in the singular, and *oka/gi oka* and *aka/gi aka* in the plural. (See Ochs this volume for further discussion of these forms.)

Exx. 5 and 6 illustrate the use of these expressions in appeals on the part of high-status persons to low-status persons.

Example 5

NIULALA (3;6) VII-2(1)-009 (video)
[Niulala is inside the house with his mother, Akenese (Ak), his younger brother, Fineaso (F), and another small child, To'oto'o (To'o). Ak is in the central room of the house. Niulala and To'o are in a side room.]

Niulala	*Others*
[Ak ⇒ To'o, arm extended toward To'o]	Ak: *ko'o mai* [= 'aumai] To'oto'o bring
	ska [= se ka] *masi,* ( ) *se* art+my+appeal cracker emph
	maiga ke a'u kago bring+nom to me touch
	vaelua divide in half (To'to'o bring me a cracker so I can divide it in half.)
[To'o gives cracker to Ak; Ak breaks off piece and gives rest to To'o]	
	(. . .)
[N comes out of side room]	
	Ak: *Niulala* Niulala (Niulala.)
uhh/	
	Ak: *sau mai sa'u masi* come bring my cracker (Come bring me a cracker.)
leai/ no (No.)	

Ak: *aisea*
why
(Why?)

laga   ke 'ai' ū/
because tns selfish
(Because I'm selfish.)

Ak: *ke 'ai' ū   iā a'u*
tns selfish to me
(Are you being selfish toward me?)

uhh/   F: [Laughs]
uhh

[N and F running around room]   Ak: *se   Niulala, ( ) Figeaso*
emph Niulala   Fineaso
(Please! Niulala, Fineaso!)

ei/
excl
(Hey!)

F: o!
Ak: *sau   la   'oe mai*
come now you give

ska   masi   e
art+my+appeal cracker emph
(Come here now and give me a
cracker.)

In this interaction, Akenese remains seated while the children move back and
forth between the side and center rooms.

Example 6

MATU'U (2;4) III-3(2)-150
[Matu'u is sitting with several older brothers, Se'emu (Se'e), Veni (V), and Gaiga (G).
She is eating a mango given to her by the researcher. Her brothers are begging for parts
of it.]

Matu'u   *Others*
[Eating mango skin]   Se'e: *mai* [= 'aumai] *se ka*
                                        give   art my+appeal

                                        ū   oi   Matu'u
                                        bite excl Matu'u
                                        (Give me a bite Matu'u.)
                          (. . .)
                                  V: *ska* [= se ka]   *ū,   mai   ma*
                                        art+my+appeal bite give for

                                        a'u legā faku mago
                                        me that seed mango
                                        (Give me a bite, give me that
                                        mango seed.)
                          (. . .)
[Gives piece of mango skin to V]

                                  ⌐ Se'e: / /mai ma a'u ga [= legā] faku
                                        give   for me that   seed

    mago
    mango
    (Give me the mango seed.)
G: / /*Tu'u mai ma ka'ika   le*
   Matu'u give for me+appeal art
   pa'u
   skin
   (Matu'u give me the skin.)

Matu'u eventually gives the partially eaten mango to another brother, Siota, who has not been present. Siota holds the mango for a few seconds and then gives it back to Matu'u when she extends her hand to him. She then finishes eating it and throws the seed away.

Exx. 7 and 8 show the use of *gi aka, ka,* and *ska* in appeals on the part of low-status persons to high-status persons.

Example 7

NIULALA (3;6) VII-1(2)-205
[Niulala's sister Moana (Mo) is trying to get a drink of water from the sink. She appeals to her mother for help.]
Mo: *mama mai* [= 'aumai] *gi   aka   vai ka   ke le au*
    mama give   some my+appeal water I+appeal tns neg reach
    (Mama, give me some water, I can't reach.)

Example 8

NAOMI (3;6) VII-1(2)-281
[Naomi is sitting at the edge of the house eating a coconut. Her brother, Aimalala (Ai), and mother, Matau'aina (M), are gathering coconut husks outside at the back of the compound. Naomi wants a spoon to scoop out the coconut meat. She calls to Ai several times but he doesn't respond.]
    alu Lala [= Aimalala] *mai* [= 'aumai] *ska* [= se ka]   *sipugi*/
    go Aimalala   bring   art+my+appeal spoon
    (Aimalala go get me a spoon.)
    ( ) *Lala   alu mai ska   sipugi*/
        Aimalala go bring art+my+appeal spoon
    (Aimalala go get me a spoon.)
    kae alu e   mai ska   sipugi/
    shit go comp bring art+my+appeal spoon
    (Shit, go get me a spoon!)
    se   alu mai ska   sipugi/
    emph go bring art+my+appeal spoon
    (Go get me a spoon!)
    ei/
    excl
    (Hey!)

The young child's appeals and demands for objects are discussed in more detail later in this chapter.

Summary

This section has focused on the hierarchical organization of Samoan society in which particular behaviors are associated with particular social statuses. These beliefs concerning appropriate behavior are evidenced in a variety of social contexts. In addition, this section has highlighted the traditional emphasis on reciprocity, which plays an important part in the early socialization of children. In particular, it has focused on the exchange and redistribution of goods between individuals and between extended families.

A semantic comparison of deictic verbs in English and Samoan

This section presents a comparison of the English verbs "come," "give," and "bring," and their Samoan counterparts *sau* 'to come' and *'aumai* 'to bring/give' in terms of their semantic properties. Table 6.1 specifies the major semantic features of the English and Samoan forms. This information indicates that "come" and *sau* are semantically less complex than "bring," "give," and *'aumai*. "Come" and *sau* are noncausative verbs, whereas "bring," "give," and *'aumai* are their respective causative counterparts. Furthermore, "come" and *sau* seem to be equivalent terms, whereas both "bring" and "give" are incorporated into the verb *'aumai*.

Differences in the use of "give" and "bring" on the one hand and *'aumai* on the other are shown in Table 6.2.

The situations in Table 6.2 differ in terms of the relative distance of speaker, addressee, and object. In Situation I, there is little distance between these three entities. The object is either in the addressee's possession or closer to the addressee than to the speaker. In a situation such as this, the English verb "give" would most likely be used to request the object, e.g., "Give me the book," whereas in Samoan the verb *'aumai* would be used, e.g., *'Aumai le tusi*. In Situation II, the speaker and addressee are relatively close together, and the object is at some distance. In this case, "bring" would most likely be used to request the object in English, e.g., "Bring me the book," whereas in Samoan the appropriate verb is again *'aumai*, e.g., *'Aumai le tusi*. Finally, in Situation III, the addressee and object are at some distance from the speaker and may or may not be close to each other. Here "bring" is most appropriate, e.g., "Bring me the book," and in Samoan the verb *'aumai* is still used, e.g., *'Aumai le tusi*.

On the basis of the semantic facts presented in Tables 6.1 and 6.2, one might predict that the semantically less complex *sau* 'to come' would be used productively before the semantically more complex *'aumai* 'to bring/give'. Such a prediction would be in line with many studies of lexical acquisition in

Table 6.1. *Semantic feature analysis of deictic verbs in English and Samoan*

English	Samoan

"Come"
    Change in location of actor
	Sau
	    Change in location of actor

"Give"
    Change in location of object
    (Gentner 1975)
    Cause to have (Lyons 1977)	

	'Aumai
	    Change in location of object/agent
	    and object
	    Cause to have/to come

"Bring"
    Change in location of agent and object
    Cause to come (Lakoff 1972)	

Table 6.2. *Comparison of the use of "give," "bring" and 'aumai*

Situation I		Situation II		Situation III	
Sp A				Sp	A
	o	Sp A	o		o
English					
Give (me) the o.		Bring (me) the o.		Bring (me) the o.	
Samoan					
'Aumai *le* o.		*'Aumai* *le* o.		*'Aumai* *le* o.	

Sp = speaker; A = addressee; o = object.

English, particularly those concerned with deictic verbs (e.g., Clark and Garnica 1974; Richards 1976; Tanz 1980). However, the present data on Samoan children indicate that *'aumai* 'to bring/give' is used before *sau* 'to come' and that it is generally used more productively than *sau* when both have been acquired. These results are presented in Table 6.3.

This contradiction ties into the major area of concern in this account, that of the influence of cultural constraints on language acquisition. What are the social constraints on the use of *sau* and *'aumai* to summon, demand, and appeal by children in traditional Samoan households? To what extent are Samoan children expected to exert (or to attempt to exert) control over others' behavior through language? In the following discussion, I present evidence

Table 6.3. *Relative productivity of* sau *'to come' versus* 'aumai *'to bring/give' in each child's speech corpus*

Child	Verb	Age at onset	Total	I	III	V	VII
Iakopo		2;1					
	sau		8% (10)	0	2% (1)	0	47% (9)
	'aumai		92% (121)	100% (9)	98% (57)	100% (45)	53% (10)
Matu'u		2;1					
	sau		44% (32)	33% (5)	25% (3)	54% (15)	53% (9)
	'aumai		56% (40)	67% (10)	75% (9)	46% (13)	47% (8)
Naomi		2;10					
	sau		18% (39)	13% (7)	3% (1)	42% (22)	11% (9)
	'aumai		82% (176)	87% (45)	97% (29)	58% (30)	89% (72)
Niulala		2;11					
	sau		33% (36)	14% (3)	18% (6)	27% (6)	66% (21)
	'aumai		67% (72)	86% (18)	82% (27)	73% (16)	34% (11)

for the operation of socially grounded restrictions on children's use of *sau* that do not hold for *'aumai*.

Social constraints on the imperative use of *sau* and *'aumai*

Social status and young children

In most societies, language-acquiring children are generally surrounded by more older persons than younger persons. Studies of English-speaking children have shown that young children are sensitive to age differences and that, for example, they modify their speech appropriately when addressing younger children (Anderson 1977; Sachs & Devin 1976; Shatz & Gelman 1973). Samoan children are also sensitive to age differences of addressees.

In traditional Samoan communities, status of individuals is based in part on their age and generation. Individuals who are older, and in particular those who belong to a higher generation, are considered higher in rank than those who are younger. The status of individuals is a crucial component in assessing the relationship between caregiver and child within the household. As discussed earlier, those who perform caregiving tasks (e.g., adults, older siblings) are treated as having higher rank relative to their young charges.

Children spend a great deal of their time interacting with other children of comparable age within the household compound. These groups of children, called *'aukegi* or *'auvaega,* form a peer group in the sense that the children participate more or less equally in various activities.

Children who are members of *'aukegi,* such as those in this study, normally have at least one younger sibling. These younger siblings are typically referred to as *si 'ou tei* 'your dear little sibling' (or *si 'ou kei* in household register). Children considered as *si 'ou tei* are distinguished from *'aukegi* members in that they are potential charges (recipients of care) of the young children who form the *'aukegi.* For example, Matu'u, one of the children focused on in this study, has a younger brother Losi. Losi is often referred to as *si 'ou kei* (or *'soukei'*) in speech addressed to Matu'u. In addition, Matu'u is on some occasions instructed to perform caregiving tasks for Losi (e.g., to get him something to eat, to fetch him from the edge of the house). Younger siblings such as Losi are considered to be of lower rank relative to their older sibling caregivers such as Matu'u.

These hierarchical distinctions (i.e., between adult and older sibling caregivers, *'aukegi* members, and *si 'ou tei*) are relevant to young children's use of *sau* and *'aumai* in imperatives. In particular, in Samoan society imperative uses of *sau* are generally restricted to the speech of high-status persons to those of low status or to speech between peers. Young children appear to acquire this sociolinguistic rule as they acquire the verb itself. On the other hand, imperative uses of *'aumai* are not restricted in this way. That is, these utterances may be directed from low- to high-status persons.

Imperative use of sau 'to come'

To assess the children's sensitivity to social constraints on the use of *sau* to summon others, their spontaneous uses of *sau* in this way were coded according to whether the addressee was of higher rank than the child (i.e., older sibling caregivers and adults), a peer (i.e., comembers of an *'aukegi*), or of lower rank (i.e., infants and other younger siblings considered to be *si 'ou tei* with respect to the child). The category of lower-ranking individuals also includes domestic animals such as cats, dogs, chickens, and pigs, since they were often the addressees of child utterances. The results of this analysis are presented in Table 6.4. The results indicate that young children tend to use *sau* to summon peers and lower-ranking individuals, in keeping with the social constraints on the use of *sau* to summon others. Exx. 9 and 10 show the imperative use of *sau* directed to a younger sibling.

Example 9

NAOMI (3;0) II-3(2)-053 (video)
[Naomi and her mother, Matau'aina (M), are sitting inside the house. Naomi has put a transistor radio on the floor in front of her. She is pretending that the radio is an infant.]

	Naomi	Others
[⇒ radio on floor]	*sau* (2×)/	
[Touches radio]	come	
	(Come! Come!)	
[Puts radio on lap]	*ia moe*/	
	ok sleep	
	(Okay, sleep.)	
	moe 'oe/	
	sleep you	
	(You go to sleep.)	
	ia moe/	
	ok sleep	
	(Okay, sleep.)	
[Patting radio]	[Soft, rhythmic, singsong]	
	moe (2×) *pepe moe* (3×)	
	sleep baby sleep	
	pepi ma moe pepi moe	
	baby ? sleep baby sleep	
	pe– pepi moe ta pi/	
	ba– baby sleep ? ?	
	(Sleep, sleep, baby sleep,	
	baby sleep, baby sleep,	
	baby sleep, baby sleep,	
	ba–baby sleep.)	

Table 6.4. *Rank of addressee of imperatives with* sau *'to come'*

Child	Age at onset	Total	Lower	Peer	Higher
Iakopo	2;1	100% (3)	0	100%(3)	0
Matu'u	2;1	100% (22)	73% (16)	0	27% (6)
Naomi	2;10	100% (29)	62% (18)	0	38% (11)
Niulala	2;11	100% (25)	8% (2)	68% (17)	24% (6)
Average		100% (19.75)	46% (9)	25% (5)	29% (5.75)

In this example, Naomi uses the verb *sau* in an imperative utterance directed to a radio that she is pretending is an infant.

Example 10

MATU'U (2;6) V-3(2)-416
[Matu'u is sitting inside the house eating a *masi* 'cracker'. She has been chopping the *masi* into pieces with a knife and eating the crumbs.]

	Matu'u	*Others*
	⟍[To Losi]	
	sau/	
	come	
	⟍(Come.)	
	sau 'i/	
	come here	
	(Come here.)	
	⟍(veni ia)/	
[L comes and sits	*sau ia*/	
near Matu'u]	come emph	
	⟍(*Come.*)	
	sau (3×)/	
	come	
	(Come, come, come.)	
[Matu'u stands and		
picks up crumbs from		
floor and eats]		
[Chops off piece of	*ia*/	
masi and gives to L]	here [used when offering]	
	(Here.)	

This example shows the imperative use of *sau* directed to a younger sibling, Losi (L).

It is also important to point out that there are many nonspontaneous instances (not included in this analysis) in which the child is instructed to ''call out'' a summons on behalf of a high-status person. The constraints that normally operate on the child's imperative utterances of *sau* are suspended in these elicited imitation sequences. This is illustrated in Ex. 11.

Example 11

IAKOPO (2;4) III-3(2)-332
[Iakopo is sitting inside the house with his mother, Āpolo (Ā). He has been eating candy (*lole*). Ā is trying to get him and several other children to eat some rice she has placed on a mat in front of her.]

Iakopo	Others
	Ā: *vala'au Iuliaga e sau*
	call Iuliana comp come
	(Call Iuliana to come.)
(lole)/	
	Ā: *fōgō Iuliaga e sau*
	call Iuliana comp come
	(Call Iuliana to come.)
loti [= lole]/	
candy	
(Candy.)	
	Ā: *a'e vala'au Iuliaga e*
	neg affect call Iuliana comp
	sau
	come
	(Come on! Call Iuliana to come.)
	'ua leai se lole
	tns neg art candy
	(There isn't any more candy.)
	Ā: *a ga 'ua 'uma ga* [= oga]
	emph there tns finish comp
	'ai 'oe
	eat you
	(*There*, you've finished eating it.)
'oe/	
you	
(You.)	
	Ā: *vala'au Iuliaga e sau*
	call Iuliana comp come
	(Call Iuliana to come.)
[Interruption]	
	Ā: *vala'au Iuliaga e ōmai*
	call Iuliana comp come,pl
	(Call Iuliana to come.)
	vala'au e ōmai e 'a'ai
	call comp come,pl comp eat,pl
	'oukou, vala'au Sasa ma Iuliaga
	you,pl call Sasa and Iuliana
	e ōmai
	comp come,pl
	(Call them to come so you (all) can eat, call Sasa and Iuliana to come.)
	Ā: *se vala'au Iuliaga*
	please call Iuliana
	(Please! Call Iuliana.)

ana [= Iuliana] *sau/*
Iuliana   come
(Iuliana come.)

Ā: *fōgō kele*
  call loudly
  (Call loudly.)

ana/
Iuliana
(Iuliana.)
ana   sau/
Iuliana come
(Iuliana come.)
ana   ana   sau/
Iuliana Iuliana come
(Iuliana, Iuliana come.)
ana   sau/
Iuliana come
(Iuliana come.)

This example illustrates the way in which high-status caregivers (e.g., mothers) tend to remain stationary and relatively detached from the activities of young children. Rather than moving and involving herself directly in the situation, Iakopo's mother directs him to summon Iuliana and Sasa.

Imperative use of 'aumai *'to bring/give'*

Restrictions on the child's use of *sau* to summon others does not hold for the imperative use of *'aumai* in making demands or appeals for objects. Ex. 12 shows the use of *'aumai* in an imperative directed to an older sibling.

Example 12

IAKOPO (2;4) III-1(2)-250
[Iakopo, his father, Siō (S), his mother, Āpolo (Ā), and two sisters, Iulia (Iu) and Iuliana (Iul) (4;5), are inside the house. Iul is playing near Iakopo with a ball that S bought in Apia (the capital city). The ball has become flat.]

Iakopo	*Others*
[⟹ Iul; extends hand] ↘*mai* [= *'aumai] polo Siō/*	
give ball Sio	
(Give me Siō's ball.)	
	Ā: [To Iak]
	'o le ā
	top art interr
	(What's the matter?)
↘*ai* [= *'aumai] polo a'u/*	
give ball my	
(Give me my ball.)	
	Ā: [To Iul]
	'avifo [= *'ave* + *ifo*]

	give+down
	le mea i
	art thing to
	sou [= si 'ou]
	your dear
↘*mai polo pu* [= pā]/	*kei*
give ball flat	younger sibling
(Give me the flat ball.)	(Give it to your little brother.)

Iu: [To Iul]
mai le
give art

pā/   *polo a   le kama*
flat   ball poss art boy
(It's flat.)

(Give the kid his ball.)

As described in the section "Exchange and Redistribution of Goods," demands and appeals for goods are crucial to the establishment and maintenance of social relationships. Young children continually witness older siblings and adults negotiate the redistribution and exchange of goods within and across households. This process takes place in a variety of social contexts, ranging from very informal to very formal. A critical feature of the redistribution of goods across many types of situations is that every individual is entitled to a share, *including the young child*. It is quite common at these times for young children to make demands for objects. This is illustrated in the following example. In this elicited imitation sequence, Iakopo's mother, older cousin, and older sister encourage him to make demands for a banana by calling out to a woman in a nearby house.

Example 13

IAKOPO (2;1) I-2(1)-446
[Iakopo is sitting inside the house with his mother, Āpolo (Ā), his sister, Iuliana (Iul), and a male cousin, Lio (L). An adult female member of Iakopo's extended family is inside another house in the compound. She is addressed as either Aponiva or Tautala.]

Iakopo   *Others*

Ā: [To Iak]
fai fia   'ai fa'i
say want eat banana
(Say "I want to eat a banana.")

L: [To Iak]
fia   'ai fa'i
want eat banana
(I want to eat a banana.)

Ā: [To L]
vai [= va'ai] *le* [= lea] *lue le*
look   now   nod art

                                   ulu
head
(Look, he [Iakopo] is nodding his
head.)

ala [= Tautala]/   Ā: *vala'au Kaukala 'aumai le fa'i*
Tautala   call   Tautala   bring   art banana
(Tautala.)

                                  (Call Tautala to bring a banana.)
ala/
Tautala
(Tautala.)

                               Ā: *ia vala'au*
                                 ok call
                                 (Okay, call her.)

ala (2×)
Tautala
(Tautala, Tautala.)

                                  Ā: *fōgō 'aumai sau fa'i*
                                  call   bring   your banana
                                  (Call her to bring a banana for
                                  you.)
ala/
Tautala
(Tautala.)

                                  Ā: *vala'au*
                                  call
                                  (Call.)
                           Iul: [High]
                                  (taua) *'aumai se fa'i*
                                         bring   art banana
                                  (( ) bring a banana.)
                                  Ā: *vala'au Pogiva* [= Aponiva]
                                  call   Aponiva
                                  'aumai se fa'i
                                  bring   art banana
                                  (Call Aponiva to bring a banana.)
                           Iul: *kopo* [= Iakopo] *fōgō Kaukala*
                                  Iakopo   call   Tautala
                                  (Iakopo, call Tautala.)
                             L: *fōgō Pogiva*
                                  call   Aponiva
                                  (Call Aponiva.)

    Unlike the use of *sau* to summon others, demands and appeals for objects using *'aumai* are made between peers (e.g., *'aukegi* members), from higher- to lower-ranking individuals (e.g., mothers or sibling caregivers to young children), and from lower- to higher-ranking individuals (e.g., young children to sibling caregivers or mothers). With this information in mind, the children's spontaneous use of *'aumai* in imperatives was also coded with respect

Table 6.5. *Rank of addressee of imperatives with* 'aumai '*to bring/give*'

Child	Age at onset	Total	Lower	Peer	Higher
Iakopo	2;1	100% (112)	0	38% (42)	62% (70)
Matu'u	2;1	100% (28)	18% (5)	29% (8)	53% (15)
Naomi	2;10	100% (161)	1% (1)	0	99% (160)
Niulala	2;11	100% (62)	15% (9)	29% (18)	56% (35)
Average		100% (91)	4% (4)	19% (17)	77% (70)

to the rank of the addressee. This is shown in Table 6.5. These results indicate that children's imperative uses of 'aumai tend to be directed to higher-ranking individuals or to peers. (Fewer of these utterances are directed to lower-ranking individuals, since, as pointed out in the section "Social Status and Young Children," there are fewer potential addressees of lower rank relative to the child.) These utterances are often appeals for objects directed to higher-ranking individuals. In addition, young children use 'aumai to demand objects as a way of asserting themselves with peers, older siblings, and adults.

Summary

The two major trends in the children's use of *sau* and 'aumai may be summarized as follows: (1) Imperatives with 'aumai tend to be directed to higher-ranking persons or to peers. These results reflect a social situation in which a young child is supported and encouraged to make demands for objects to a range of addressees. (2) Imperatives with *sau* tend to be directed to lower-ranking persons or to peers. These results reflect the fact that within the household it is higher-ranking persons (i.e., adult and sibling caregivers) who generally issue such imperatives, rather than young children. The fact that children's imperatives with *sau* tend to be directed to lower-ranking individuals or peers evidences their sensitivity to sociolinguistic knowledge.

These norms for the imperative use of *sau* versus 'aumai indicate why a Samoan child uses *sau* less productively than 'aumai (as shown in Table 6.3). Since young children are surrounded by more older (i.e., higher-ranking) than younger (i.e., lower-ranking) individuals, then from the point of view of the child as speaker, the range of appropriate addresses for *sau* is more restricted than the range of appropriate addressees for 'aumai (in the child's everyday environment). Children's more productive use of 'aumai relative to *sau* is additional evidence for their sensitivity to social constraints on the use of these forms.

Trends in spontaneous production: semantic constraints versus social constraints

In this paper, I have examined certain developmental trends in the production of deictic verbs from two perspectives. The first perspective, the one that has received the most attention in research in this area, concerns the semantic structure of deictic elements and the constraints this structure imposes upon the child's production (and comprehension) of these forms. In this view, properties of deictic elements are determined independently of the use of these items in particular contexts by particular individuals. These properties are treated as inherent characteristics that are presumably true for deictic forms in any speech context. This aspect of the Samoan child language data was presented in the section comparing deictic verbs in English and Samoan.

The second perspective concerns certain pragmatic characteristics of deictic verbs as they are evidenced in the spontaneous speech of children. This perspective focuses on the social function of utterances with deictic verbs. In this view, properties of deictic elements are determined by their use in particular contexts by particular individuals relative to the behavioral norms of a community. A major assumption of the present study has been that this latter perspective must be taken into account when language production is observed in relatively naturalistic settings, where the situation of utterance does not remain constant.

I have proposed that, in Samoan, imperative utterances used to summon, demand, and appeal are sensitive to different social constraints on production. I described certain restrictions that apply to Samoan children's use of *sau* to summon others but not to the child's use of *'aumai* to make demands or appeals for objects. Specifically, I described the fact that imperative utterances with *sau* tend to appear in the speech of high-status individuals to low-status individuals and in speech between peers. This restriction is based in large part on the fact that high-status persons tend to carry out more stationary tasks and to direct low-status persons to perform more active tasks. Imperative utterances with *'aumai* are not restricted in this way. These utterances appear in the speech of low-status to high-status persons, in speech of high-status to low-status persons, and in speech between peers. This pattern of use is based on the fact that demands and appeals for objects are ways of establishing and maintaining social relationships.

In addition to semantic considerations, these differences in social functions and contextual constraints affect and account for the developmental trends in the use of *sau* 'to come' and *'aumai* 'to bring/give' by young Samoan children interacting with familiar household members. The intent of this study has been to demonstrate that it is essential to consider not only the semantic structure of young children's utterances, but also the social role of the child as a user of language within a particular culture.

Appendix: Abbreviations used in the English glosses

art   article
comp   complementizer
dx   deictic particle
emph   emphatic particle
excl   exclamation
foc   focus particle
incl   inclusive
interr   interrogative
neg   negation
nom   nominalizer
pl   plural
poss   possessive marker
pro   pronoun
tns   tense marker
top   topic particle

Notes

This research was supported by National Science Foundation Grant no. 53-482-2480; Principal Investigator: Elinor Ochs.
1   An utterance was considered spontaneous if it did not occur in the same form in the previous speech of the child or another within several minutes of recording time or within the same interaction.
2   Household compounds are clusters of individual houses belonging to an extended family. A compound is situated on land owned by the family and managed by the *matai* of that family (i.e., the person who holds the chiefly title for the family). A household compound usually includes one or more houses in which the daily activities of eating, sleeping, and socializing in general take place. In addition, there is a separate smaller structure used for cooking only (the *umu kuka*). Compounds will also often have an outhouse and, at a separate location, a pipe (with faucet attached) to provide cold running water for washing and drinking.
3   These descriptions do not refer to inherently good or bad qualities of speech.
4   *Kava* is a mildly intoxicating beverage made from a dried and pulverized pepper root and water.
5   The transcription conventions used in this paper are derived from those outlined in Sacks, Schegloff & Jefferson (1974) and Ochs (1979). In the following example, only major pauses are indicated. In later examples, => is glossed as "looks at."
6   The expression *'ua e iloa* often has the effect of softening the force of an utterance.
7   When village laws are violated, the offending party is normally required to pay a fine, which varies in amount depending upon the severity of the transgression.

References

Andersen, E. S. 1977. Learning to speak with style: a study of the sociolinguistic skills of children. Unpublished Ph.D. dissertation, Stanford University.

Clark, E. V. 1978. From gesture to word: on the natural history of deixis in language acquisition. In J. S. Bruner & A. Garton, eds., *Human growth and development: Wolfson College Lectures 1976*. Oxford: Oxford University Press, pp. 85–120.

Clark, E. V. & Garnica, O. K. 1974. Is he coming or going? On the acquisition of deictic verbs. *Journal of Verbal Learning and Verbal Behavior* 13:559–572.

Duranti, A. 1981. *The Samoan fono: a sociolinguistic study*. Pacific Linguistics, ser. B, no. 80. Canberra: Australian National University, Linguistic Circle of Canberra.

Gathercole, V. 1978. More on the acquisition of *come* and *go*. In D. Lance & D. Gulsted, eds., *Proceedings from the 1977 Mid-America Regional Linguistics Conference*. Columbia: University of Missouri Linguistics Area Program, pp. 65–80.

Gentner, D. 1975. Evidence for the psychological reality of semantic components: the verbs of possession. In D. A. Norman, D. E. Rumelhart, & the LNR Research Group, eds., *Explorations in cognition*. New York: Freeman, pp. 211–246.

Keller-Cohen, D. 1973. Deictic reference in children's speech. Paper presented at the Annual Meeting of the Linguistic Society of America, San Diego, Calif.

Kernan, K. 1969. The acquisition of language by Samoan children. Unpublished Ph.D. dissertation, University of California, Berkeley.

Korbin, J. 1978. Caretaking patterns in a rural Hawaiian community, ch. 1: Sibling caretaking in Polynesia. Unpublished Ph.D. dissertation, University of California, Los Angeles.

Lakoff, G. 1972. Linguistics and natural logic. In D. Davidson & G. Harman, eds., *Semantics of natural language*. Dordrecht: Reidel, pp. 545–665.

Lyons, J. 1977. *Semantics*. 2 vols. Cambridge: Cambridge University Press.

Macrae, A. J. 1976. Movement and location in the acquisition of deictic erbs. *Journal of Child Language* 3,:191–204.

Mead, M. 1928. *Coming of age in Samoa*. New York: Morrow (Quill Paperbacks).
1930. *Social organization of Manu'a*. B. P. Bishop Museum Bulletin 76. Honolulu.

Milner, G. B. 1978. *Samoan Dictionary*. Manila: Samoan Free Press.

Ochs, E. 1979. Transcription as theory. In E. Ochs & B. Schieffelin, eds., *Developmental pragmatics*. New York: Academic Press, pp. 43–72.
1982. Talking to children in Western Samoa. *Language and Society* 11:77–104.
In press. *Culture and language acquisition: acquiring communicative competence in a Samoan village*. Cambridge: Cambridge University Press.

Richards, M. M. 1976. *Come* and *go* reconsidered: children's use of deictic verbs in contrived situations. *Journal of Verbal Learning and Verbal Behavior* 15:655–665.

Sachs, J. S. & Devin, J. 1976. Young children's use of age-appropriate speech styles in social interaction and role-playing. *Journal of Child Language* 3,:81–90.

Sacks, H., Schegloff, E., & Jefferson, G. 1974. A simplest systematics for the organization of turn-taking in conversation. *Language* 50,4:696–735.

Schieffelin, B. 1979. Getting it together: an ethnographic approach to the study of the development of communicative competence. In E. Ochs & B. Schieffelin, eds., *Developmental pragmatics*. New York: Academic Press, pp. 73–108.

Shatz, M. & Gelman, R. 1973. *The development of communication skills: modifications in the speech of young children as a function of listener*. Monographs of the Society for Research in Child Development 38, serial no. 152. Chicago: University of Chicago Press.

Shore, B. 1982. *Sala'ilua: a Samoan mystery*. New York: Columbia University Press.

Tanz, C. 1980. *Studies in the acquisition of deictic terms*. Cambridge: Cambridge University Press.

Weisner, T. & Gallimore, R. 1977. My brother's keeper: child and sibling caretaking. *Current Anthropology* 18,2:169–190.

7. The acquisition of register variation by Anglo-American children

ELAINE S. ANDERSEN

Firth noted many years ago that "Every human being is a bundle of institutionalized roles. He has to play many parts, and unless he knows his lines as well as his role he is no use in the play" (quoted in Verma 1969:293). The research described in this paper was designed to examine how and when preschoolers in middle-class Anglo-American cultures learn their "lines," i.e., how they acquire full *communicative competence* (Hymes 1972). As children become active members of any language community, they must learn to speak not only grammatically but also appropriately. Children in all societies must, at some time during acquisition, learn a variety of sociolinguistic and social-interactional rules that govern appropriate language use. Even where the language addressed to 2-year-olds may be of highly specialized nature, by the time these children reach age 4 or 5, they have experienced diverse speech settings: They go to the doctor, to preschool, to birthday parties, to the grocery store. They participate in a variety of speech situations, with people who differ in age, sex, status, and familiarity, and whose speech will therefore vary in a number of systematic ways. This type of language variation has been described for a number of situations in American English under the rubric of *register variation* (see Andersen 1977, in press or Ferguson 1977 for more detailed summaries of work on registers). The range of registers examined in the study described below included "babytalk," "foreigner talk," "teacher talk," and "doctor talk." In addition, male/female distinctions were noted across the various registers.

Are young children aware of sociolinguistic and social-interactional differences of this type? What do they know about the appropriateness of varied linguistic forms available to indicate particular situations and particular roles and relationships? Role-play is one of the means available to them for experimenting with linguistic aspects of social interaction (Grimshaw & Holden 1976). Ervin-Tripp (1973) has noted that when nursery-school children role-play they often adopt consistent speech patterns in accordance with the social categories involved – mothers and babies, doctors, etc. One way to elicit use of such speech patterns, then, would be to set up specific role-playing situations for the children. However, since I found in a pilot study that the attention span of 4- and 5-year-olds was very short under such conditions, in this research I used a number of role-specific puppets for whom children had to "do the voices." In this way, I was able to obtain longer, more fluent speech in several different settings, discourse that revealed the nature of the language styles, or registers, in the children's repertoires.

I recorded the speech of twenty-four children (half boys, half girls) ranging in age from 3;9 to 7;1, in three different role-playing situations (Andersen 1977, in press). In one session (the family setting), for example, a child would speak for puppets representing a father, a mother, and a baby; in another session (the school setting), that same child would role-play as a teacher, a student, and a foreign student; in the third (the medical setting), he or she would speak as a doctor, a nurse, and a patient. The child was asked to play two roles at a time – so as to elicit contrasting "styles" – while the experimenter played a third, mainly to keep the session going. Elsewhere (Andersen 1979, 1984) I have referred to this technique as "controlled improvisation," where I set up the roles and the context, but the subjects are free then to improvise as they wish.

In this paper I concentrate on the most familiar setting, the family situation, and provide a brief overview of what 5-year-old children (i.e., those just about to enter the school system) know about the registers appropriate for different family members.[1] I shall first give a brief overview of the speech these children ascribe to the roles of father, mother, and child, and then concentrate on quantitative analyses of a small subset of distinctions.

First, *fathers:* Fathers' speech was straightforward, unqualified, and forceful. They all used deep voices, frequently spoke louder than any other family member (sometimes yelling), and showed a marked tendency to produce shifted vowels. They backed and lowered vowels in a manner that produced an almost sinister "accent": e.g., Yes → /yʌs/; Bad → /bad/. Their sentences were shorter than the mothers' but longer than those of the children they portrayed.[2] Speech as father contained the greatest proportion of direct imperatives, and – even excluding one-word answers to yes/no questions – a large proportion of their turns were single-utterance turns. Unlike the mothers, they did not usually explain the rationale behind the directives and other speech acts they addressed to their children. Also, just as Gleason (1975) found for real fathers, their language clearly demarcated their role within the family. In my corpus, fathers talked mainly about going to work, "firing the secretary," having meetings, or building a new "repartment" building. Consider Ex. 1:

(1) Em:[3] What would you like for lunch?
    Sf: I'm supposed to go to work now anyway.

Em: All right, dear.
Sf: I'm gonna have a meeting there, so I won't see you late tonight.

and Ex. 2, where the discussion has been about needed groceries:

(2) Em: Why don't you pick some up on the way home from work?
Sf: Maybe. No I don't think I will have any time. 'Cause I'm going to a meeting after I come home from work.

Moreover, in addition to showing the limits of their own responsibilities, the language as father also makes explicit the role of the mother in the family, as in Ex. 3:

(3) Sc: Should I have [bwɛkfɪs] now?
Sf: Ask your mother.

Similarly, when asked for a bedtime story, these fathers were likely to respond as in Ex. 4:

(4) Ec: Tell me a story.
Sf: Mommy will.
Ec No, I want you to ———
Sf: I'm going to sleep.

In a similar case, when the child had requested a story the father initially responded like the father in Ex. 4, but when pressed further he reluctantly agreed with the minimal:

(5) Sf: All right. Sit down. "Once upon a time. The end."

In contrast to this direct, forceful speech of fathers, the general impression one gained from the role-play as *mother* was that mothers were more talkative, more polite, and their speech was qualified and softer. They spoke with higher pitch than fathers and often used exaggerated intonation but rarely approached the volume that marked the fathers' utterances. They used more endearments and babytalk terms, but fewer direct imperatives than fathers. Their utterances were longer than any other family members' (see note 2), and they tended to have more multiutterance turns.[4] In addition, these turns were longer than the multiutterance turns of the fathers – largely because the mothers qualified or explained almost everything they did or requested. Ex. 6 is a fairly typical illustration of some of these characteristics in the mothers' speech to child and to father:

(6) Sm: Gotta get the baby tucked into beddy bye. She's not a sleepy. [To baby] Go to sleep, sleep, sleep, darling. Go to sleep. [Turns to father] Don't you think it's time to go to bed? It's midnight – we should go to bed.

The content of the mothers' speech revolved around family care. Mothers talked about putting children to bed, as in the example just cited and in Ex. 7:

(7) Sc: Mommy, I'm all done.
Sm: OK, sweetie. Now it's time for your naptime.

They told fairly long, involved bedtime stories, with great expression, and they were responsible for everyone's food, as illustrated in Ex. 8:

(8) Ef: What did you do today?
  Sm: I had a little bit of a treat.
  Ef: What was that?
  Sm: Ravioli.

    .
    .
    .

  Ef: Didn't you go out?
  Sm: No I didn't.
  Ef: You spent all day making ravioli?
  Sm: Yes.

and they took seriously matters like birthday parties, as in Ex. 9:

(9) Sm: It's gonna be her birthday tomorrow.
  Ef: Whose birthday is tomorrow?
  Sm: Oh, Honey's.
  Ef: Oh. Do I know her?
  Sm: Yes, you do! Just the child that you put to bed.
  Ef: Oh, I was just kidding.
  Sm: Stop kidding me. [Laughter]

Speech as young *child* is probably the easiest of the three roles to distinguish apart from context, largely because of a number of phonological, prosodic, and lexical characteristics that systematically mark the register and are unique to it. Most of the children in the study began the child role by marking it with a "goo-goo," "gaga," or "a, a," until told, "This child is a little older than that." They then adjusted to more "normal" English in a high pitch, with: (1) a babytalk overtone that might be characterized as palatized speech (i.e., the tongue seems to be kept higher in the mouth and the vocal cavity made smaller); (2) some nasalization; and (3) some whining utterances, in which vowels are lengthened, often on heavily stressed syllables, as in Ex. 10:

(10) Sc: I *wa:n* go to the park and *plei:*.
  Em: Your daddy will take you.
  Sc: *Ma:ma*.

In addition to the "goo-goo's" and "gaga's" that appeared so frequently, there were other sound effects such as the fairly frequent "waah" /wæ:/, indicating dissatisfaction, as in Ex. 11:

(11) Sc: Now, I want carrot.
  En: Why don't we wait 'til lunchtime for that?
  Sc: Waa-h! [See also Ex. 14.]

A number of phonological substitutions also occurred in this role. These included:

$$/\theta/ \;\rightarrow\; \left\{\begin{array}{l}[f]\\ [d]\end{array}\right\} \text{ e.g., } \quad\text{``. . . birfday at fwee-firty'' (birthday at three-thirty)}$$
$$\text{``. . . wid de flowers'' (with the flowers)}$$

[ð] → [ʒ]   e.g., "[ʒɪʃ] one" (this one)

/d/ → [g]   e.g., "googie googie" (goody-goody) [assimilation]

$$/s/ \;\rightarrow\; \left\{\begin{array}{l}[\theta]\\ [\int]\end{array}\right\} \text{ e.g., } \quad \begin{array}{l}\text{``Yeth'' (yes)}\\ \text{``[g\varepsilon\int]'' (I guess)}\end{array}$$

$$\left\{\begin{array}{l}/l/\\ /r/\end{array}\right\} \;\rightarrow\; [w] \text{ e.g., } \begin{array}{l}\text{``aw weady'' (all ready)}\\ \text{``jump wope'' (jump rope)}\end{array}$$

$$C \;\rightarrow\; [\emptyset] \quad /\underline{}\# \text{ e.g., bwekfis (breakfast) [consonant cluster} \\ \underline{} \qquad\qquad\quad \text{pwoduc 19 (Product 19) simplification]}$$

As child, the speech contained a higher proportion of names (mostly vocatives) than in the other roles – mainly "Mommy" and "Daddy" – that were frequently pre- or post-posed to questions and requests, as in Exx. 12 and 13:

(12) Sc: Mommy, come back here [soft voice].
(13) Sc: Daddy, can you help me get dressed?

The mean length of utterance (MLU) was shortest in this role, though there were some long, very unbabylike utterances used by children portraying a baby.[5] Omission of function words also occurred, though it was infrequent in these data. Ex. 14 is an instance of an omitted auxiliary and preposition:

(14) [Child doesn't want to go to the park with Daddy]
    Sc: Mama, I not going that. Waa-h!

In line with the earlier discussion of mothers' role as caretaker, it is interesting to note that the child roles included two and a half times as many turns addressed to mother as to father.

I turn now from this general description and present the results of some quantitative analyses of the distribution of, first, a small set of lexical items, and, second, certain directive types.

In examining the transcripts to see who used such possible register markers as babytalk words (e.g., "night-night," "doggie"), endearments (e.g., "honey," "sweetie"), and placeholders or boundary markers (such as "well," "now," "uh"), I found that whereas there were some differences in the number of each of these items by role, there were also striking frequency differences of a more subtle linguistic nature that were revealed only through a finer-grained analysis. In the case of boundary markers, not only were there almost ten times as many of these in both mother and father speech as in child speech, but there was also a clear difference in the distribution of particular types. If we consider the two most common markers in the family context, "well" and "uh," we find that the marker "well" almost never appeared in the speech of child to parent. Parents, on the other hand, used "well" frequently, one and a half times more often than "uh" in the total corpus. If we look only at the utterances of parents to children, "well" was twice as frequent as the marker "uh." The overall difference in the distribution of these markers suggests that children considered "well" an adult term, and its greater use in speech to child suggests it is a more authoritative marker than "uh" (i.e., it is used downward in rank).

In the case of endearments, there was a similar distributional difference. Only mothers and fathers used endearments, with mothers using slightly more of them. But again at a finer level, there was a distinction in the distribution of certain endearment terms, including "honey," "sweetie," "darling," and "dear." For example, "honey" seemed to be a nonspecific endearment; it was the most frequent of the terms, and was used by both mothers and fathers in addressing either each other or the child. "Sweetie" was the second most frequent endearment, but it was found only in mothers' speech to children. This suggests that "honey" is a general, all-purpose endearment, expressing only affection, but that "sweetie" expresses an additional dimension (e.g., downward in age or status), and it might also be a term that marks female speech. With regard to the latter point, it is interesting to note that all endearments discussed here came from the role-playing of the female subjects: All the girls in this 5-year-old group used endearments in their family role-playing, and none of the boys did.

Another lexical indication of status differences in family roles was observed in the use of the word "yes" and its informal variants "yeah" and "yep." In parent-to-parent speech, where the speakers have more or less equal status, the formal and informal versions of the affirmative occurred with equal frequency. However, in the speech of parent to child, where differences in age and rank exist, the more formal "yes" occurred two and a half to three times more frequently than its informal variants. In contrast, the subjects' speech as child contained three times as many informal tokens as formal ones – an almost exact inverse of the parent-to-child ratio.

I now turn briefly to the findings concerning the kinds of directives used with each role. As part of a speech-act analysis of the data, I examined the directives (as opposed to, say, representatives – see Searle 1975) used in each of the family roles. Part of this analysis is summarized in Table 7.1. A comparison of the proportion of directives in the speech of mother to child, father to child, and child to child suggests there was only a small difference between roles – that parents addressed somewhat more directives to their children than vice versa. If we go one step further and, on syntactic grounds, compare all the directives requesting an action, the data appear more interesting: These pretend-fathers used many more imperatives than mothers or children – a finding that matches the real-life observations of Gleason (1975). Mothers used an equal number of declarative and imperative forms as directives, and children used a mix of declarative, imperative, and interrogative

Table 7.1. *Percentage of directives used in each role[a] and the syntactic expression of directives requesting action[b]*

		Father to child	Mother to child	Child to parent
	Directives	33	38	25
	Imperative	88	46	31
Directives for action	Declarative	12	54	46
	Interrogative	0	0	23

[a]Based on the total number of speech acts in that role.
[b]The analysis of syntactic form presented here excludes all information-seeking directives, i.e., questions requiring only a verbal response.

forms. Moreover, children's interrogative forms were often imbedded imperatives that tended to be polite "upward in age or rank" forms, as in Ex. 13.

Although mothers and children used a similar proportion of directives that were declarative in form, these directives were qualitatively different. Mothers tended to use hints, such as "Dinner's ready," "Baby's sleepy," or, as in Ex. 7, "Now it's time for your naptime," whereas children used many more need-statements, such as "I need breakfast" (see also Exx. 10 and 11). These distinctions are reminiscent of the Sachs & Devin (1976) finding that children distinguished between internal-state questions used when addressing babies and external-world questions used to mothers and peers. (See Andersen 1984, in press for a more detailed analysis of directives in children's role-play speech.)

Conclusion

The data discussed in this paper show the importance of going beyond standard measures of linguistic development in assessing what preschoolers know about their language. The findings suggest that, even before they begin formal schooling, children have a fairly sophisticated knowledge of the rules governing appropriate language use. By age 5, they make subtle distinctions among types of speech acts, and choose sentence structures, lexical items, and phonological features to "fit" the different roles in their sociolinguistic repertoire. In addition, the results of this study demonstrate that the examination of children's role-playing speech is a useful and feasible way to tap their implicit knowledge of social uses of language and its appropriateness for different social roles that they would not have the opportunity to reveal in more naturalistic contexts.

Notes

The preparation of this paper was supported in part by National Science Foundation Grant no. BNS75-17126 and in part by grants from the Spencer Foundation and the March of Dimes. An earlier version of the paper was presented at the Ninth Annual Stanford Child Language Research Forum. Eve Clark, Charles Ferguson, and Catherine O'Connor provided valuable comments on that earlier version. The paper was completed while I was a guest fellow at the Max-Planck Institüt fur Psycholinguistik. Address for correspondence: Dr. Elaine S. Andersen, Department of Linguistics, Grace Ford Salvatore 301, University of Southern California, Los Angeles, Calif. 90089-1693.

1 A more complete description of children's register knowledge related to these and other roles is provided in Andersen in press.

2 The mean lengths of utterance (in words) for the three roles in this group of subjects were: mothers 6.4, fathers 4.8, children 2.3.

3 The following code is used in all the examples cited in this paper: E = experimenter; S = subject, m = mother; f = father; c = child.

4 An *utterance* here is the conversation equivalent of a written sentence, with boundaries determined by prosodic markings; included in this category are phrases that express a complete idea. A *turn* is made up of all the utterances that form a speaker's uninterrupted contribution to the discourse.

5 Sachs & Devin (1976) found a similar inconsistency in their role-play data.

References

Andersen, E. S. 1977. Learning to speak with style: a study of the sociolinguistic skills of children. Unpublished Ph.D. dissertation, Stanford University.

1979. Register variation in young children's role-play speech. Paper for symposium "Communicative Competence: Language Use and Role-Play," SRCD Biennial Meeting, San Francisco, March.

1984. The acquisition of sociolinguistic knowledge: some evidence from children's verbal role-play. *Western Journal of Speech Communication* 48,2:125–144.

In press. *Speaking with style: sociolinguistic development in children.* London: Croom Helm.

Ervin-Tripp, S. 1973. Children's sociolinguistic competence and dialect diversity. In A. Dil, ed., *Language acquisition and communicative choice.* Stanford: Stanford University Press, pp. 262–301.

Ferguson, C. A. 1977. Babytalk as a simplified register. In C. E. Snow & C. A. Ferguson, eds., *Talking to children.* Cambridge: Cambridge University Press, pp. 209–235.

Gleason, J. B. 1975. Fathers and other strangers: men's speech to young children. In D. P. Data, ed., *Georgetown University round table on languages and linguistics.* Washington, D.C.: Georgetown University Press, pp. 289–297.

Grimshaw, A. D. & Holden, L. 1976. Postchildhood modifications of linguistic and social competence. *Items* 30,3:33–42.

Hymes, D. 1972. On communicative competence. In J. B. Pride & J. Holmes, eds., *Sociolinguistics: selected readings.* Baltimore: Penguin Books, pp. 269–293.

Sachs, J. & Devin, J. 1976. Young children's use of age-appropriate speech styles in social interaction and role-playing. *Journal of Child Language* 3,1:81–98.

Searle, J. 1975. A taxonomy of illocutionary acts. In K. Gunderson, ed., *Minnesota studies in the philosophy of language.* Minneapolis: University of Minnesota Press, pp. 344–369.

Verma, S. K. 1969. Towards a linguistic analysis of registral features. *Acta Linguistica Scientiarum Hungaricae* 19:293–303.

Part III

Expressing affect: input and acquisition

8. Teasing and shaming in Kaluli children's interactions

BAMBI B. SCHIEFFELIN

Introduction

An important issue facing researchers interested in language socialization is how children learn to use culturally appropriate rhetorical means to negotiate and accomplish certain pragmatic ends. For example, how do young children acquire the culturally specific routines and affective displays necessary to manipulate others to obtain what they want and keep what they do not wish to give up?

This chapter examines exchanges in which Kaluli adults verbally tease and shame children to achieve a variety of ends. Teasing and shaming, two related speech acts and speech events, figure prominently in Kaluli adult–adult and adult–child verbal interaction. Kaluli adults try to avoid physical intervention when trying to influence others, especially small children. Instead, they prefer verbal manipulation through teasing and shaming, and socialize their children to do the same. As in many other Pacific cultures, such as Samoa (Ochs in press), one of the major ways in which social control is achieved is through members' fear of being publicly confronted and shamed. This is especially the case when individuals take something that is not theirs to take, as in cases of theft or adultery. When members feel that the risk of getting caught is low, they may attempt such acts, and, if they are not caught, there may be little consequence for them. However, if they are caught, confrontation can occur, and shaming, which is serious, will be public. Throughout these affectively marked exchanges individuals try to preserve their social relationships, while at the same time attempting to get what they want. Ideally, once compensation is paid and balance is restored, relationships can continue as before. While adults may teasingly shame young children, shaming is taken very seriously by adults among themselves, and is not made light of. One question that this chapter addresses is: How do children acquire the necessary cultural

165

and linguistic knowledge to participate in these communicative contexts? To understand this process, we must consider social, cultural, and linguistic factors that organize this domain of language socialization.

Most studies of child socialization have taken the view that socialization is an internalization process by which a person acquires attitudes, values, and social and personal attributes. The focus of most socialization studies has been to relate what is done to the child in order to understand the behavior and personality of the adult. Wentworth (1980) has criticized this mechanistic view of socialization, which focuses primarily on outcomes, and offers a different perspective, one that takes socialization as an actual interactional display of the sociocultural environment. From this perspective, socialization is seen as a demonstration or presentation to a novice of the rules whereby appropriate behavior might be constructed. In addition, it is a presentation of techniques, procedures, modes of interpretation, and information. Like speech, which is shaped according to the addressee, members' culture is always presented to someone. Thus, as Wentworth points out, the context of any socializing activity is modified by the structure of the interaction, as well as by the participants and their relations to one another.

The analysis of teasing and shaming presented here is compatible with the interactional framework suggested by Wentworth. To understand some of the ways in which children learn how to interpret and appropriately respond to teasing and shaming, I examine spontaneous interactions between Kaluli care-givers (almost exclusively mothers) and their young children. It is in these interactions that caregivers display to their young children the appropriate ways to both understand and eventually respond to these frequent routines. For this analysis, teasing and shaming will be taken as sequences or speech acts with a particular rhetorical force where speakers attempt to inhibit or change a person's actions as well as convey a particular affective message about the relationship between those individuals involved and an audience or potential audience of family, peers, and community. Of prime importance is to understand not only the forms and functions of these particular speech acts, but to detail the social process of these acts and the type of social universe in which these interactions frequently occur. In particular, I consider the linguistic resources and turn-taking and sequencing conventions that constitute the particular discourse strategies used in teasing and shaming. These strategies vary according to the age of the addressee. Children must learn how to participate in interactions involving these two related speech acts or events, as well as learn how to distinguish them from one another when linguistic forms are similar. Only then can they treat teasing and shaming as part of a cultur-ally conventionalized system of social control.

Teasing is pervasive in everyday social interactions: Kaluli seems to enjoy various degrees of verbal provocation. Teasing creates tension, as one is never completely sure which way an interaction might swing, owing to the unstable nature of many of the teasing frames. Although teasing may appear to be an act of serious consequence, it ranges in terms of key (Hymes 1972) from having few serious immediate consequences (*ba madali* 'to no purpose') to being playful, controlling, or pointedly malicious. Kaluli distinguish between teasing and tricking and between what is done among adults and between adults and children. Kaluli name different kinds of teasing based on the desired outcome of the speech act or speech event. For example, *enteab* 'tease to make angry' and *kegab* 'tease in mock anger' mark different affective keys. There are also terms to name responses in teasing routines. For example, *a:la:nyab* 'does not care' describes the turn when one is not provoked during teasing; it contrasts with *debab* 'teases back' and with *wa:l* 'return', which indicates a comeback that matches the initial teasing move.

Duranti (1984) has pointed out that much of contemporary speech-act theory has focused on the centrality of the recognition of a speaker's intentions as a crucial aspect of interpretation. The implication of this is that "meaning is already fully defined in the speaker's mind BEFORE the act of speaking. The addressee is little more than a passive recipient who can either guess it right or wrong. The role of context is that of a mere adjunct that may help the hearer if conflicting interpretations seem possible" (p. 1). As Duranti makes clear from his analysis of the *fono* (a Western Samoan speech event involving political oratory) and from the cross-cultural research of others (for example, Kochman 1983; Ochs & Schieffelin 1984; Rosaldo 1982), this view of intentionality and interpretation is ethnocentric and ignores the interactive role that language plays in mediating and negotiating social relations.

In understanding Kaluli teasing and shaming, it is important to take into account a Kaluli view of interpretation. According to Kaluli, one doesn't know what another thinks or feels. The most obvious manifestation of this orientation is that Kaluli prefer not to talk about or guess what might be in another's mind, but talk about or act on what has been already said or done. This suggests that Kaluli do not focus on figuring out or trying to recognize the intentions of a speaker as the sole determinant of a response, but instead provide a response that helps shape the hearer's desired outcome in any interaction. In many cases, the desired outcome of teasing is ambiguous or has several possible and acceptable outcomes. How any particular teasing utterance is taken is up to speaker, addressee, and even audience. In a given interaction, a speaker may be less than committed to a particular position and may wait for an addressee's response (as an indication of one possible outcome). A particular type of response can help negotiate and shape the meaning of an initial utterance. For example, unless the addressee takes an utterance as a challenge, it does not become one. The same goes for an utterance intended to tease or shame. In these situations, the meaning of the exchange is co-constructed in an ongoing manner by participants. Given the potential ambiguity of the tone or key of teasing situations, an addressee might provide an equally ambiguous response to push the speaker to make a more serious commitment to his or her utterance. The exchange can continue in this manner for some time as each member takes an equal share in attempting to define what is going on.

Kaluli tease each other using a rich repertoire of linguistic devices that figure importantly in a variety of relationships (adult–adult, adult–child, and child–child) and social contexts including domestic activities such as food preparation and sharing, work situations, casual play, and disputes. Furthermore, teasing sequences may be initiated by children as well as by adults.

Cultural and linguistic setting

The Kaluli people[1] live in a rain forest on the Great Papuan Plateau in the Southern Highlands Province of Papua New Guinea (E. L. Schieffelin 1976). They number approximately 1,200 and live in about twenty longhouse communities. Kaluli society is generally egalitarian, lacking in the "big man" pattern of social organization so common in the Papua New Guinea highlands. Men utilize extensive networks of obligation and reciprocity in the organization of work and the accomplishment of major social transactions such as bridewealth.

The majority of the Kaluli are monolingual speakers of Kaluli, a non-Austronesian verb-final language (B. B. Schieffelin 1986). Kaluli everyday life is overtly focused in verbal interaction. Talk is thought of and used as a means of expression and manipulation. In this generally egalitarian society, it is difficult to compel anyone to do something that he or she does not wish to do. Teasing and shaming can be important means of persuasion, in addition to being crucial for social control and critical in the public management of others. Among the Kaluli, where individuals must make their own way and move others to act, verbal skills get you what you want, need, or feel owed. Extensive demarcation of kinds of speaking and speech acts further substantiate the observation that Kaluli are energetically verbal. Talk is a primary way to be social, and a primary indicator of social competence (B. B. Schieffelin in press).

Kaluli use two culturally significant and opposing strategies in face-to-face interactions: assertion and appeal (E. L. Schieffelin 1976). Assertion involves putting oneself forward in a strong, self-confident manner; appeal draws on verbal strategies of begging in an attempt to make someone feel sorry for the speaker and act on his or her behalf. Kaluli say that even very small children are able to beg and elicit feelings of pity from others, but as they get older they must be shown how to be verbally assertive. Teasing (*dikideab*) and shaming (*sasideab*) are found only in the assertive modality of interaction, and consequently they must be explicitly taught to young children.

Teasing and shaming in childhood

From about 6 months of age, infants are involved in teasing and shaming routines. These sequences are usually short and involve calling the infant a name such as *wa:fi* or *wa:fi fo* 'retard' or 'retard fruit'. After calling the infant such a name, the adult will usually laugh or smile to mark the event as not serious. Adults are careful not to frighten small infants and therefore tease them gently. As the child gets older, additional names are added, such as the proper names of the few individuals known to act in strange and undesirable ways.

When children reach the age of 3 or so, more serious name-calling begins. This usually occurs when an adult is angered or frustrated by the actions of a child who is expected to know better. For example, a caregiver might say to a child who has taken more than his or her share of food, *Gasa ge!* 'You are a dog!', referring to the habit of dogs to take what is not theirs. Other names refer to undesirable physical characteristics and are also applied situationally. These names do not stay with an individual over time or contexts. Such names include: *kuf aba* 'extended stomach' (from eating too much), *migi bamu* 'flat nose', *migi sambo* 'long nose', *bo badiyo:* 'big breasts', and *gumisiyo:* 'short thing'. However, it should be emphasized that children are not stigmatized by these names, nor are they used in order to traumatize or hurt the child. These names are often used when an adult is exasperated or frustrated by a child's inappropriate behavior. As in all teasing in Kaluli childhood, no one is ever marginalized or pushed out. One's familial relationships are enduring, and, given that, they are both taken for granted and constantly exercised.

In addition to name-calling, there are sets of formulaic phrases used only in teasing older children. For example, one set is used in mock offers to trick or provoke the addressee into thinking that he or she can eat or take something the child in fact cannot. These forms make use of a second person pronoun (*gi*) followed by a verb inflected for third person minus the final consonant. Even though there is no explicit negative marker, forms such as *gi na!* and *gi dia!* mean 'you don't eat!' and 'you don't take!' respectively. These forms are productive for future tense as well as for dual and plural addressee marking. Speakers use *gi na!*, for example, when another person requests (either ver- bally or nonverbally) what they are eating. The speaker, while offering the food to the other, says, *"Gi na!"* and withdraws the food. This type of exchange infuriates people, as it tricks them into thinking that the food will be shared, when in fact it will not be. Adults begin instructing children of 22 months or so to use these expressions with older children or adults who are begging for their food. (One way that adults can tease each other is to use children in the middle.) By the time children are about 30 months old, they are able to direct these expressions to older children and adults, and are continually encouraged to do so.[2] Once children are over 3 years, adults direct these formulaic expressions to them to tease them when they are begging inappropriately.

Teasing occurs over a range of situations, but the most frequent involve sharing and rights to food. Every claim seems to be negotiable, since who gets what to eat often depends on the situation at hand and what individuals can get away with, not on strict rules of ownership. Since individuals rarely make direct statements of authority, interactions such as the ones that follow are frequent in families, and are among the frequent contexts for teasing. Within such contexts as taking or sharing food, Kaluli use rhetorical questions, third-party threats, formulaic expressions, and sarcastic statements to tease and shame.

Example 1

[Mother is in the house with a number of people, including her daughters, Yogodo (age 7) and Waye (age 9). Yogodo has taken *uka,* a wild nut, that does not belong to her.]

Waye → Mo: Yogodowo: ukayo: nab.
             Yogodo   uka   eat (3d pers. pres.)
             Yogodo is eating the uka.

[*No response*]

             No:! Yogodowo: ukayo: nabo!
             Mother! Yogodo is eating the uka!

Mo → Waye: Ni wangalo?!
             What should I do?!

Example 2

[Mother, Yogodo, Abi (age 3), and Waye find a packet of salt belonging to another member of the household, Eyobo. The children begin to eat it, and one asks who it belongs to. There is no answer. Yogodo takes it away and Abi starts to beg for it.]

Mo → children: Salanga:!   Salana:!!
             Someone could say something! Someone could say something!!
             Eyobo-wa: salana:
             Eyobo (erg.) could say something.

In situations such as these, children will be teased in order to prevent or challenge action so shaming will not occur. Children may be shamed, for example, if they refuse to share food with their parents, who almost always give it to them. In such situations, parents will use sarcastic utterances such as *Gelo: mo:mian!* 'I don't give to you!', meaning the opposite, of course: "I always give to you!" If a child takes too much, to shame him or her a parent might say, *Ge ha:lula:su diab!* 'You are taking such a little bit!'

Other types of teasing routines occur especially between siblings and cousins. Some interactions are basically playful and involve telling a child that a desired object (that has been hidden) is in plain sight or threatening to touch a child with stinging nettles while telling the child that they are harmless leaves. Older siblings become very skillful at managing these situations, increasing the tension just enough to keep up the interest and agitate the young child while at the same time making sure that the child does not lose control, thus terminating the interaction. However, away from the watchful eye of the mother, older children may tease younger ones in less benign ways, telling them to eat bad or uncooked food or items that Kaluli don't usually eat or telling a young child that Mother has gone away. Older children have been observed to be relentless in their torment of younger children, provoking them to crying tantrums. When mothers do find their small children provoked beyond a manageable limit for no good reason, they will become angry at their older children, yelling, among other things, *Dikidia:sabo!* 'Don't tease!'

Whereas adults are gentle in their teasing of preverbal children, they will purposely provoke a 2-year-old to tears. For example, in trying to discourage her 28-month-old daughter from nursing, one mother told her that she had to nurse the dog. At first the child found this funny, but the teasing continued, and the mother eventually pressed the dog to the child's face. This resulted in a frustrated and angry child, reduced to tears, which ended only when the mother offered the breast to calm her down. In another situation a mother teased her 30-month-old daughter when the little girl, not seeing her infant brother, asked where he was. The mother's reply was that the baby had died. The little girl did not believe her and continued asking, and her mother was insistent. Provoked to tears, her loud crying woke up the baby, who had been sleeping in a dark corner. Her mother quickly distracted her and she was calm.

These acts of verbal provocation, variations of which were observed repeatedly in every family, have a dramatic contour: sudden initiation and increased provocation to tears, with just as sudden calming and changing focus. These interactions help lay the foundation for culturally salient and culturally specific emotional responses to grief that have been documented for adults (E. L. Schieffelin 1976).

Teasing, shaming, and "turned-over words"

Many languages in Papua New Guinea draw on a variety of linguistic devices (like lexical substitutes) and manners of speaking (sarcasm, rhetorical questions, euphemisms) to achieve a variety of ends (Franklin 1972; Laycock 1977; Strathern 1975). In Kaluli they are known as *bale to* 'turned-over words' (Feld & Schieffelin 1982). Kaluli use *bale to* in joking, challenging, teasing, and shaming among other speech acts. *Bale to* is the most significant complex of linguistic resources for the Kaluli, necessary and salient across modes of language use (conversation, stories sung-texted weeping and song), speech acts, and contexts (Feld 1982). Expressions that either are or make use of *bale to* have a *hego:* 'underneath' or symbolic meaning. Hearers must have particular types of social and linguistic knowledge to understand these forms and make sense of what a speaker may be conveying.

An important aspect of the extensive use of teasing and shaming in every-day interactions is the use of these linguistic devices whose meanings are not solely available from the surface syntactic form of the utterance. Through continuous use and display of these forms, young children acquire both pro-duction and comprehension of these "turned-over words." One of the most pervasive and in many ways least complex of these linguistic devices said to have an underneath (*hego:*) is the rhetorical question (RQ). RQs are used widely in interactions involving teasing, which ranges in tone and manner from the playful and benign to the provocational and angry. In addition, RQs are used in interactions with the intention of confronting and potentially shaming an individual.

RQs are different from information-seeking questions even though they may use the same lexicon and syntactic forms. Information questions have a perceptible rise and lengthened final vowel, and the speaker usually waits for the addressee to respond before taking the next turn. In contrast, RQs have a perceptible fall and clipped final vowel, and a speaker may fire off several in rapid succession, leaving no space for the addressee to respond. Given that RQs call for no answer, this turn-taking procedure is not surprising. Informa-tion-seeking questions are for the most part unambiguous; the meaning (*hego:*) of RQs may not be. The *hego:* of RQs is always different from the literal proposition contained in the information question. For example, "Is it yours?" means "It is not yours!" and "Did I say + proposition" means "I did not say + proposition." RQs are used to challenge claims, propositions, and actions in order to redirect or terminate the actions of an addressee. Of importance in their effectiveness are the sequencing and mode of their delivery.

Speakers frame RQs through various linguistic means, some of which render the RQ partially ambiguous, leaving the assignment of meaning to the addressee. This sets up the way in which the addressee will proceed as next speaker. After assessing the addressee's reaction, the speaker may adjust for the desired effect of the next turn.

Such teasing and shaming situations contrast with contexts where speakers are decidedly unambiguous in their intended tone and message. For example, within the *ada:* relationship in which Kaluli mothers convey to their young children how they are to feel sorry for younger siblings and give them food, they use formulaic verbal constructions and nonverbal expressive behaviors strictly associated with these meanings (B. B. Schieffelin 1981). In these situations speakers use a set of contextualization cues (Gumperz 1977) that signal how the message is to be interpreted. These contextualization cues and affect keys include aspects of surface form, prosody, paralinguistic features, sequencing order, situational and discourse history, and context of the talk.

In teasing and shaming situations, contextualization cues do not set up a single simple interpretive frame or affective key, and participants must pay close attention to what is going on to interpret often shifting or ambiguous cues. This close monitoring is especially critical in teasing and shaming, where, within the context of kinship relationships, alliances may momentarily shift or reorganize. The boundaries of key shift as speakers and addressees assess face-saving needs in exchanges where what constitutes entitlement, access, and ownership is negotiable.

The socialization of rhetorical questions in teasing and shaming

What in the verbal environment of young Kaluli children may facilitate the learning of teasing and shaming forms that lay the foundation for the learning of more complex *bale to* 'turned-over words' as well as the social and linguistic inferencing pervasive in Kaluli talk?

The foundations for learning how to understand these verbal forms of social control are laid down in the early interactions between caregivers and children, before infants are capable of verbalization. The earliest pattern is as follows.

Example 3
[Seligiwo: (9 months) has crawled to the woodpile and is pulling himself up.]
Mo → S: Aba   fa:la:naya?!
              Where are you climbing?!
[Mother takes baby off the woodpile]

In dyadic interactions, a caregiver's utterance (usually a RQ) followed by her action sets up a sequence consisting of a verbal message followed by the appropriate consequential behavior. In sequences such as the one above, the caregiver physically intervenes and provides the child with a model of the desired outcome. Such sequences frequently occur between caregivers and their preverbal children, as small children tend to act in objectionable ways; for example, putting objects in their mouths that are not considered safe, and crawling near potentially dangerous areas.

However, a great many interactions involving Kaluli caregivers and their young children are organized triadically. Triads typically involve the mother, her language-learning child, and another sibling or member of the household. As part of teaching their 2-year-old children how to use language in interactions with others, mothers tell them what to say, using an imperative *a:la:ma* 'say like that' following the utterance to be repeated. The intended (third-party) addressee may be an infant, an older child, or an adult. The utterance that the 2-year-old is expected to repeat is shaped according to the intended addressee.

Example 4

[When her son Seligiwo: (7 months) was crying, Mother speaks to her daughter Ma:li (24 months).]

Mo → Ma:li →> S: Wanga ya:laya?!   A:la:ma.
                          Why are you crying?! Say like that.
Ma:li → S: Wanga ya:laya?
Mo → Ma:li →> S: Ya:la:sabo!   A:la:ma.
                          Don't cry!
Ma:li → S: Ya:la:sabo!

Both utterances (RQ and negative imperative) are said in such a way (high volume, exaggerated intonation) as to startle the infant, get his attention, and change his behavior. Thus in using a RQ to a preverbal child in this way (to stop him crying) the mother is attempting to distract (*ha:nulab*) the child from his crying. She is also involving her 2-year-old daughter in this caregiving situation and instructing her in what she will say when taking care of the infant by herself. However, there is an underlying proposition to the RQ "Why are you crying?!" namely, "There is no good reason for you to be crying; therefore, you should not cry." This is made explicit in the negative directive that follows. While it is unlikely that the preverbal addressee understands the proposition that is implied in the RQ, the 2-year-old who is in the process of learning the underlying proposition comes to understand the rhetorical force of such utterances and the desired outcome.

A sequence using similar linguistic forms (negative imperatives and rhetorical questions) towards achieving somewhat different interactional ends is found in situations of control that are the precursors of situations that will eventually be used to threaten a child with shaming.

Example 5

[As Seligiwo: (11 months) takes something belonging to Babi, Mother speaks to Ma:li (28 months).]

M → Ma:li →> S: Dia:sabo!   A:la:ma.
                          Don't take! Say like that.
Ma:li → M: Huh?
M → Ma:li →> S: Dia:sabowo:! A:la:ma.
                          Don't take!
Ma:li → S: Dia:sabo!
M → Ma:li →> S: We Babiya:no! A:la:ma.
                          This is Babi's!
Ma:li → S: We Babiya:no!
M → Ma:li →> S: Ga:nowo:?!   A:la:ma.
                          It is yours?!
Ma:li → S: Ga:nowo:?!

The participants in these situations (both mothers and their 2-year-old children) make no demands on the preverbal infant to respond verbally – only nonverbally, as these utterances are intended to change the infant's action. Again, the immediate desired ends on the part of the adult is to change the infant's actions through explicit verbal instruction. Such sequences are composed of three components. Initially there are negative imperatives explicitly indicating the immediate desired action or outcome (*Dia:sabo!* 'Don't you take!'), an assertion indicating the reason (in this case, ownership by another individual), and finally, an RQ supporting the preceding assertion that turns the interaction back to the addressee in the form of a question. Utterances such as *Ga:nowo:?!* 'Is it yours?!' are to be read "It is not yours (to take)." In this example, as in the majority of others, the object that is in question belongs to none of the speakers, but to a third person who may or may not be present. Sequences of this type are repeatedly found in Kaluli families.

Though the preverbal child may not understand the individual utterances, hearing the routine formulation of these relatively short, syntactically simple emphatic utterances across a variety of contexts minimally conveys the message that one's action should be changed or terminated. At least the infant may be distracted from the course of action. Caregivers always separate each proposition into a single utterance, avoiding the use of more complex clause-chaining constructions. This pattern of using a single proposition per utterance in teasing and shaming sequences continues well beyond the child's own productive use of complex syntactic constructions and becomes part of the key of the speech event itself. These same routines continue to be used in family interactions with children of all ages. They are not simplified for young children or made more complex for older ones.

At the interactional level, caregivers leave no "turn space" to the infant, since in these situations, as in all others, the infant is not expected to respond. No interpretation is expected. Speakers are usually unambiguous about their desire to control the situation. They select linguistic forms appropriate to the situation, using as much volume and repetition and as many emphatic markers as are needed to achieve their ends. Using both verbal and nonverbal means, they must reorganize a situation in which behavior needs to be changed. There is no expectation that the infant will actually comprehend what is said, just that he or she change the current behavior.

By the time infants are about 14 months old, mothers add an additional component to such verbal sequences involving social control. Often framed as either an RQ, *Go:no: mo:sindilowaba?!* 'Aren't you ashamed?!', or a directive, *Sindiloma!* 'Be ashamed!', children are told explicitly how they are supposed to feel when confronted about taking something that is not theirs to take. In addition, at this time caregivers make extensive use of third-party threats to add emphasis to these sequences in situations when children are acting inappropriately. Such utterances take the form *Ge sama:ib!* 'Someone will say something to you!' or *Dowa: sama:ib* 'Your father will say something (to you)'. The threat is of being publicly and verbally confronted and consequently shamed. The "something" that someone will say is "Is it yours?!" or a similar RQ. Mothers and other caregivers never threaten children with what they themselves might or could do, but always refer to a third person who is not present, or someone (like the researcher) who would not actually do anything at all. (Reference to the researcher as punitive agent was actively discouraged!)

The pattern of using third-party threats was consistent with language used with older children as well as between adults. Given the organization of social relationships in Kaluli society, first-person threats are potentially too dangerous and explosive. One might be pushed to act on his or her threat, which would defeat the point of the exchange. To be called on one's threat could shut the interaction down, when the point is to continue using verbal means of social control to achieve a particular end. In any case, given the difficulty individuals in this society have compelling one another to do something, regardless of their age, verbal manipulation with threats that speakers cannot act on reduces the direct confrontational nature of social control while maintaining a high level of drama. Thus, well before infants are using language themselves, mothers are speaking to them (as well as directing their older siblings to speak to them) with the use of a specific set of single-proposition linguistic devices to control or alter their behavior. As they get older, these same linguistic devices begin to take on the specific affective keys of teasing and shaming them.

Discussion

Several issues have come out of these data. First, a particular form conveys a different type of rhetorical force or accomplishes a different outcome depending on the age of the addressee. For younger preverbal infants, the desired effect may be distraction caused by utterances being directed to them to startle them. For the older preverbal infants, the caregiver may believe that the child can understand the direct imperative, and the remainder of the sequence in which it occurs holds the child's attention without the child fully comprehending the utterances. Or finally, as children mature and begin to acquire a fuller range of linguistic expression, the caregiver may believe that they will also understand how they are expected to feel about the actions that are taking place.

Second, with the same addressee, teasing routines may themselves shift in ways that are purposefully intended to trick or confuse, play or test, put down or mock-threaten the individual. Therefore, we see how linguistic forms in interactional routines have different meanings or rhetorical force according to who the addressee happens to be, as well as having speakers using similar routines and forms to obtain varying affective outcomes from the same addressee.

Third, from the data examined (eighty-three hours of tape-recorded and transcribed spontaneous family interactions) one can find the following sequential combinations. These are directed to infants who have not yet begun to speak (under 20 months) and occur the majority of the time with *a:la:ma* in triadic situations with older siblings.

(1) Claim/RQ ("This is B's! Is it yours?!")
(2) RQ/claim ("Who are you?! This is your brother's!")
(3) RQ/negative directive ("Why are you crying?! Don't cry!")
(4) RQ/negative habitual ("What are you eating?! One doesn't eat it!")
(5) Negative directive/claim/RQ/RQ ("Don't take it! It's father's. Who are you?! Aren't you ashamed?!")

In all of these sequences RQs are used confrontationally. Kaluli call these RQs *sasideab* 'someone shames'. By using these forms speakers challenge or attempt to terminate the action performed by the addressee. The RQs used are the very ones that speakers claim would be said in third-party threats, such as "Someone will say something." No Kaluli child wants to be challenged, teased, or shamed. Yet interactions involving children are marked by the pervasive use of these forms. They serve the caregivers' needs to control their young children and socialize them to display culturally appropriate behaviors. There is no expected response to these utterances and therefore no negotiated interpretation on the part of a listener. The speaker is unambiguous about the intended meaning, using these forms to control the young child's behavior.

Notably absent in these interactions are negative statements (such as "It isn't yours!" or "You shouldn't eat it") followed by a RQ. Thus the listener has to learn to make the logical connection between the RQ and another utterance in order to understand the meaning and pragmatic force of the RQ and the interaction. That is, the sequences of claims, negative directives, and negative habituals with the RQ provide discourse-based propositional supports for inferring how the RQ is to be interpreted by the preverbal child.

In addition, these interactions aid the older language-learning child in mastering the appropriate sequencing and delivery style of RQs in teasing or shaming routines. Through triadic routines using *a:la:ma,* they participate in and talk through sequences directed to the younger child. The younger child may not understand what is being said, but he or she will see the social interaction displayed. Children must learn, for example, that RQs are not to be answered like information questions. In interactions, children under 24 months occasionally answered RQs. When this happened, everyone would laugh at the child's response, then quickly through direct instruction using *a:la:ma* tell the child the appropriate way to talk back. Young children must learn that RQs are meant to change their behavior, but also that they might try to renegotiate the claim or challenge the speaker with another RQ. Over time they learn that they should feel ashamed when confronted with RQs if compliance with directives is not forthcoming.

The discourse structure involving RQs in teasing and shaming is somewhat different when older children are the third-party addressees in direct instruction sequences using *a:la:ma*. In these sequences, the supporting material for the RQs is largely dropped. That is, the mother instructs the child in using a series of RQs (and other linguistic devices such as formulaic expressions), building sequences of these forms alone. One such example follows.

Example 6

[Wanu (27 months), his sister Binalia (5 years), cousin Mama ($3\frac{1}{2}$ years), and Mother are eating salt that belongs to Isa, another sister.]

Mo → W →> M & B: Aba:nowo:?! A:la:ma.
                  Whose is it?! Say like that.

W → M & B: Aba:nowo?!

Mo → W →> M & B: Ga:nowo:?! A:la:ma.
                  Is it yours?!

W → M & B: Ga:nowo:?!

Mo → W →> M & B: Ge oba?! A:la:ma.
                  Who are you?!

B → W →> Mo: Ga:nowo:?! A:la:ma.
              Is it yours?!

Mo → W →> M & B: Na:noka:! A:la:ma.
                  It's mine!

In sequences using *a:la:ma,* caregivers usually insist that the child use the correct form, and not paraphrase or innovate. If the child does not repeat what the caregiver provides, other attempts will be made to get the child to do so. In her speech directed to the young child, the mother (and other adults) also comes to rely solely on the special forms used for teasing and shaming. Thus by the time children are 2 years old, speech directed to them draws on a variety of expressions that tease or shame them for the purposes of social control.

Language directed to the child changes as the child gets older, from more explicitly stated claims to ones that are less so. Because of constant exposure to these forms across contexts and their use by caregivers in triadic situations to assist young children in getting control over what caregivers see as theirs, it should come as no surprise that children use RQs spontaneously and appropriately in certain contexts by the time they are 2 years old. Even when they do not fully articulate all of the words, they convey the rhetorical force of their utterance with the correct intonational contours and other contextualization cues. At this age, RQs appear both in challenges and in teasing, especially in situations involving the distribution of food and the possession of desired objects. Children use a range of teasing expressions by the time they are 30 months old; their use of explicit reference to shaming appears much later. Kaluli consider the ability to tease and shame through the use of RQs to be a sign of social competence in young children. These are the verbal means through which young children can be strong and independent.

I can summarize some of the ways in which valences of different factors involved in teasing and shaming change and shift over developmental time. These are illustrated as sets of continua.

Preverbal infants ——————————→   3-year-old children

(1) Structure:
   Triadic interactions ——————————→   Dyadic interactions
(2) Means of control:
   Nonverbal + verbal control ————→   Verbal control
(3) Meaning:
   Literality of forms ——————————→   Nonliterality of forms
(4) Context:
   Increase in importance of situational and discourse history to the interaction
(5) Key:
   Increase in key variation
(6) Interpretation:
   Increase in co-construction of interactions

Teasing and shaming in Kaluli society

Having taken a developmental perspective, it is important to be cautious when linking the ways in which teasing and shaming are used in interactions involving children with interactions between adults. For one, the stakes are different for adults than for children. For adults, motives are an important issue, whereas young children often act because they don't really know or understand. Whereas teasing and shaming are pervasive in family interactions, the affective key is not usually heavy or traumatic, in that children are not subjected to serious or permanent consequences resulting from being teased or shamed. For the Kaluli, teasing and shaming are systematically part of interactions with children, and as such, they operate on many levels, are structured dyadically and triadically, and are expressed both verbally and nonverbally. They are used to teach children how to be part of Kaluli society, to include them rather than set them apart.

However, these modes of interaction do even more, and it is important to consider why they are so pervasive in this egalitarian society, where any person may try to control another and where people usually do not want to appear to deny each other anything. In several senses, RQs provide an interactional context in which both speaker and addressee have some choice in what the outcome will be. RQs maintain the speaker/addressee relationship while allowing one person to try to control another. In producing an RQ in response to an action or claim, the speaker is not boldly denying the requester. Unlike negative directives, RQs put the ball back in the addressee's court, providing him or her with the option to respond (in a limited number of ways) or to remain silent. RQs call for no answer, but they do keep communication open and acknowledge the other. An RQ (with its *hego:* 'underneath') provides the addressee with some face-saving protection, a great deal more than one would have after negative directives, which increase status differentiation and change the speaker/addressee relationship. The message may be similar, but the metacommunication is not.

Yet another reason that teasing and RQs in general are so common in Kaluli interactions may have to do with the fact that Kaluli enjoy interactions that have some creative tension in them, where the outcome is potentially unpredictable and dependent on the individual's ability to be clever. The forms of talk used in teasing and shaming, especially RQs, can create a dramatic tension in an interaction, a tension that keeps the channels of communication open and the outcome unpredictable.

Whereas the Kaluli value assertiveness and directness, they value their social relationships even more. Given the Kaluli sense of individual autonomy, it is not surprising that these modes of social control are used at the beginning of social life, in interactions that involve preverbal infants.

Notes

Thanks go to those who supported the research on which this chapter is based: the National Science Foundation and the Wenner-Gren Foundation for Anthropological Research. Buck Schieffelin, Steve Feld, Peggy Miller, Lawrence Carrington, and Elinor Ochs offered other types of invaluable support.
1   The data on which this analysis is based were collected during the course of two years' ethnographic and linguistic fieldwork (1975–7) among the Kaluli in the Southern Highlands Province of Papua New Guinea. This study on the development of communicative competence among the Kaluli focused on four children who were approximately 24 months old at the start of the study. However, an additional twelve children (siblings and cousins) were included in the study; their ages ranged from birth to 10 years. The spontaneous conversations of these children and their families were audiorecorded for one year at monthly intervals, with each monthly sample lasting three or four hours. Detailed contextual notes accompanied the audiotaping, and these annotated transcripts, along with interviews and observations, form the data base.
2   The acquisition of these teasing forms by young children is discussed in Schieffelin 1986.

References

Duranti, A. 1984. Intentions, self, and local theories of meaning: words and social action in a Samoan context. Center for Human Information Processing, Technical Report 122. University of California, San Diego.

Feld, S. 1982. *Sound and sentiment: birds, weeping, poetics and song in Kaluli expression.* Philadelphia: University of Pennsylvania Press.
Feld, S. & Schieffelin, B. B. 1982. *Bale to:* 'Turned over words' in Kaluli. Paper presented at the 1982 Georgetown University Round Table on Languages and Linguistics.
Franklin, K. 1972. A ritual pandanus language of New Guinea. *Oceania* 43:66–76.
Gumperz, J. 1977. Sociocultural knowledge in conversational inference. In M. Saville-Troike, ed., *Linguistics and anthropology.* Georgetown University Round Table on Languages and Linguistics. Washington, D.C.: Georgetown University Press, pp. 191–211.
Hymes, D. 1972. Models of the interaction of language and social life. In J. Gumperz & D. Hymes, eds., *Directions in sociolinguistics: the ethnography of communication.* New York: Holt, Rinehart & Winston, pp. 35–71.
Kochman, T. 1983. The boundary between play and nonplay in Black verbal dueling. *Language in Society* 12:329–337.
Laycock, D. C. 1977. Special languages in parts of the New Guinea area. In S. A. Wurm, ed., *New Guinea area languages and language study,* vol. 3. Pacific Linguistic series C, no. 40. Canberra: Australian National University, pp. 133–150.
Ochs, E. In press. *Culture and language acquisition: acquiring communicative competence in Western Samoa.* Cambridge: Cambridge University Press.
Ochs, E. & Schieffelin, B. B. 1984. Language acquisition and socialization: three developmental stories and their implications. In R. Shweder & R. LeVine, eds., *Culture theory: essays on mind, self and emotion.* Cambridge: Cambridge University Press, pp. 276–320.
Rosaldo, M. 1982. The things we do with words: Ilongot speech acts and speech act theory in philosophy. *Language in Society* 11:203–237.
Schieffelin, B. B. 1981. A sociolinguistic analysis of a relationship. *Discourse Processes* 42:189–196.
1986. The acquisition of Kaluli. In D. Slobin, ed. *The cross-linguistic study of language acquisition.* Hillsdale, N. J.: Erlbaum, pp. 525–593.
In press. *How Kaluli children learn what to say, what to do, and how to feel.* Cambridge: Cambridge University Press.
Schieffelin, E. L. 1976. *The sorrow of the lonely and the burning of the dancers.* New York: St. Martin's Press.
Strathern, A. 1975. Veiled speech in Mt. Hagen. In M. Bloch, ed. *Political language and oratory in traditional society.* London: Academic Press, pp. 185–203.
Wentworth, W. M. 1980. *Context and understanding: an inquiry into socialization theory.* New York: Elsevier North-Holland.

9. Teasing: verbal play in two Mexicano homes

ANN R. EISENBERG

Teasing a child is a behavior that seems specifically designed to create uncertainty in the recipient of the tease. Although the teaser does not actually intend the literal content of his or her utterance to be accepted as true, teasing creates the possibility that the child will believe the utterance to be true. According to Grice's (1975) maxim of quality, speakers should not say anything they believe to be untrue; yet in teasing children, adults intentionally violate this maxim. The question to be addressed in this chapter is why adults choose to tease children and thereby create this type of uncertainty in them.

Although descriptions of teasing are rare in the literature on interactions involving young children, there are enough data to indicate that explanations of teasing must focus on a particular cultural or subcultural group (Coles 1977; Heath 1981; Miller this volume; Schieffelin this volume; Simmons 1942). Teasing has been shown to vary across groups in its structural characteristics, assignment of roles permissible for children, and association with other speech forms, such as criticism, joking, and assertion. Thus, the specific focus of this chapter will be the teasing that occurred in the interactions of two Mexican immigrant families living in northern California.

The suggestion to be made is that while there are common characteristics shared by all teasing sequences, at any particular time the specific goal of the teaser may vary. Specifically, the adults in the current study teased for two primary, and sometimes overlapping, purposes: to control the behavior of children and to have fun with children. Some teasing sequences were simply for fun; others incorporated social messages into a playful context. Although these two forms were not entirely distinct, viewing teasing from these two perspectives provides a useful framework for understanding the complexity of the behavior.

Although adults primarily teased to have fun and to control children's behavior, teasing also emphasized the relationships existing between the par-

182

ticipants involved in the interaction sequence. Those relationships were emphasized both by the verbal messages used in teasing and in the alignments created as teasing sequences evolved. Thus, in addition to asking why adults tease children, the paper also addresses the question of what children may be learning within the context of such interactions. What were the children learning about the nature of talk and the way in which relationships were expressed through talk? In addition, how did the children learn to become active participants in teasing?

The data base

The data were part of a study on the acquisition of communicative competence by two monolingual, Spanish-speaking girls living in the metropolitan area near Oakland, California. Both girls were born in the United States, but their parents were all immigrants from central Mexico who had lived in the United States for less than six years when the study began. All the adults spoke only Spanish at home. Both girls were first-born, each with a younger sister born during the course of the study.

The two girls, Nancy and Marisa, were audiotaped every three weeks in two two-hour sessions. Taping continued for approximately a year: from 21 to 32 months for Nancy and from 24 to 38 months for Marisa. The investigator made extensive contextual notes during each recording session, and transcriptions were made within two to four days. When it was unclear what was occurring in a recorded interaction sequence, portions of the transcripts were shown to the mothers and they were asked for their interpretations. The mothers were also frequently asked why they or their children had acted in a particular fashion.

The events recorded included a number of different situations and individuals. Most recordings were made in the home or outside in the yard or courtyard where the women of the neighborhood would often congregate. All the recording sessions included the mother, and most also included other relatives or neighbors. Nancy lived with her parents, infant sister, two maternal uncles, an aunt, and, for a few months, her grandfather and a male family friend. She also interacted on a daily basis with her 3-year-old neighbor Pablito, his family, and other slightly older cousins and neighbors. Marisa lived with her parents and infant sister and, during the summer, her maternal grandmother and 12-year-old uncle. Next door lived her mother's sister, two uncles, and her 4-year-old cousin Laura, who was her constant playmate. Thus, the situations in which the girls were teased (or involved in teasing others) could also be compared with how older children and other adults were teased.

A teasing sequence was defined as any conversational sequence that opened with a mock challenge, insult, or threat. A key feature of the teasing sequence was that the teaser did not intend the recipient to continue to believe the utterance was true, although he or she might intend the recipient to believe it initially. This is an important distinction, because teasers do often hope to "trick" their listeners into believing them so as to enjoy the results when the latter realize that they have been duped. Using the criterion of eventual intent is also useful in distinguishing teasing from another type of untrue utterance the adults often used when attempting to control the behavior of young children – namely, threatening them with the appearance of a witch or bogeyman (el CuCui) who would spirit them away. In teasing sequences, that the teaser did not intend the tease to be understood as true was always eventually made apparent, either by a disclaimer (for example, *No lo creas* 'Don't believe it'; *Estoy jugando, no más,* 'I'm just playing') or by the use of contextualization cues, such as exaggerated intonation, laughs, or winks, which signaled "This is play." No such cues accompanied threats that children were expected to believe.

Within teasing sequences, adults threatened to inflict bodily harm ("We're going to throw Marisa in the garbage!"), disrupt important relationships ("I'm going to take your baby away!"), and withhold affection ("I'm not going to love you any more!"). Affectional bonds between the child and someone else were also frequently threatened ("Nancy, Aunt Sonia says she doesn't love you!"). Valued abilities (e.g., singing, dancing) and attributes (e.g., attractiveness, sanity) were also attacked and adults used their knowledge of the children's fears, likes, and dislikes to threaten them playfully with events they knew would provoke dismay in the child ("I'm going to dress you as a witch for Halloween, right, Nancy?", said when the child was known to be afraid of witches).

The most common teasers were the girls' mothers, probably because they were most frequently with the children. After mothers, men – particularly uncles – were most likely to be teasers. Female relatives other than the mothers were much less likely to incorporate teasing into a relationship with a child. Hopper, Sims & Alberts (1983) have suggested that men are more likely to tease children than are women. Although this sex difference was not entirely supported in the current study, teasing did represent a larger proportion of men's conversations with young children. In one or two cases, nearly all of a specific uncle's interactions with a niece involved teasing and joking. In addition, men and women tended to tease in slightly different ways. Mothers were most likely to tease children about being crazy (or being locked up with the crazies) or with the withdrawal of love or disruption of a relationship (e.g., "I'm going to take your baby"), whereas uncles were more likely to tease girls about being ugly or to threaten them with bodily harm.

From a discourse standpoint, the typical teasing sequence began with the adult issuing a challenge directly to the child. At that point, the child could either defend herself or another adult could help the child with the defense. In other cases, the challenge was not actually addressed to the child, but was formed as a statement about the child and directed to a third party. Essentially, the teaser attempted to solicit the other individual's participation in teasing the child. In this type of sequence, the younger child could also be invited in as the co-teaser of another child or adult. In a similar type of sequence the very young child could also be given lines to repeat to help tease someone else. Most of the sequences in which the tease was directed to the child as addressee could be characterized as purely playful episodes. In contrast, while they incorporated elements of play, sequences in which the child's role was that of intended overhearer or invited co-teaser generally also involved a message about appropriate behavior.

Teasing as play

Telling jokes, describing comical situations, and teasing are important forms of fun and amusement in Mexican homes, and members of the culture place a high value on verbal playfulness. Humor is important because it is entertaining, serves as a time filler, and brings group members together (Castro 1982). Interpersonal relationships are important to Mexican people, and a vital aspect of those relationships is humorous communication and verbal interplay.

Children become a part of these noisy times at a very early age. From infancy they are drawn into interactions with others. Mothers talk to infants as if they can understand and interpret their babbling, gestures, and cries for others. With the instruction *díle* 'say to him/her', they tell preverbal infants what to say to others, and the others respond as if the infants had repeated the parent's utterance. Once children begin to speak, they are expected to repeat what they are told to say and thus begin to use language to conduct interpersonal relationships (see Eisenberg 1982 for a more complete description of the use of *díle*). Conversations with young children are also highly routinized, allowing children to participate despite a lack of sophisticated linguistic resources. The content of such interactions is less important than simply having the interaction. The goal is simply to have children participate and to enjoy interacting with them.

Teasing provides another context in which adults and children can converse and thereby act out a social relationship, despite the limited linguistic resources of the child. Teases are uttered under circumstances and within relationships where it is most plausible for the antagonistic statement to be framed and understood as play (Bateson 1972; Goffman 1975). In the context of the study, many aspects of the situation in which teasing occurred suggested that, in its simplest form, teasing was a type of social play. First, teasing was most common when adults were taking a break from the routine chores of the day and were relaxing in the courtyard or sitting out front on the stoop. Teases also most commonly clustered together in discourse involving other playful forms, jokes, and laughter. The laughter and accompanying winks, play faces, provocative tones, deep sighs, and exaggerated or singsong intonation acted as "contextualization cues" (Gumperz 1977), signaling the playful nature of the attack.

In addition, the adults frequently repeated the same initiations over and over again so that the repetitiveness provided a background for interpreting the challenge as nonserious. Having participated in a very similar interaction before, the child knew what the outcome would be. Teasing also generally occurred in a context in which the child could feel safe. Teasers were almost always someone known to the child and someone who frequently engaged her in such interactions. Further evidence that the adults perceived teasing episodes as play was that when they were shown the sequences and asked what was going on, they would respond, "I was just playing." That children were allowed to talk back and challenge adults during teasing also marked the sequences as play, since speaking assertively was clearly inappropriate for children in other contexts. Children who challenged adults or were heard doing so with their young visitors were considered *malcriados* 'poorly raised' or *groseros* 'rude'.

Teasing "works" because of its inherent ambiguity. The recipient must decide whether the speaker is serious or whether he or she is "only joking." Once the teaser opens a teasing episode, a successful interaction can take two forms. In the first, the recipient immediately recognizes the tease and plays along, either defending himself or counterteasing. In the second, the recipient fails to understand that the teaser was not serious and thus becomes the "butt" of the tease. This second type of sequence is most successful when the recipient joins in the fun once he or she eventually realizes that the original statement was just a tease. The first type works because all the participants play together; the second works because someone's vulnerability is exposed.

The adults in the study began teasing a child to amuse themselves, but that amusement could either be shared with the child or be at the expense of the child. Although teasing could and did occur in dyadic situations, it was most common when three or more people were present, particularly when those other individuals were other adults. Within dyadic situations, adults used teasing to play *with* the child. Teasing initiations were highly ritualized and clearly accompanied by playful contextualization cues. The type of teasing initiation used in dyadic contexts was also quite easily responded to, making it simple for a child without sophisticated linguistic skills to play along.

Within triadic or multiparticipant contexts, however, there were many indications that teasing was intended to amuse the teaser and the audience rather than the teaser and the recipient of the tease (although eventually the recipient might join in the laughter at his or her own expense). Provoking an angry or confused response from a child was considered funny, particularly if another adult was present to share in the amusement over the child's anger or frustration. The teaser often played to the audience, signaling his or her expectation concerning the child's reaction with a smile or wink:

Example 1[1]

Nancy (N, 26 months) and her mother (M) are watching TV with the investigator (I) shortly before Halloween. They have just watched a commercial for Halloween candy and have discussed what Nancy will say when she goes trick-or-treating. Nancy's mother knows she is afraid of witches.

M: La voy a disfrazar de bruja, ¿verdad, hija?
   (I'm going to dress her as a witch, right, honey?)
   [Winks at I and speaks softly]
   Le da miedo.
   (It scares her.)
   [To N] ¿Disfrazo de bruja?
   (A witch costume?)
[N shrieks]   no!
M and I: [laugh]

In such situations, the adults responded with laughter to the child's anger or distress.

Because the adults often teased to amuse themselves and other adults, the joke was sometimes at a level of complexity that the child might not understand. In fact, it was often the child's nonresponse – the lack of awareness that someone was teasing – that amused the adults. The relationship between Nancy and her friend Pablito was the focus of this type of joking. The two were frequently teased about being boyfriend and girlfriend. Similarly, Marisa's father would tease her about the Anglo boy living upstairs, asking if she were going to kiss him and if she liked *los hueros* 'the fair ones'.[2] No matter how Marisa responded, he and her mother would laugh.

Children, as immature and unsophisticated speakers, were easy victims[3] of this type of tease. They were not, however, the only victims; ideal victims included both those who could not defend themselves and those who could be counted on to defend themselves well. Quick-witted adults frequently teased others who were less witty, including the investigator in the study, who was a nonnative speaker of Spanish and, like the young children, a less sophisticated speaker, who could therefore also be counted on to miss some of the nuances of the conversation.

The various adults in the study differed somewhat in the extent to which they felt upsetting a child through teasing was appropriate. Nancy was more likely than Marisa to be teased to the point of upset, particularly by her uncle Ramon, who was frequently criticized by Nancy's mother for angering the children. Ramon, it seems, was likely to go beyond the "bounds defined by custom'' (Radcliffe-Brown 1940:186). Exactly when one "goes too far," however, seemed to be a situated accomplishment (Hopper, Sims & Alberts 1983): There were no general rules, although it was obvious that all participants knew when it had happened.

The multiparticipant context in which teasing most frequently occurred was also exploited in other ways. Teasing was "safe" when others were present because those others could help defend a child who could not yet defend herself. Alternatively, they could assure the child that the teaser was playing or that what he or she was saying was not true. Supporting the child in the interaction helped the child understand that teasing was a form of play and helped her learn to play along, enacting the role of self-defender. In the case of the youngest children, the second adult frequently gave the child the appropriate lines to repeat in response to the attack:

Example 2

[Marisa (M, 27 months) is having her hair braided by her Aunt Amalia (A) while her Uncle Carlos (C) looks on.]
C: [Wrinkling his nose and shaking his head]
   ¡Fea, fea!
   (Ugly, ugly!)
A: "No es cierto," díle. "Soy bonita."
   ("That's not true," tell him. "I'm pretty.")
                            soy bonito/
                            (I'm pretty/)
C: [Imitates her speech] "No nonito."
   ¿No estás bonita?
   (You're not pretty?)
A: "Sí," díle, "soy bonita."
   ("Yes," tell him, "I'm pretty.")
C: Estás fea.
   ("You're ugly.")
                            bonita/
                            (pretty/)

Throughout Ex. 2, Marisa's aunt gives her the appropriate reply to someone who accuses her of not being pretty – an important attribute for little girls. Telling Marisa what to say in response gave her the opportunity to assert important, positive characteristics about herself. In similar situations, Nancy's mother would tease her about her aunt not loving her and if Nancy became upset (rather than responding, for example, *No, a tí no te quiere* 'No, she doesn't love *you*'), her aunt would reassure her that she did love her. A secondary effect of the mother's challenge was that it put the aunt in the position of affirming the fact that a loving relationship existed between her and Nancy. Whatever the focus of the attack, the resolution of the episode almost always yielded a positive statement in response: "Yes, I am pretty" or "Yes, she does love me."

Teasing as social control

While all of the teasing episodes were playful (by definition), many of them also seemed to involve something more than "just play." In many of the episodes, the adults' teasing also had an underlying message concerning the inappropriateness of someone's behavior. In these cases, the challenge was used as a subtle form of criticism to convey a message of disapproval when the offense did not seriously threaten the adult's authority. The most common offenses to provoke teasing were the child's silliness or failure to perform well, although minor offenses, such as refusing to greet someone, also led to teasing. These episodes of social control were similar to those described by Schieffelin (this volume) in which Kaluli mothers in Papua New Guinea teased children to shame them into behaving in accordance with their wishes.

Occasionally, the third party, often another child, was enlisted as co-teaser in the interaction. An utterance could be addressed to a third party, but the butt of the tease was the child, who was expected to overhear. Challenges were frequently issued to the third person, who was invited to agree about the shortcomings of the individual being teased: "Ah, Laura's crazy, isn't she?" or "We're not going to take Marisa to her grandpa's, right, Monica?" The adults manipulated the multiparticipant context to "gang up" on a child. The children were given the opportunity to play both the role of the indirect recipient of the tease and that of the individual asked to participate in the teasing.

The following sequence illustrates some of these discourse features:

Example 3

[Nancy (N, 24 months) and her mother (M) are sitting on the stoop with their neighbor, Ceci (C), an older woman. Nancy pulls away when Ceci tries to hug her.]
M: Oye, Nancy. Dále un besito a Ceci.
   (Listen, Nancy. Give Ceci a kiss.)
[N whines and pulls away]
 C: Un besito. [Sighs heavily, shaking head] Ah, pues, ya no te voy a querer.
   (A kiss. Ah, then, I'm not going to love you any more.)
M: [To C, shaking her head, clicking tongue] No le de manzana ni nada lo que quiere.
   (Don't give her an apple or anything she wants.)
 C: [Shakes her head] Ya, no. Pues, porque ya no me quiere.
   (Not any more. Because she doesn't love me any more.)

   [To N] ¿Verdad que ya no me quieres?
   (Isn't it true that you don't love me any more?)

Talking about the behavior of a child who was expected to overhear was common, both when the message was intended to be taken literally and when it was not. In their conversation with each other ("Don't give her an apple or anything she wants"; "No, not any more, because she doesn't love me anymore"), Doña Ceci and Nancy's mother were doing what Clark & Carlson

(1982) called "talking laterally." In talking laterally, the speaker does not appear to be speaking to the indirect addressee, an appearance that is often useful. There would, however, be no point in discussing not giving Nancy what she wants unless Nancy were there and intended to overhear. Similarly, when a teaser says to Erica, "Marisa's ugly, isn't she?", he is not seeking confirmation of his statement for his own sake, but is doing so for the sake of Marisa, the third party. With the use of the tag question, the adult is not asking Erica the question, but is letting Marisa know she is asking Erica the question and inviting her to agree.

Yet the use of playful contextualization cues in Ex. 3 – the exaggerated head-shaking and sighing and the clicking of tongues – also signaled that the adults did not intend these social-control messages to be taken too seriously. They did, however, intend to make Nancy uncertain about their intent. By teasing Nancy with the withholding of love, the two women were able to make a couple of points: that Nancy should give a kiss when asked for one; and that loving (and the giving of gifts that accompanies it) is contingent upon the child's demonstrations of affection.

In other related sequences, the young child was used as a foil to influence someone else. Older children who misbehaved also found themselves becoming the recipients of a group attack, as adults and other children joined together as attackers. Even other adults could be the recipients of a joint teasing venture, most commonly when one adult would give a young child lines to repeat to another adult. Having the child repeat lines to tease another individual enabled adults to communicate messages that might have been inappropriate to communicate directly. This type of teasing frequently involved potentially volatile issues, such as an uncle's laziness or a grandfather's drinking. As Abrahams (1962) pointed out, this form of verbal play is perilously close to real life. Having the child issue the challenge and invoking the teasing mode created a safe context for the communication of a potentially threatening message. By virtue of the communicative situation created, the recipient of the tease was in a position where it was difficult to respond as if the attack were actually serious. Becoming angry with the adult issuing the teasing statements was inappropriate because involving the child clearly signaled that the sequence was play – at least on the surface. Becoming angry with the child was even more inappropriate, because the child was clearly not the one issuing the challenges. This type of pointed teasing works for the teaser because he or she can always deny any intent to convey a message. Thus, the message is conveyed without fear of immediate retaliation.

Teasing and relationships

Thus far, teasing sequences have been discussed as examples of play with language and as attempts to control the behavior of young children. Yet at the same time the teasing sequences conveyed a number of underlying messages to children, especially messages concerning the nature of social relationships. Teasing sequences reinforced relationships both through the content of the episodes and through the structural relationships created as the sequences developed.

The content of teasing episodes addressed issues of relationships in many ways. Resolution and development of many of the sequences involved naming a series of family members who might protect, help, or defend a child in the face of an attack. For example, a teasing routine that Marisa and her mother frequently engaged in involved Marisa's mother threatening to leave Marisa behind when the family went to visit Grandpa in Mexicali. The episode would continue with Marisa listing individuals who might take her if Mama did not and her mother responding with reasons why those others would not or could not take her either. The theme of visiting Grandpa in Mexicali and the listing of relatives appeared in many other conversations as well and was an important strategy for scripting Marisa's interactions with her mother. Relationships with extended family members were extremely important to the families, and it was considered important for children to know who their relatives were and what those relationships involved (Eisenberg 1982).

The existence of important relationships was also emphasized through threats to those relationships. An important consequence of such threats was that the threat required a verbal statement acknowledging the existence of the relationship and often another verifying its continuation. For example, when an adult threatened to steal a baby sister, the child was supposed to counter, "No, mine!", stating that the baby was hers and could not be taken away. Similarly, in the following example, Nancy's mother placed Nancy's aunt Sonia in the position of affirming her love for Nancy:

Example 4

[Nancy (N, 27 months) wants Ana (A) to take her to the park, so her mother (M) tells her to ask Ana if she wants to go. Since "want" and "love" are the same verb in Spanish, Nancy misunderstands and asks if Ana loves her. Nancy's aunt Sonia (S) is also present.]

[To A]   me llevas?/
                                        (will you take me?/)

M: Díle a Ana, "Quieres?"
   (Say to Ana, "Do you want to?")
                                        me quieres?/
                                        (do you love me?/)

A: Sí.
   (Yes)

M: Sonia no te quiere. Oye, Nancy, Sonia no te quiere. Quiere
   a Os:car, a la Bi:bi, y a Chape:tes.
   (Sonia doesn't love you. Listen, Nancy, Sonia doesn't love
   you. She loves Oscar, Bibi, and Chapetes.)

[N screams angrily]   cállate!/ mensa!/
                                        (shut up!/stupid!/)

M: [Shaking head sadly] No, Sonia no te quiere.
   (No, Sonia doesn't love you.)
S: Nancy, sí te quiero.
   (Nancy, I do love you.)
M: Oye, no te quiere, dice.
   (Listen, she doesn't love you, she says.)
                                        sí quiere a mi!/
                                        (she does love me!/)
[M tells her not to tip the chair over]

Ex. 4 reinforces the relationship between Nancy and her aunt in two ways. First, the mother's challenge elicits the clear statement that Aunt Sonia does love Nancy, both from Nancy and her aunt. Second, the mother's challenge puts Nancy and her aunt in a position where they unite by both playing the role of contradictor to the mother's role as challenger.

Other messages about relationships concern the nature of specific relationships, particularly those between men and women. As Hopper et al. (1983) suggested, many of the themes that appear in teasing sequences involving fathers and uncles seem to involve issues related to courtship. Men tease about attractiveness or they threaten girls with restraint or injury, suggesting the ideas that girls must be attractive and perhaps also that females can expect males to restrict their movement. Within the context of the play frame, males may also threaten to withdraw affection or to trade affection or a favor for the freedom from restraint. For example, typical teasing episodes involving Marisa and her uncle began with the challenge *Estás fea, ¿verdad?* 'You're ugly, right?', led to Marisa's counterassertion that she was pretty, and concluded with the uncle's willingness to accept the counterassertion if she would "show him" she was pretty with a kiss.

Teasing also reinforced relationships through the alignments created within the episodes. Many times when an adult provoked a child by teasing, the outcome was an alignment between the child and her co-defender, as in Exx. 2 and 4. Mothers "forced" children into interacting with others by giving them lines to repeat in conversation with others or by teasing them so that the other person would help the child negotiate the resolution of the mock conflict. Adults also invited children into special relationships with them by using teasing to make another child (or adult) the "outsider." When teasing works – either because two people have fun with each other or because they share the enjoyment over frustrating someone else – the result is an increase in feelings of closeness and solidarity.

Successful teasing episodes remind one of Blount's (1972) description of the use of whispering among Luo adults and children:

Whispering, in time, comes to be an intensifier within the dyadic addressor–addressee relationship. Third parties are excluded from sharing the message, as indeed, one dimension of the message is that only one particular receiver is intended as the recipient. Furthermore, there is the implication that a special relationship holds between the two participants, and the shared knowledge of this relationship sanctions the appropriateness of the code. In one sense, the parent and child establish collusion, bracketing off their relationship from the remainder of the environment and thereby intensifying the interaction routine. (pp. 239–40)

In a similar fashion, teasing intensifies the relationship between those involved. That it is "safe" to tease a particular individual indicates that a special relationship exists. The knowledge that the relationship exists also "sanctions the appropriateness of the code." Teasing can also establish collusion by creating alignments; inviting a child to help tease creates a special and valued closeness between that child and the adult who invites her into the relationship. The other child must then work to gain entry into that relationship. In fact, the Mexican immigrant adults in the study also used whispering – the telling of secrets – to bracket off relationships. They would invite young children to come close with the statement *Te voy a decir una cosa* 'I'm going to tell you something', and would whisper something into the child's ear when she approached. Aunts were more likely to invite a child (and not the others) to share a secret; uncles were more likely to establish the special relationship by teasing.

Children's participation in teasing

The remaining question concerns the children's own developing abilities to participate in teasing sequences. Over time both children became more adept at interpreting teasing as play and at participating in teasing sequences on their own. At first, however, neither child participated much in teasing sequences, unless supported in self-defense by another adult. Throughout the course of taping, most of their responses tended to be very simple, consisting of either a rapid denial ("No!") or, less frequently, the offer of an alternative to the threat or challenge.

Gradually, the girls began to recognize more different teasing initiations and to make more counterassertions. Rather than simply replying "No," they began rephrasing the challenge, changing the identity of the recipient of the tease. Thus, "Marisa's crazy," became "No, you" or "No, *Laura's* crazy." Over the year in which they were observed, each of the girls developed particular teasing routines with specific individuals and within those routinized sequences increased the extent to which they were able to participate. In the last few taping sessions, the girls also began to tease others, although their initiations were still infrequent, highly routinized, and usually occurred when they themselves had just been teased or had observed someone teasing someone else. Nancy, for example, would ask if someone wanted something she had, would hold it out, and then at the last minute would snatch it away, roaring with laughter. Marisa also made announcements that various people were crazy and would greet the sighting of every neighborhood dog with "Doggie, bite *X!*" uttered in singsong intonation.

As Miller (this volume) indicated, singsong intonation was most important in determining whether a child recognized teasing as play and was the first of the contextualization cues the children learned. Even when the content of a child's retort was not quite appropriate, often the tone of the utterance was. Singsong intonation was not limited to teasing or responding to teasing, but appeared frequently in statements of possession, making those statements sound like taunts. From the adult standpoint, a singsong utterance like "I have playdoh, ah-ha, ah-ha!" may have been inappropriate or an over-generalization, but for the child it may have been a way of determining when such taunts were appropriate and who was likely to respond to them. It may have been a means of learning which taunts and teases would work with adults and which would work with other children.

Toward the end of taping, Marisa was also able to manipulate singsong intonation and other contextualization cues associated with teasing to defuse the impact of a threat she had made – a threat that would have been inappropriate had it not been playful. In other words, Marisa could use the cues to say, "I was just playing":

Example 5

[Marisa (Ma, 34 months) protests when her father (F) teases her by offering her a taco with chile in it when he knows she does not like chile. Her mother (M) and grandmother (G) are also present.]

[Ma shakes her head]
          chile no, Papi/ te pego, Papi/
          (no chile, Daddy/ I'll hit you, Daddy/)

F: [Sternly] ¿A quién le vas a pegar?
   (Whom? Whom are you going to hit?)

[Ma laughs]
          mi mami/
          (my Mommy/)

F: [Still stern] ¿Porqué?
   (Why?)

M: [Laughs] ¡Mira!
   (Look!)

          mi Maya/
          (my Grandma/)

[Ma laughs again]

F: [Laughs] ¿Porqué?
   (Why?)

          mi Tata 'lente/
          (my Grandpa Valente/)

F: Oh tu tata Valente.
   (Oh, your Grandpa Valente.)

M: [Laughs]

G: [Laughs] A tu Papa Valente ahorita no le alcanzas. Está muy lejos.

(Right now you can't reach your Papa Valente. He's very
far away.)
[All laugh]

Marisa was probably not teasing when she first said, "I'll hit you," but once
her father responded, she realized from his tone of voice that she should not
have said that to him. Rather than pursue her original statement – and face
punishment – she laughed to indicate that her threat was not serious and made
it more outlandish (and hence, more playful) by adding her mother, grandmother, and grandfather to the list of those to be hit. (Listing the names of
relatives is also an appropriate conversational theme no matter what the context.) Once her mother laughed, indicating that she accepted that Marisa was
playing, her father accepted her threat as playful. Thus, Marisa was able to
use teasing to get herself out of trouble.

Marisa's facility with teasing is even more interesting in view of the fact
that, overall, Marisa's abilities lagged behind Nancy's. Although Nancy's
knowledge of syntax was more sophisticated at 28 months than Marisa's was
at 38 months, Marisa was more adept than Nancy both at responding to
teasing and recognizing that teases were not serious. While Nancy continued
to become angry when teased, Marisa could taunt back and work out excep-
tions to the challenges, as well as manipulate teasing to avoid punishment.
Her facility with teasing, despite the limitations in her syntax and pronunciation, suggests that the acquisition of some speech genres may not be entirely
dependent on grammatical development. The ability to distinguish between
the surface meaning of an utterance and its intended meaning may not depend
entirely on other linguistic abilities.

There are a number of possible explanations of why Marisa was more at
ease with teasing than Nancy, despite her lack of grammatical sophistication.
One is that the ability to recognize nonliteral meaning is more dependent on
cognitive development that comes with age than are specific linguistic abilities. Thus, since Marisa was slightly older, she was somewhat better at
participating in teasing. Another possible explanation may have to do with
personality differences. Not all adults are equally good at teasing or at recognizing that they are being teased (hence, the sense that certain individuals
make good victims), and this difference may first arise in early childhood as a
result of temperamental or other factors.

Alternatively, differences in experiences with teasing may create these
individual differences. Marisa's facility with teasing may have stemmed from
having more experience with teasing and, in particular, more experience with
the form of teasing that was fun for both participants. In Nancy's home,
Nancy was more often the butt of the tease, and half the fun was upsetting her.
In Marisa's family, however, teasing was not only more frequent but was
more commonly marked with laughter. In addition, when Marisa was teased,

she was given more help in responding to the teasing. Furthermore, Marisa's cousin, Laura, was the recipient of teasing as often as Marisa was, and the adults often invited Marisa to help tease Laura. Thus, Marisa received more practice and help both in responding to teasing and learning to tease others.

Summary

A number of observations can be made about the use of teasing in these two Mexican immigrant homes. First, teasing was primarily a means of playing with a child, either for the amusement of the adult (or adults) or the adult and the child. Adults could tease children to establish or maintain an interaction with them when there was little information to share. Although the content of teasing often touched on important conversational themes (e.g., love, grandparents), the content was usually less important than simply having the interaction. Interpersonal relationships with intimates were extremely important in the families, and an important component of those relationships was verbal contact. Teasing was a way to interact – and to have fun with interaction – without being dependent on the exchange of information. Teasing also reinforced relationships in the alignments it created between individuals. When adults helped children respond to teasing or invited children to help them tease someone else, they created an additional close and special bond between themselves and the child.

Teasing could also be used as a means of social control. Although many of the adults' threats were not intended seriously (e.g., "I'm not going to love you any more"), there was a thin line between this type of empty threat and other empty threats that children were supposed to believe – or, at least, fear might be true. For example, the adults often warned the children that the police or a witch or the bogeyman might come take them away if they misbehaved.

Finally, teasing is also a linguistic skill that children may have to learn to manipulate to speak like the adult members of their particular cultural group. Learning to participate in teasing and to recognize that one is being teased requires sensitivity to nonverbal cues and an ability to go beyond the surface meaning of a message to determine the intentions of the speaker. Learning to tease without overstepping the boundaries of behavior appropriate for small children requires learning complex social rules. Children have to determine who can be teased and in what contexts. The differences between Marisa's and Nancy's ability to participate in teasing sequences suggest that the ability to play with language in this manner may not be closely related to the child's ability to discover the rules of syntax.

Language use is embedded in a complex system with culturally specific functions and meanings. In order to understand the meaning behind cultural variation in conversation and its effects on development, we must give careful attention to the ways of speaking across societies and the acquisition of both linguistic and sociocultural knowledge that is influenced by those ways of speaking. Since cultural and social values are continually expressed through social interaction, the examination of those interactions can furnish information about the relationship between language and culture and what children are being taught about them.

Notes

The research for this paper was supported by grant NIE-G-81-0103 from the National Institute of Education. I would like to thank Shirley Brice Heath, Robert Hopper, Bambi Schieffelin, and Elinor Ochs for participating in many conversations about teasing, and Susan Ervin-Tripp and Dan Slobin for their comments on an earlier version of this paper.

    The term "Mexicano" is the Spanish word for "Mexican" and was chosen over "Chicano" or "Mexican-American" because all members of the families still thought of themselves as Mexican and called themselves "Mexicano."

1 Transcription conventions follow Bloom, Lightbown & Hood (1974). The child's speech appears in the right-hand column and the speech of all others on the left. Slashes (/) indicate the end of a child's utterance, and question marks in parentheses (?) indicate unclear or inaudible utterances. A colon indicates that the previous syllable of a word received exaggerated or unusually long intonation. All contextual information and nonverbal behavior is described in brackets on the left side of the page. Translations are meant to convey the gist of the conversation, although the English versions of the children's speech are closer to exact translation.

2 The word *huero* often has the added connotation of "empty."

3 In general, the term "recipient" is used for the target of the tease. The term "victim" is reserved for the target of a tease that a teaser hopes will at least momentarily confuse the addressee.

References

Abrahams, R. D. 1962. Playing the dozens. *Journal of American Folklore* 75:209–220.

Bateson, G. 1972. *Steps to an ecology of mind.* New York: Ballantine.

Bloom, L. M., Lightbown. P. M., & Hood, L. 1974. *Conventions for transcription of child language recordings.* Unpublished manuscript. Columbia University.

Blount, B. 1972. Aspects of socialization among the Luo of Kenya. *Language in Society* 1:235–248.

Castro, R. 1982. Mexican women's sexual jokes. *Aztlan* 13:275–294.

Clark, H. H. & Carlson, T. B. 1982. Hearers and speech acts. *Language* 58:1–74.

Coles, R. 1977. *Eskimos, Chicanos, Indians.* Vol. 6 of *Children of crisis.* Boston: Little, Brown.

Eisenberg, A. R. 1982. Language acquisition in cultural perspective: talk in three

Mexicano homes. Unpublished Ph.D. dissertation, University of California, Berkeley.

Goffman, E. 1975. *Frame analysis.* New York: Macmillan.

Grice, H. P. 1975. Logic in conversation. In P. Cole & J. P. Morgan, eds., *Syntax and semantics,* vol. 3: *Speech acts.* New York: Academic Press, pp. 41–58.

Gumperz, J. J. 1977. Sociocultural knowledge in conversational inference. In M. Saville-Troike, ed., *Linguistics and anthropology.* Georgetown University Round Table on Languages and Linguistics. Washington, D.C.: Georgetown University Press, pp. 191–212.

Heath, S. B. 1981. Teasing talk: strategies for language learning. Presented at the American Anthropology Association Meeting, Los Angeles, December.

Hopper, R., Sims, A. L., & Alberts, J. K. 1983. Teasing as Daddy's classroom. Presented at the Child Language Conference, Glasgow.

Radcliffe-Brown, A. R. 1940. On joking relationships. *Africa* 13:195–210.

Simmons, L. W., ed. 1942. *Sun Chief: the autobiography of a Hopi Indian.* New Haven: Yale University Press.

10. Teasing as language socialization and verbal play in a white working-class community

PEGGY MILLER

In the following narrative a young mother from the working-class community of South Baltimore recalls an incident that occurred when she was in junior high school:

When I got free lunch, you know, we went through the cafeteria, and the group in the table would all stand up and say, "You got free lunch tickets" [singsong intonation], you know, and they, all of em around the room start hittin the tables and everythin. And I would stand up and I says, "Well, well, you all think you're really teasin somebody. At least I know I'm agettin somethin free and youse ain't. Hahaha. What do you think of that?" And they shut their mouths, boy.

They did. And the ladies that give the food out, they just laughin their tails off back there. They say, "Did you hear that little girl, she stood up there." And I sit down and I says, "You see, I'm gonna enjoy my free lunch." I was eatin, boy, eatin.

And I says, "I even got 15 cents to buy me a fudge bar" [laughs]. They come in there with boloney sandwiches in them bags. I'd say, "You can eat that stale boloney. I'm gettin jello on the side of my plate" [laughs].

Nora tells this tale with pride and pleasure. Her proficiency in the art of teasing enabled her to outwit her peers and to transform a potentially painful experience into an occasion for self-display.

Teasing, as practiced by three families from South Baltimore, is a complex form of verbal play, marked as such by modifications of the normal pattern of speech. Although teenagers and adults are the most imaginative practitioners of this genre, even 2-year-olds show some understanding of the elements of teasing. Like other local varieties of social play, for example, pretend play with dolls (Miller & Garvey 1984) and rhymes and verbal games (Miller 1982), teasing occurs first at home in interaction with mother and other caregivers.

Teasing is not just a type of play, however. It is also a key to language socialization in these families. In every community particular themes are

199

emphasized in the socialization of the young. In South Baltimore one theme in the socialization of girls has to do with affection, sympathy, and the loving care of babies. Teasing manifests this theme insofar as most teasing of young children is done affectionately. But teasing is more revealing of another theme – the high value placed on interpersonal skills of self-assertion and self-defense. Teasing is related to the ability to stand up for oneself, to speak up in anger, and to fight if necessary.

Teasing thus represents the intersection of several important questions in the study of language development and socialization: What are the beliefs and values that caregivers hold about language and the social world? What kinds of language socialization strategies do they use with novice speakers? How do caregivers' beliefs and practices affect language learning? And which aspects of the child's developing communicative system are exploited for playful purposes? The objective of this paper is to address these questions through an examination of teasing as practiced in one urban working-class community.

The study

The study is part of a larger investigation of early language development in South Baltimore, a community of mixed German, Polish, Irish, Italian, and Appalachian descent (Miller 1982). Amy, Wendy, and Beth were first-born children of mothers who had completed from eight to twelve years of schooling. Two of the mothers received public assistance; one was employed as a machine operator in a factory. Although the children had important, often daily, contacts with members of an extended family, the mother was the primary caregiver in every case.

The study was longitudinal in design and ethnographic in approach, combining intensive observations of the children in the contexts of everyday life with an inquiry into the beliefs and values of their families. A series of twelve video recordings was made during the third year of life (age at outset varied from 19 to 25 months). Each child was observed in the rowhouse living room as she interacted with her mother and other family members. The mothers were interviewed periodically throughout the study.

The videotapes were transcribed in detail, with each transcript including a record of what the child said, a record of what other speakers said, a running description of the child's nonverbal behaviors, and a description of contextual features and of other speakers' behaviors. (See Miller 1982 for transcription procedures.)

The present analysis was based on samples I to VI for each of the children, encompassing a mean length of utterance period of about 1.5 to 2.2 morphemes and an age range of 19 to 22 months for Amy, 24 to 27 months for Wendy, and 25 to 28 months for Beth.

Teasing as language socialization

A previous analysis led to the identification of direct instruction as a strategy of early language socialization in South Baltimore (Miller 1982). This analysis revealed that the mothers of Amy, Wendy, and Beth believed in the importance of teaching 2-year-olds to talk and that they routinely gave direct instruction in various aspects of language and speaking during the mean length of utterance period of 1.5 to 2.5 morphemes. That is, they explicitly told the child what to say or how to say it or quizzed her on these matters, using such teaching devices as elicited imitation, prompts, directions to ask or tell, and tutorial questions. These interactions provided opportunities for the child to acquire various kinds of social and linguistic knowledge – to answer and ask what-questions; to assert and comply verbally and nonverbally; to participate appropriately in conversation; to take care of "babies" in mothering play with dolls; and to rhyme, sing, and play verbal games. In addition, a developmental analysis of one category of direct instruction (naming people and things) for one of the mother–child pairs revealed that the mother's instructions were well adapted to the child's level of understanding about naming.

These findings concerning direct instruction tell part – but by no means all – of the story of language socialization in South Baltimore. One question that remained concerned the finding of differences across families in the frequency of direct instruction. Although all three families used this strategy on an everyday basis, there was individual variation in the incidence of direct instruction. A second question concerned the possibility of complementary types of socialization strategies. Did caregivers engage novice speakers in other types of patterned interactions that did not involve explicit instruction in language and speaking?

Teasing is one such type of patterned interaction. In the first six samples twenty teasing sequences were identified for Beth, twelve for Amy, and nine for Wendy. A sequence consisted of at least two turns (where one could be nonverbal) concerning a single disputed issue. Caregivers initiated teases as a way of redirecting the child's activity or securing her obedience. They playfully disputed the child's claim to valued objects (e.g., toys, food), relationships (e.g., attachment between mother and child), abilities (e.g., dancing, fighting, building), or qualities (e.g., prettiness, maturity).

From a discourse standpoint, the typical teasing sequence began with the caregiver issuing a mock threat, challenge, or insult and the child responding with a denial, counterclaim, or nonverbal counteraction. Following this initial exchange, mother and child exchanged a series of denials, counterclaims, or counteractions. The interaction then continued until one speaker yielded to the other, they reached a stalemate, negotiated a mutually acceptable resolution, escalated the argument into an exchange of ritual blows, or lost interest and changed the subject.

Example 1[1]

Amy II, 19 months

	Amy	*Marlene (mother)*
[A has been drinking M's soda]		
	gimme cup/	
[A reaches for cup in M's hand]		
[M gazes at A, pushes A away with fist against A's belly]		You're gonna get punched right in the gút [Provocative tone].
[A returns M's gaze]		
[A smiles]		
[A raises fist toward M, smiles]	mm/	
[A turns in circle]	look/	
		Ya wanna fight? [Loudly]
[A strikes fighter's pose, legs apart, arms at shoulder level, fist raised toward M]		
[M smiles at A]		Huh?
[A swats at M, kicks sofa next to M]		Do ya? [Laughs]
[A turns around and runs down hallway]	[Laughs]	
		Peggy: She knows how obviously [Laughs].
[A runs back into living room]		Amy.
		Do ya?
[A turns away]	[Laughs]	
		Lemme see your fist?
[A turns and faces M, raises chin defiantly]		
[A falls to floor]	oh uhp/	
[A jumps toward sofa]	[Shrieks]	

In this example Marlene pushes Amy away and threatens to punch her for drinking her soda. Amy responds by raising her fist – in effect a nonverbal threat. The two then exchange a series of threats; the mother's are verbal (e.g., "Ya wanna fight?"; "Do ya?"); Amy's are nonverbal (e.g., raised fist, raised chin). That these threats are not intended to be serious is indicated by the accompanying smiles and laughter, and the tease eventually dissolves into exuberant physical play.

Another example, this one involving Beth and her mother, Nora, revolved around conflicting claims to my doll.

Example 2

Beth VI, 28 months

	Beth	Nora (mother)
[N has been trying to redirect B's activity]		
		I'm gonna get the baby [Singsong intonation].
[Very short switching pause between N's utterance and B's] [B wheels around toward doll]	ḿy/	
		No, it ain't your baby. That's ḿy baby [Very rapidly].
[B kneels next to doll, looking at N]	that Peǵgy baby/	
[B picks up doll]		It's Peggy's baby?
[B holds doll to chest, looking at N]	yes/	
		Well, where's mine?
[B walks away into adjoining room]	I find yours/	
		No, that's all right. You don't have to find it. Come here. That's all right. I got a baby in my belly.

This sequence opens with Nora threatening to seize a doll that Beth has a special right to play with. Beth replies, "my," asserting her claim to the doll. The two then exchange counterclaims. Nora: "No, it ain't your baby. That's my baby." Beth: "that Peggy baby." In the remaining turns Nora and Beth negotiate a settlement: Nora concedes that the doll is Peggy's (and by implication Beth's to play with) and Beth offers to find a doll for Nora.

In addition to having a characteristic discourse form, teasing was set apart from the surrounding stream of talk by a variety of contextualization cues. Gumperz (1977) defined contextualization cue as any aspect of the surface form of utterances – such as prosodic and paralinguistic features and lexical and phonological choice – that signals how message meaning and sequencing patterns are to be interpreted. Several of the cues that allow for the contextualization of teasing are illustrated in Exx. 1 and 2. These include singsong intonation, emphatic stress, unusually short switching pause, loud delivery, rapid delivery, provocative tone of voice, frequent use of words related to fighting (e.g., punch, fight, fist), frequent use of possessive words, and use of the modal particle "well." Although teasing sequences tended to be redundantly marked, no one sequence contained all of these cues, and in fact the distribution of cues tended to vary across the three mother–child pairs. For example, Beth and her mother were much more likely than the others to use singsong intonation and possessive words.

Other contextualization cues that marked teasing sequences were formulaic expressions, such as "hahaha," "heeheehee," "yeayeayea," and "heck on it." In addition, nonverbal accompaniments to teasing included gestures (e.g., rubbing one index finger over the other, raised fist, raised chin); repeated or prolonged mutual gaze; and hitting or swatting at the other speaker.

This, then, is a general description of interactions in which the mothers teased the children. From a language socialization standpoint, it is necessary to ask what these interactions meant to the mothers. One source of evidence in this regard comes from the interpretive comments and asides that one of the mothers made spontaneously during three of the sequences. In all three cases Nora referred approvingly to Beth's anger. For example, "I like her when she gets mad. I'm tellin you, she'll, she'll take that ashtray and throw it, dump it all over the floor and she'll tear up stuff like this. She's got a temper."

Additional data were obtained at the end of the study (after all the videotapes had been collected) when Nora offered interpretations of various interactions, including teasing sequences. For example, in response to one teasing sequence she explained as follows her reasons for teasing: "Teasing will make her want to learn on her own, it encourages her to be independent, it makes her mad, gives me a chance to encourage her if she has trouble (defending her claims or displaying her ability). I say, 'You're still little. It's all right.' " Nora added that one can't tease too often because Beth will just give up; she'll be too insulted.

The evidence, then, from Nora's spontaneous comments during teasing sequences and from her reactions upon later viewing video recordings of teasing sequences provide some clues about her understanding of teasing per se. In addition, remarks made by all three mothers during the interviews help us to fit teasing into the broader picture of their beliefs about child rearing, language learning, and affective socialization.

Each of the mothers repeatedly expressed her intention to equip her daughter with the values and skills she would need as she grew older and ventured out into the world. This meant teaching her the names of people and things, helping her to participate in conversation, and encouraging her to be affectionate and sympathetic (Miller 1982). It also meant instilling strength, pride, and independence and helping the child to learn how to control hurt feelings, how to defend herself, and when to speak up in anger (Miller & Sperry in press). Teasing sequences provided one context in which these valued skills and qualities could be transmitted. Or, as Amy's mother, Marlene, explained it, teasing prepares the child to stand up for herself in real-life disputes:

That's why a lot of times when we used to play little games together, I'd take my fist and like punch her in the chest. You know, not hard enough to hurt her, but, you know, to knock her down. She'd get back up. She'd think it was funny, right? Or I'd take my fist and I'd hit her in the arm and then she'd hit me back and I'd pretend it hurt and I'd (say), "Oh," you know, but it toughened her up. When she got out there to where somebody really meant it, then she realized, you know, "Hey, this is it, they're really pickin on me." And she just, you know, punch back. So, I think that helps too, if you sit down and try to tell your kid, you know, "Hey" you know, "they're gonna punch you, you punch them." And by acting this out with them. By pushing them down and lettin them feel theirself hit the floor, whatever. I think it toughens them up. And I think that's good for a girl nowadays, anyway, because with everything that's goin on, even a girl has to defend herself. And, yeah, I think that's good.

Thus, teasing interactions had, in part, a serious intent: to impart to the child essential survival skills. However, the mothers did not associate teasing with language learning in the same straightforward way that they associated teaching with language learning. In their view, children are taught to talk; they are teased to talk back.

The children as novice teasers

At the age of 2 Amy, Wendy, and Beth already knew how to respond nonverbally to mock threats, challenges, and insults. They raised fists, gave defiant looks, rubbed one index finger over the other, and swatted at the opponent. They also showed some ability to respond verbally and with appropriate content, using such words as "fight," "punch," "beat," "shut up," "dummy," "punk," and "fat." In the following sequence, for example, Wendy says, "I beat you" after her mother has repeatedly made fun of her powdered face.

Example 3
Wendy II, 25 months

	Wendy	Liz (mother)
[W has put powder on her face]		Look at your face.
.		
.		
.2		
[W buries head in L's neck]		[Laughs]
	mommy/	[Laughs]
[W hits playfully at L]		
[W leans back on L's legs, facing L, smiling]	[Laughs]	

[L points at W's face]		[Laughs]
[L points again]		Haha.
[L points again]		Hee.
[W tries to sit up but is laughing too hard]	[Laughs]	
[Both laughing together]	[Laughs]	[Laughs]
[L points at W's face]		
[L pokes W's stomach]	[Laughs]	
		Look at your face. You got powder.
[W lunges for L]		
	I beat you/	
[L shakes W]		
[W buries face in L's chest]	[Noises]	
[L pushes W up; rubs W's cheeks]		
[W lunges for L]		
[W and L playfully slap and hit one another, laughing]	[Laughs]	[Laughs]

.
.
.

There is also some evidence that the children were beginning to assume the role of teaser, initiating sequences by issuing mock threats, insults, or challenges. For example, Amy smiled at her mother and said, "Shut up, punk" (Amy III, 20 months). Wendy struck playfully at her mother's hand, laughing and saying, "Um bad! um bad!" (Wendy II, 25 months).

It is Beth, however, who provides the most evidence of a developing understanding of teasing. She engaged in the largest number of sequences (twenty) and achieved the most proficiency in teasing. Microlevel analysis across the six samples revealed advances in Beth's understanding of various aspects of teasing. She became more adept at interpreting her mother's messages and at producing her own.

For example, in the early samples Nora's openers in teasing sequences were often repeated or rephrased several times before Beth responded. When she did reply, her responses were limited to denials or counterclaims. By the final sample Beth responded promptly to a single opening utterance. This is illustrated in Ex. 2. The mother says, "I'm gonna get the baby." and Beth very rapidly retorts and takes possession of the doll. From this we can infer that Beth understood her mother's utterance as a threat requiring immediate counteraction, both verbal and nonverbal. By the final sample Beth had also added several dispute tactics to her repertoire: She could yield to her mother's argument, contribute escalating claims, and take an active part in negotiating a resolution of the conflict.

In addition, the final sample contained three sequences in which Beth responded with marked counterclaims or challenges to her mother's preceding utterance, which was unmarked or unclearly marked as a teasing opener. Whatever Nora's original intention, Beth transformed the interaction into a teasing sequence. Interestingly, all of these interactions were preceded by commands from Nora to which Beth refused to comply. These sequences suggest that Beth was beginning to try out the role of teaser and that she did so first in contexts of defiance.

There were developments, too, in Beth's use of contextualization cues. From the very beginning and consistently throughout the samples, she used a large proportion of possessive constructions and marked her utterances appropriately with emphatic stress.

Singsong intonation underwent particularly dramatic change. In the first three samples Beth used singsong only once and this in imitation of her mother's preceding utterance. In Sample IV she produced a total of thirty-three utterances with singsong intonation, and only five of these occurred within teasing sequences. An examination of the remaining twenty-eight instances revealed that the majority were formulaic expressions such as "yeayeayea," directed at no particular person and occurring in contexts of self-expression or display, as Beth reveled in her own physical agility. Less frequently, singsong intonation occurred in contexts of defiance or as Beth seized possession of some object. From the adult standpoint, Beth's use of singsong was an instance of overgeneralization. She had not yet narrowed down the contexts of appropriate use. From Beth's standpoint, this explosion of singsong was a form of practice play, pleasurable for its own sake but also a way of understanding this type of intonation. In Sample V singsong was used in much the same way but much less frequently.

Finally, in Sample VI Beth used singsong intonation appropriately in the course of a teasing sequence.

Example 4

Beth VI, 28 months

	Beth	*Nora (mother)*
[N has been urging B to ask Grandma for paper to write on]		
[B puts pen under arm, pouts]	nó-oh/ [Provocative tone]	
		Well, then, I don't care. Well, then, don't ask her.
[B holds Peggy's pen, pouts, gazes defiantly at N]		

		Don't look at me like that.
[B gazes at N]	Peǵgy pen/	
[B reaches for tape box]	that/	I don't care.
[B gazes at N]	Peǵgy pen/	I got a pen too, hear?
[B approaches N, extends pen toward N, chin raised defiantly]	Peggy pen/ [Singsong]	[Laughs]
[B sticks pen under arm, pivots, walks away]		Wanna see how fast I get it? [Rapidly]
[B faces N again, nods once emphatically on "Peggy," gazes at N]	that Peǵgy pen/	
		Give it here! [Very rapidly, loudly]
[B clutches pen to her, nodding, gazes at N]	I hold it/	
		Well, then you better be quiet. [To Peggy] I like her when she gets mad . . .

Singsong intonation marks the climax of this sequence. Until this point Beth has simply reiterated her challenge that the pen is Peggy's, implying that she (Beth), not her mother, has a special right to use it. The mother, for her part, has used a variety of dispute tactics (demanding that Beth cease being provocative, claiming indifference, asserting that she too has a pen). Beth then intensifies the provocation by marking her utterance with singsong intonation and by thrusting the disputed pen in her mother's face. Her mother threatens to take the pen, Beth stands her ground, and the mother reiterates her threat. The sequence ends on a more conciliatory note: Beth retains the pen but claims merely to *hold* it.

Although Amy, Wendy, and Beth used a variety of dispute tactics in teasing episodes, it was uncommon for them to fret or whine in response to a tease. On the few occasions in which such responses did occur, the mothers' reactions varied from sympathy to shaming the child for being a "sissy." In Heath's (1981) report of teasing as practiced in a black working-class community, she noted that the only option not open to young boys was to assume the role of a baby or younger child in response to a tease.

Teasing as verbal play

So far I have described teasing from the perspective of language socialization. Different facets emerge if we look at teasing as a form of verbal and social play. Following Schwartzman (1978), one might say that teasing is characterized by *allusion* to arguments, fights, and displays of anger. In teasing one modifies or plays with the pragmatic resources of language. To tease is to convert a dispute into a mock dispute.

Garvey (1977) has shown that social pretense requires a considerable amount of communication. Each player needs to convey to the other that she has adopted a playful attitude. This may be accomplished by enacting a role or identity, that is, by assuming the appropriate voice quality, content of speech, gestures, and so on. The pretend state may also be indicated by signals such as laughter or giggling or by referring explicitly to the pretend transformation (e.g., "I'll be the *x*"; "Let's play *x*").

In teasing sequences the mothers – and the children to a limited extent – enacted the functional role of contestant. They issued threats, insults, and challenges and used various tactics to sustain, escalate, and resolve the dispute. They marked their utterances with emphatic stress, provocative tones, and rapid delivery; pouted, stared, and raised chins defiantly. They seized possession of disputed objects, made fighting gestures, and swatted and lunged at the opponent.

The players communicated the playful nature of these disputes in a variety of ways. Perhaps most obvious were the accompanying smiles and laughter. Amy and Wendy used these signals in the earliest recorded teasing sequences, that is, at 19 and 25 months, respectively. Beth gave no such signals in the early samples, suggesting that she did not yet understand that teasing was not to be taken literally. By 27 months, however, she too signaled her appreciation of teasing as play, and during one sequence her mother explicitly drew attention to this: "She knows I'm playin. Look at those eyeballs. Get out of here. Look. she wants to laugh. I see her wanna laugh. She wants to laugh. I could see that smile startin to come on."

With the exception of asides such as this, the playful transformation was not explicitly referred to in teasing interactions. To propose at the outset "Let's tease" (as one might say "Let's play house") would be to violate the basic rule of a tease that dictates the deliberate creation of conflict or tension (Heath 1981). There were other ways of distinguishing (playful) teases from (nonplayful) disputes, however. Teasing singsong and teasing gestures were two such markers. Also the mothers encouraged their daughters to aggress against them only in play, not, for example, when the mother was disciplining the child. A child might be threatened for disobedience, but she would not be threatened with a punch in the face or challenged to put up her fists. It is as though the mother, as teaser, assumed the rule of an older, bullying child and chose the content of her utterances accordingly. Content was thus an important marker signaling the playful nature of teases.

One of the reasons why social play, such as teasing, requires considerable metacommunicative work is because of the unstable nature of the frame "this is play" (Bateson 1972). If one is not careful, a tease can slip into a real dispute. Nora was acknowledging this aspect of teasing when she said that one should not tease too often or the child will become insulted and stop trying. On another occasion she complained that another adult teased unkindly: "(He was) teasin her, but still that can go through a child's mind."

Teasing exists, then, in intimate relation to real disputing. In this it is similar to "playing the dozens," as practiced in poor urban black communities. Playing the dozens is a type of ritual insult, often sexual in content, and tightly constructed out of rhymes or puns. According to Abrahams (1962), the strict formal structure of playing the dozens is necessary because of the highly volatile nature of the issues. This type of verbal play is, in his words, "perilously close to real life." For this reason it is practiced first in safe situations, that is, in interaction with other adolescent males. Among adults it can lead beyond the verbal to physical fights. Teasing too is learned initially in safe contexts, in interaction with caregivers who do not retaliate for real. By the time Amy, Wendy, and Beth ventured beyond the rowhouse stoop to more dangerous encounters, they had had extensive experience of teasing.

This preparation for life in their own community did not necessarily equip them for interactions with outsiders, however. The close connection between teasing and real disputing renders it particularly susceptible to misinterpretation by persons who are not familiar with the local norms of communication. Speech genres such as teasing and playing the dozens depend not only on an understanding of the general rules of face-to-face interaction but on specific cultural knowledge (Philips 1973). One has to be able to read the subtle cues that distinguish a tease from a literal dispute. When children from non-mainstream groups, for example, black migrant children (Lein 1975) and American Indians (Philips 1973), take their varieties of teasing into the classroom, teachers may mistake a tease for a deliberate display of disrespect.

In conclusion I would like to address one final question, raised by Sachs (1980). She asked what, if anything, children learn about language structure or use from playful interactions. She concluded that pretend play between adult and child provides a good opportunity (though not a necessary one) for learning to use language to structure the world. Teasing provides a different kind of learning opportunity. Teasing reveals the close connection between language and action and sensitizes the child to the potential of language for argument, self-assertion, and self-defense. Teasing demands that the child be alert to nuances of speech and demeanor. She must be able to think on her feet, to deliver the swift retort or counteraction. Teasing also sensitizes the child to the possibility of playing with the rules of language use, of extracting a communicative act or event from its ordinary context and treating it non-literally. The child whose verbal imagination takes root in teasing gains not only a survival tool but an appreciation of some of the playful and transforming possibilities of language.

Notes

This work was supported in part by National Institutes of Mental Health Grant no. 1ROlMH34413-01.

1 The following format is used in all examples: The sample is identified by roman numeral, indicating the number of the sample, and by the child's age in months. Column 1 contains a description of nonverbal behaviors, with the actor identified by first initial. Column 2 contains the child's utterances; Column 3, other speakers' utterances. Paralinguistic information (e.g., intonation, rate of delivery) is given in brackets immediately after the utterance.
2 The three vertical dots indicate that material has been omitted from a lengthy episode.

References

Abrahams, R. D. 1962. Playing the dozens. *Journal of American Forklore* 75:209–220.

Bateson, G. 1972. A theory of play and fantasy. In *Steps to an ecology of mind*. New York: Ballantine, pp. 177–193.

Garvey, C. 1977. *Play*. Cambridge: Harvard University Press.

Gumperz, J. J. 1977. Sociocultural knowledge in conversational inference. In M. Saville-Troike, ed., *Linguistics and anthropology*. Washington, D.C.: Georgetown University Press (Georgetown University Round Table on Languages and Linguistics), pp. 191–211.

Heath, S. B. 1981. Teasing talk: strategies for language learning. Paper presented at the American Anthropological Association Meeting, Los Angeles, December.

Lein, L. 1975. "You were talkin though, oh yes, you was": black American migrant children: their speech at home and school. *Anthropology and Education Quarterly* 6:1–11.

Miller, P. 1982. *Amy, Wendy, and Beth: learning language in South Baltimore*. Austin: University of Texas Press.

Miller, P. & Garvey, C. 1984. Mother–baby role play: its origin in social support. In I. Bretherton, ed., *Symbolic play: the representation of social understanding*. New York: Academic Press, pp. 101–130.

Miller, P. & Sperry, L. L. In press. The socialization of anger and aggression. *Merrill-Palmer Quarterly*.

Philips, S. U. 1973. Teasing, punning, and putting people on. Paper presented at the American Anthropological Association Meeting, New Orleans, November.

Sachs, J. 1980. The role of adult–child play in language development. In K. H. Rubin, ed., *Children's play*. San Francisco: Jossey-Bass, pp. 33–48.

Schwartzman, H. B. 1978. *Transformations: the anthropology of children's play*. New York: Plenum.

11. The acquisition of communicative style in Japanese

Patricia M. Clancy

One of the most striking meeting places of language and culture can be found in communicative style. The notion of communicative style has been defined by Barnlund (1975) to include the topics people discuss, their favorite forms of interaction, the depth of involvement sought, the extent to which they rely upon the same channels for conveying information, and the extent to which they are tuned to the same level of meaning, such as factual versus emotional content. Obviously, communicative style is one aspect of "communicative competence," relating, in particular, to the "rules for use" that govern speakers' production and interpretation of language appropriately in context (Hymes 1972). Communicative style, which I will define loosely here as the way language is used and understood in a particular culture, both reflects and reinforces fundamental cultural beliefs about the way people are and the nature of interpersonal communication. As Scollon (1982) has argued, children's acquisition of culture-specific patterns of communication is an extremely important part of their socialization, since such patterns serve as one of the primary sources of information on cultural values concerning social relationships and interaction. Thus acquisition of communicative style plays a part in the development of children's social cognition, thereby helping to shape their world view (Whorf 1956) or "reality set" (Scollon & Scollon 1981).

Japanese communicative style

It is widely recognized that the communicative style of the Japanese is intuitive and indirect, especially compared with that of Americans. As Azuma et al. (1980) have said, verbal expression among the Japanese is "context dependent, indirect, rich in connotation and evasive in denotation." The basis

213

of this style is a set of cultural values that emphasize *omoiyari* 'empathy' over explicit verbal communication. A striking example of these values can be found in the Japanese attitude toward speech itself. As Ito (1980) points out, verbosity has traditionally been looked down upon in Japan, especially for men; this is revealed in traditional sayings such as *Iwanu ga hana* 'Silence is better than speech'. The Japanese have little faith in verbal expression or in those who rely upon it. As Nitobe has written, "To give in so many articulate words one's innermost thoughts and feelings is taken as an unmistakable sign that they are neither profound nor very sincere" (cited in Barnlund 1975:133). The Japanese apparently do talk less than Americans; Barnlund found that a large sample of Japanese and American students characterized the Japanese as "silent" much more frequently than Americans, who were seen as "talkative." Doi (1973) notes that upon arriving in the United States, he found that the incessant talk of Americans, even during meals, made them sound "hypermanic." My own experience after a few months of assimilating Japanese norms was that, indeed, I seemed to be talking endlessly and compulsively, perhaps stimulated to even greater volubility to compensate for the comparative silence of my conversational partners.

When verbal communication does enter in, it will often be inexplicit and indirect. As Doi (1974) has pointed out, the structure of the Japanese language fosters ambiguity in various ways. For example, in Japanese it is grammatically acceptable to omit overt reference to any element in a sentence that the speaker assumes to be "understood"; frequent use of nominal ellipsis in Japanese discourse results in a much higher rate of potential ambiguity than in English (Clancy 1980). Since Japanese is a left-branching verb-final language, with negation appearing as a verb suffix, speakers may negate a sentence at the last moment, depending upon the addressee's expression (Doi 1974). They may also nominalize and negate entire sentences upon their completion to make assertions less direct; when this is done with negative predicates, multiple embedded negations are created. Loveday (1982:4) cites the following example from Gibney, which reflects Westerners' perception of this usage:

"It isn't that we can't do it this way," one Japanese will say.

"Of course," replies his companion, "we couldn't deny that it would be impossible to say that it couldn't be done."

"But unless we can say that it can't be done," his friend adds, "it would be impossible not to admit that we couldn't avoid doing it."

The average American is likely to find Japanese multiple negation mind-boggling to process syntactically, and maddeningly roundabout as a way of expressing opinions. The structure of the Japanese language and speakers' exploitation of all its potential for ambiguity and indirection probably play an important part in Americans' perception of the Japanese as "reserved," "cautious," and "evasive" (Barnlund 1975).

The Japanese rely upon indirection in many common social situations especially when they are trying to be polite. Japanese who have had contact with Americans quickly become aware of their comparatively greater use of indirection, as a result of many misunderstandings. For example, Japanese visitors to the United States often point out that in Japan an offer of food should ideally be refused three times before accepting. Of course, the host must realize that the guest is actually hungry and merely exhibiting appropriate *enryo* 'reserve'. From the reports of my own acquaintances, it appears that most Japanese who come to America can expect to suffer a period of hunger before learning that offers of food will be made only once (cf. also Doi 1973), and may raise a few eyebrows by their unseemly boldness in accepting offers quickly upon returning to Japan.

The Japanese reliance upon indirection is consistent with their attitude toward verbal conflict. As Barnlund points out, in Japan conversation is "a way of creating and reinforcing the emotional ties that bind people together" with the aim of social harmony. Therefore, overt expression of conflicting opinions is taboo. Even conference participants, for example, in contrast to their argumentative American counterparts, tend to express their views tentatively, in anticipation of possible retraction or qualification depending upon how they are received; they try to feel out the positions of their colleagues, seeking a common ground for establishing unanimity (Barnlund 1975; Doi 1974).

However, the value placed upon unanimity does not prevent individuals from harboring their own thoughts and feelings. Doi (1974) discusses this phenomenon in terms of *honne to tatemae,* roughly "real feeling versus (socially) accepted principle." This distinction, which was also pointed out to me by Japanese friends, is not, ideally, regarded as involving hypocrisy, although the potential for this interpretation exists and is sometimes made even by Japanese. Americans tend to feel that acting and speaking in accordance with one's *honne* is a matter of personal integrity, but, according to Doi (1974), in Japan the discrepancy between *honne* and *tatemae* is generally seen, in good conscience, as merely reflecting the way society works. Individuals may hold their own view, but, in the interests of group harmony, should not express it if it conflicts with the opinions of others.

One outcome of this system is that in Japan it can be extremely difficult to find out what is on someone's mind. Americans discover to their frustration that yes may well mean no, but cannot figure out when. Reluctant to disagree with another's opinion or refuse a request, the Japanese feel pressured to give their consent, even when they actually disagree or are unable or unwilling to comply. Ueda (1974) discusses "sixteen ways to avoid saying 'no' in Japan," which include silence; ambiguity; expressions of apology, regret, and doubt; and even lying and equivocation. Ueda's subjects reported using direct no at home, but very rarely in public; in fact, lying was the most frequent means of declining requests reported by the subjects. According to Ueda, the reasons underlying avoidance of no include empathy with the addressee, whose feelings would be hurt, and concern about the potential negative results, such as retaliation by a person in a position of power relative to the speaker. In interpreting the response to a direct question or request, therefore, one must be ready to guess what the speaker probably means, even in spite of what may actually be said.

Clearly, the Japanese style of communication can work only in a rather homogeneous society in which people actually can anticipate each other's needs, wants, and reactions. Japanese society is, in fact, extremely homogeneous, and more group-oriented than American society, which has much greater ethnic diversity and places a much higher value on individualism. Of course, all socialization by definition entails teaching children to conform to the expectations of the social groups in which they are being raised. But in Japan, where interpersonal communication relies so heavily upon intuition and empathy, conformity to group norms can be seen as an essential aspect of communicative style. For the system to work, people must be interpretable, which means that their thoughts and feelings must fall within the range of others' ability to imagine and understand, even without any explicit verbal expression.

One striking aspect of language use in Japan that is related to conformity is the existence of a great number of fixed verbal formulas that are used extensively in daily interactions. These expressions cover a much broader range of situations than English verbal formulas, including, for example, *Itadakimasu* 'I will receive it', which must be said before starting to eat, and *Ojama shimasu* 'I will get in the way', said upon entering someone's house. As Loveday (1982) points out, in Japan formulas are used very frequently, and apparently without fear of sounding unoriginal and therefore insincere. In contrast, Americans tend to prefer individualized expressions. Loveday reports that when asked what they would say upon receiving a birthday present, Americans gave a variety of answers, including "It was very thoughtful of you to remember my birthday"; when asked what they would say to someone who had saved them from drowning, they responded, "What can I say . . .", "I don't know how to thank you," etc. The Japanese used the same formula of thanks in both cases. It is as if the Americans are relying upon the words themselves to communicate their feelings to the listener, and therefore find the verbal formulas inadequate. In Japan, there seems to be an extensive codification of contexts in which particular feelings are expected; speakers need only indicate, by means of the right formula, that they are experiencing the appropriate reaction, without expressing any more personal, individualized response. An important goal of socialization in Japan is to promote the unanimity in feeling that will support the norms of verbal agreement and empathy.

As this summary shows, the characteristics of Japanese communicative style reveal a very different view of verbal interaction from that shared by Americans. Reddy (1979) proposes that English-speakers' view of communication rests upon the "conduit metaphor": speakers "put their ideas into words," which they "exchange" with the listener, whose task is merely to extract the ideas from the words again. The main responsibility for successful communication rests with speakers, who must know how to "get their ideas across." This view of communication is explicitly espoused in much of popular American psychology; for example, one goal of assertiveness training is to teach people to express their thoughts and feelings explicitly in words, rather than relying upon indirect or nonverbal messages. In contrast, in Japan the ideal interaction is not one in which the speakers express their wishes and needs adequately and listeners understand and comply, but rather one in which each party understands and anticipates the needs of the other, even before anything is said. Communication can take place without, or even in spite of, actual verbalization. The main responsibility lies with the listener, who must know what the speaker means regardless of the words that are used. In this view of communication, mind-reading is seen as both possible and desirable, rather than a misguided expectation of those who have not learned to express themselves adequately.

The Japanese view of communication arises from, and contributes to, *amae,* a concept that Doi (1973) regards as basic to both individual and social psychology in Japan. To *amae* is to depend upon and presume upon another's benevolence (Doi 1974). The prototype of a relationship based upon *amae* is that between mother and child, which serves as a model for many other social relationships in Japan, such as the paternalism of employers towards employees. According to Doi (1974), all interpersonal communication in Japanese society has the emotional undertone of *amae.* In fact, an analysis of Japanese communicative style suggests that it is a style that *amae*s, with the speaker presuming upon the listener's willingness to cooperate, empathize, and intuit what he or she has in mind. Thus Japanese communicative style places speaker and hearer in the prototypical social relationship, namely, one that is based on *amae;* the values reflected and reinforced by this mode of communication constitute an integral part of Japanese culture.

Acquisition

How do Japanese children learn this intuitive, indirect style of communication? Study of early mother–child interaction has revealed patterns emphasizing nonverbal communication at an extremely early stage. In their investigation of thirty Japanese and thirty American infants 3–4 months old interacting with their mothers, Caudill & Weinstein (1974) found that Japanese mothers talked to their children significantly less often than American mothers, and that Japanese children had significantly lower rates of "positive vocalization" than the American children. On the other hand, the Japanese mothers were together in the same room with their children, even while they were sleeping, significantly more often than American mothers, and responded quickly to soothe and care for their children's needs upon any negative vocalization. This finding is consistent with Vogel (1963), who reports that in his study of middle-class mothers in a Tokyo suburb, one of the first things the mothers did after birth was to find out under what circumstances their children cried and to satisfy them so that they never cried for more than a few seconds. The Japanese mother's goal is to empathize with her child's needs; one result of this goal is that the motivation for vocalization is reduced. Caudill & Weinstein (1974:8) conclude that "It is as if the majority of the American pairs had reached an 'agreement' to be talkative, while the majority of the Japanese pairs had reached an 'agreement' to be silent." By as early as 4 months of age, American and Japanese children are already being socialized into different patterns of communication.

Looking at a much later stage of development, Matsumori (1981) has also found interesting differences between the communicative styles of Japanese and American mothers. In her study, Matsumori analyzed the directives used by ten Japanese and ten American mothers interacting with their children, aged 3–6 years, and their responses to a set of hypothetical situations calling for directives. The American mothers tended to express their own feelings and opinions when reacting to socially disapproved behaviors, e.g., "I don't like the way you're speaking." They used polite expressions, such as "Could/would you" when requesting personal favors, and wanted their children to address them with polite formulas such as "please" and "thank you." In contrast, the Japanese mothers tended to appeal to social norms in correcting misbehavior, e.g., *Otona no hito ni soo iu hanashikata shicha dame yo* 'Speaking that way to a grown-up won't do'. They used directives reflecting the intimacy of the mother–child relationship when requesting personal favors, rather than forms which could also be used to strangers, and insisted that their children use polite forms in addressing others, but not when speaking to their mothers. Matsumori concluded that these differences reflect differences between Japanese and American social structure and the nature of the mother–child relationship in each culture. Like the research of Caudill & Weinstein, Matsumori's work provides evidence that mothers' communicative style is an important factor in the socialization of children to culture-specific values.

In this paper, I will focus on a stage of development intermediate between those considered by Caudill & Weinstein and Matsumori: approximately 2 years of age. At this stage a good deal of mother–child communication is taking place through, or is at least accompanied by, language, but the acquisition of grammar is still not very advanced. The study of mothers' speech to young children has been popular for many years, and many suggestions have been made about the potential effects of "motherese" on semantic and syntactic development, but as yet little is known about aspects of mothers' speech to children of this age that could foster acquisition of culture-specific communicative styles. I will focus on those features of Japanese mothers' speech that might be shaping the development of communicative style, such as their use of indirection in giving directives and in saying no to their children, and their reliance on verbal strategies that foster empathy and conformity. Japanese children's exposure to this kind of verbal interaction is probably one of the earliest and most important means by which they are socialized to Japanese culture.

The data for this paper consist of tape-recorded interactions between five mother–child pairs, which were collected as part of a study of early grammatical development in Japanese (see Clancy 1986). Three children from that study will be discussed here: two boys, Yoshinobu (hereafter Y), who was recorded twelve times, usually at one- or two-week intervals, from the age of 1;11 to 2;4 years, and Masahiko (MK), who was recorded twice, at 2;4 and 2;5 years of age; and one girl, Maho (M), who was recorded four times between the ages of 2;1 and 2;3 years. M and MK were only children at the time of the recordings; Y had a 5-year-old sister who was attending kindergarten. All three were children of college-educated, middle-class parents living in a suburb of Tokyo. The fathers held white-collar positions; the mothers were not employed outside the home. The linguistic development of the three children was consistent with the literature on Japanese acquisition for their age group.

The recording sessions were each one hour long. The children were recorded in interaction with their mothers, and Y occasionally also with his sister; in some of the early sessions with Y and M, a young Japanese woman who was assisting me also participated. During the recording sessions, I interacted only minimally, devoting myself to taking contextual notes. The mothers were asked to interact with the children as they did when alone. A variety of activities were recorded, including playing with dolls and toys, reading storybooks, drawing, eating, and make-believe role-playing routines. Largely because of the presence of outsiders interacting with the mother–child pairs, there were many occasions when the mothers tried to shape the children's use and interpretation of language, and so these recordings were in certain ways ideal for the analysis of incipient communicative style. It is interesting that each of the mothers in this study seemed to seize upon these visits as occasions for socializing their children into appropriate patterns of polite interaction with people outside the family circle.

Listening and responding

One of the most basic features of communicative style is when to speak and when not to speak. The data for this study cannot be used for an analysis of the normal frequency of verbal interaction, since the goal of the recording sessions was to collect speech samples for grammatical analysis, and an effort was made to keep the children engaged in conversation as much as possible. However, the transcripts do provide clear evidence for at least one context in which the mothers consistently trained their children to speak, namely, when they are spoken to. I have suggested that Japanese communicative style places the main burden for successful communication upon the listener; obviously, the first rule for good listeners must be to notice and pay attention to speech that is addressed to them. And in Japan, as elsewhere, a basic rule of politeness is to respond to questions, comments, and requests.

Studies of young American children have shown that they often ignore the speech of others (Wetstone & Foster 1982) and fail to respond even at an age when they presumably have no difficulty understanding what is being said (Dore 1978). In my data as well, the three children would sometimes become engrossed in their own actions and either would fail to notice attempts to engage them in conversation or would choose not to reply. Their mothers did not allow this to continue; they consistently focused the unresponding child's attention upon the person who was trying to interact and repeated the utterance that had been addressed to the child, as in the following example (M 2;1):

[Child is pretending to eat imaginary food from a toy dish]
  Adult: *Mahochan wa nanika tabeten no? Koko nani ga haitten no?*
        'Are you eating something? What is in there?'
  Child: [No response]
  Mother: *Nani ga haitteru no ka naa. Oneesan nani ga haitten no tte kiiteru yo.*
        'I wonder what could be in there. Older sister[1] is asking, "What is in there?"'
  Child: *Purin.*
        'Pudding.'

Such repetitions were a frequent part of the mother–child interactions in my sample, occurring in every transcript of each child.

Sometimes mothers' repetitions may be necessary for the child's comprehension, especially when the child is first interacting with an unfamiliar person, and there were a few cases in which mothers simplified the speech in their repetition for the child. However, most repetitions did not paraphrase or simplify the original utterance; they were intended to elicit a response from the child by adding the mother's authority to the request for an answer or a favor. The great consistency with which the three mothers repeated unanswered questions shows that they felt it was very important for their children to learn to reply when spoken to. In the following example, the mother explicitly refers to the rule she is trying to teach (M 2;1):

> Adult [looking at a character in a storybook]:
> *Kore wa dare desu ka?*
> 'Who is this?'
> Child: [No response]
> Mother: *Nani! Dame ja nai, kotaenai de. Dare desu ka to yuu n deshoo. Doo yuu no? Hai to. Hisakochan to doobutsuen.*
> 'What! Isn't that bad, not answering. She says, "Who is it?" What do you say? Say, "Yes. It's Hisako and the zoo."'

Requests were repeated by the mothers with even greater insistence. In fact, mothers often reacted with great concern if a child failed to comply with a request immediately. In the following example, the mother attempts to communicate a sense of urgency, even alarm, at the discovery that a guest's wish is going unfulfilled (Y 2;3):

> PC: *Yotchan no shooboojidoosha misete.*
> 'Show me your fire engine.'
> Child: [No response]
> Mother: *Shooboojidoosha da tte.*
> 'She said, "Fire engine".'
> PC: *Shooboojidoosha.*
> 'Fire engine.'
> Mother: *Sa, hayaku. Patricia-san misete tte yutteru yo. Isoganakucha. Isoganakucha. A! A!*
> 'Well, quickly. Patricia is saying, "Show me it." You must hurry. You must hurry. Oh! Oh!'

On another occasion, when I had made a similar request, Y's mother exclaimed, *Hora! Taihen da! Motte konakucha!* 'Listen! This is terrible! You must bring it' (Y 2;3). In such cases the mothers were most probably exaggerating the degree of concern they felt in order to make an impression on their children. However, it is interesting to compare this feigned alarm with the very real concern (*ki o tsukau*) and solicitousness that the Japanese show their guests. Behind the mothers' alarmed reactions, we can sense the Japanese feeling that, ideally, a guest's needs should be met even before a direct request becomes necessary.

Repeating the speech addressed to their children was one strategy that these mothers used in socializing their children to the rules for interacting with others. All direct questions and requests must be answered; in fact, it is in light of this general rule that an addressee's silence becomes meaningful to the speaker who has asked a question or made a request. Since both questions and requests reveal that the speaker is in need, either of information or of some desired object or action, Japanese mothers' insistence that their children pay attention and respond to such utterances may be viewed as one early instance of "empathy training."

Directives

Given the Japanese emphasis upon consideration for others, it is not surprising to find that indirection is one of the hallmarks of Japanese communicative style. As Brown & Levinson (1978) have pointed out, certain speech acts are intrinsically "face threatening" to the addressee; directives, which seek to impose the will of the speaker upon the listener, constitute a prime example. Obviously, trying to get the listener to do something could easily lead to a violation of the right to "freedom from imposition" (Brown & Levinson 1978) and hence to violation of the Japanese ideal of empathy. One solution to this problem, in Japan as elsewhere, is to resort to indirection as a less coercive means of conveying imperative intent. In this section, I will examine the directives used by the Japanese mothers in my sample to their 2-year-old children to discover whether, and to what extent, very young children are exposed to indirect imperatives.

Directives of various types were extremely common in the speech of all three mothers; the average frequency across mothers and samples was 113 directives per one-hour sample. Directives frequently occurred in a series of highly repetitive utterances, with the same content being expressed several times, often in different grammatical form, either within or across speech turns. This kind of self-repetition and paraphrase seems to be one feature of an interactive style that is concerned with mutual comprehension. Newport, Gleitman & Gleitman (1977) and Cross (1977) have described a similar pattern for English-speaking mothers. They report that paraphrases were especially common in sequences of directives, where they served to ensure comprehension or, as Gleason (1977) has discussed, to guide and direct the child's behavior.

Table 11.1 summarizes the directive strategies found in the present samples of mothers' speech, in roughly decreasing order of directness,[2] and gives typical examples of each type. The strategies are divided into positive directives, which aim at getting the child to perform some action, and negative ones, which are intended to prevent or stop undesirable behavior. As the table shows, Japanese mothers use a very wide range of directives, which vary greatly in their strength of imperative force and their degree of explicitness about what the child is to do.[3] Accordingly, the different strategies also vary in what Azuma et al. (1980) have referred to as "psychological space," the amount of room a directive leaves for noncompliance. In Table 11.2, the frequency of the different directive strategies in the three mothers' speech is presented.[4] In general, the mothers had very similar directive profiles, employing the same range of strategies in similar frequency. As Table 11.2 shows, the most common directives were also the most direct and forceful, namely, those using imperative verb forms such as -nasai or the milder -te.[5] Individual lexical items, such as hayaku 'quickly', also served as very direct imperatives. Statements of obligation, for example, *Moo sukoshi ushiro ikanakya dame* 'You must go back a little more' (lit. "Not going back a little more is no good" – M 2;1), and statements of prohibition, for example, *Sonna nagetara dame* (lit. "If you throw that kind of thing, it's no good" – MK 2;4), were also quite explicit and coercive in tone. However, they may be regarded as less direct than imperatives, since on the surface they merely inform the child that certain behaviors are *dame* 'no good' or *ikenai* 'won't do'. Somewhat milder in tone were sentences without surface subjects of the form "(You) will/won't do *x*" or "(One) does/doesn't do *x*," which may be regarded as instructions (cf. Matsumori 1981) or generalizations about social norms intended to convey such instructions.[6] Taken together, these directive strategies, which allow very little "psychological space," constitute 58.3 percent, on the average, of all the utterances with imperative intent each mother addressed to her children.

The next three strategies in Tables 11.1 and 11.2 allow the child more freedom of response. In statements of permission/preference, mothers simply categorized a particular course of action as *ii* 'good/all right'. Suggestions took the form of "cohortatives" with verbs inflected in *-oo* 'let's' (although the child was usually expected to perform the action alone), conditionals in *-eba* and *-tara* 'if', and questions, such as the requests, reminders, and suggestions given on the left side of Table 11.1 beside "Questions."[7] Although as explicit about the desired action as more forceful imperatives, these suggestions leave it up to the child whether to comply with the directive or not. The children in this sample often responded to suggestions in question form by performing or refusing to perform the action, revealing that they were able to interpret them as directives. As Table 11.2 shows, suggestions, including "positive" questions, accounted for an average of 15 percent of the directive input to children.

The remaining 27 percent of directives used by these mothers were indirect in that they did not specify clearly what the child was supposed to do and/or were not addressed directly by the mother to the child, but rather were attributed to a third party. Thus Japanese children are already hearing indirect imperatives as early as 2 years of age.

Many of these indirect imperatives had the surface form of questions. There were several examples of indirect requests in question form, such as *Sooseeji arimasu ka?* 'Is there any sausage?' (Y 2;2). These "situated conventional directives," which explicitly mention the desired object, if not the action to be performed (cf. Ervin-Tripp 1977), were readily understood by the children. Y and M had even begun to use such questions themselves in the context of eating.

The most frequent type of indirect question used by these mothers was the rhetorical question with negative directive intent. Some typical examples are given on the right side of Table 11.1. These questions expressed a variety of

Table 11.1. *The directive strategies of the three mothers*

	Positive	Negative
Imperative forms	*V-nasai* *Nuginasai.* (MK 2;5) 'Take it off.' *V-te* *Nuide.* (MK 2;5) 'Take it off.' *X tte* *Doozo tte.* (Y 1;11) '(Say), "Help yourself."'	*V-naide* *Sonna koto iwanaide.* (Y 1;11) 'Don't say that kind of thing.'
Statements of obligation/prohibition	*V-nakucha/-nakya (dame/ikenai/naranai)* *Pantsu hakanakucha.* (MK 2;5) 'Not putting on your pants (won't do).' *Zembu tsukanakya ikenai no ne.* (MK 2;5) 'Not using all of them won't do.'	*V-cha/-tara dame/ikenai/naranai.* *Irecha ikenai.* (Y 2;0) 'Putting it in won't do.' *Sonna nagetara dame.* (MK 2;4) 'If you throw that kind of thing, it's no good.'
Instructions	*V-u/-ru* *Koko de kaku no.* (Y 2;3) '(You) will draw here.'	*V-nai* *Ashi de shinai.* (M 2;1) '(You) won't do it with your foot.'
Generalizations	*Arigatoo tte yuu ne.* (M 2;1) '(One) says, "Thank you."'	*Sonna koto yuwanai no.* (Y 2;2) '(One) doesn't say that kind of thing.'
Statements of permission/preference	*V-te/-tara/-eba ii* *Asonde ii yo, Yotchan.* (Y 1;11) 'Playing is all right, Yotchan.' *Motte nondara ii no.* (M 2;2) 'If you hold it and drink, it's good.' *. . . hoo ga ii* *Sore no hoo ga ii wa yo.* (Y 1;11) 'That way is better.'	*V-nakute ii* *Omikan no kawa motte konakute ii.* (Y 1;11) 'Not bringing the tangerine peels is all right.' *V-nai hoo ga ii* *. . . ima wa narasanai hoo ga ii.* (Y 2;4) '(Lit.) The side of not turning it on is better.'

224

Suggestions

V-oo
Maachan, chotto oshikko shi ni ikoo. (MK 2;4)
'Maachan, let's go make peepee.'
V-tara/-eba
Odotte agetara? (M 2;2)
'(Lit.) If you danced for them?'

Questions

Requests: V-te kureru?
Kashite kureru no? (Y 2;4)
'Will you lend me it?'
Suggestions: V-u/-ru?
Bubu Pandachan ni kashite ageru no? (Y 2;2)
'Will you lend a car to Panda?' (Y 2;2)
Reminders: V-ta?
Oishii tte kiita? (M 2;2)
'Did you ask, "Is it delicious?"'

Rhetorical:
Nani shiteru no? (Y 2;0)
'What are you doing?' (= Stop doing it.)
Dooshite tereten no? (M 2;1)
'Why are you being shy?' (= Stop being shy.)
Mada sore taberu no? (M 2;1)
'Are you still eating that?' (= Stop eating that.)

Desire statements

Mama mo nomitai naa. (M 2;1)
'Gee, I want to drink too.'

Need/problem statements

Mama onaka suite imasu yo. (Y 1;11)
'I'm hungry.'

Attributed directives

Ano oneechan mo hoshii tte itteru yo. (M 2;1)
'That girl is also saying, "I want some."'

Appeals to feelings

Tottara itai yo, oneesan itai yo. (M 2;1)
'If you pull it off, it will hurt, it will hurt her.'
(= So don't pull off her earring.)

Kikochan yamete choodai tte. (MK 2;5)
'Kikochan says, "Please stop."'

Hikooki kawaiisoo. (Y 1;11)
'I feel sorry for the airplane.'
(= So stop banging it.)

Rationales/hints

Ippai aru deshoo. (Y 2;3)
'There are lots of them, aren't there.'
(= So bring some.)
Omeme aru n ja nai. (Y 2;4)
'You have eyes, don't you.'
(= So find a place to draw.)

Oneechan no deshoo. (Y 2;1)
'It's your sister's, isn't it.'
(= So don't play with it.)
Dete konakunachau yo. (MK 2;4)
'They won't come out.'
(= So stop putting them in.)

225

Table 11.2. *The frequency of different directive strategies in the speech of the three mothers*

	Y's mother		M's mother		MK's mother	
Imperative forms	0.42	(423)	0.55	(227)	0.39	(92)
Lexical	0.01	(14)	0.01	(5)	0.02	(4)
Obligation/prohibition	0.10	(97)	0.07	(29)	0.06	(14)
Instruction/generalization	0.08	(81)	0.02	(9)	0.02	(4)
Permission/preference	0.02	(25)	0.02	(9)	0.004	(1)
Suggestions	0.08	(83)	0.02	(9)	0.13	(30)
Questions (positive)	0.04	(38)	0.07	(29)	0.06	(15)
Questions (rhetorical)	0.05	(51)	0.05	(22)	0.01	(3)
Desire/needs/problems	0.02	(18)	0.04	(17)	0.03	(7)
Attributed directives	0.03	(29)	0.04	(18)	0.06	(14)
Rationales/hints	0.15	(148)	0.10	(42)	0.23	(54)
Total directives		(1,007)		(416)		(238)

negative attitudes, ranging from amused skepticism, *Isu ni nokkeru no? bubu o* 'You put the car on a chair?' (Y 1;11), to frustration, *Ohanashi outa mo nashi?* 'Is there no speech, no song at all?' (M 2;1), and annoyed disapproval, *Mada sore taberu no?* 'Are you still eating that?' (M 2;1). In rhetorical questions, it is the disapproved action that is mentioned explicitly, and it is up to the child to figure out what to do. Given the context and the mother's obvious negative attitude and tone of voice, this was probably not too difficult for the children, although comprehension did not, of course, ensure compliance.

The least direct imperatives used by these mothers were hints, which require inference to figure out the intended directive (cf. Ervin-Tripp 1977). Some hints were very similar to rhetorical questions in that the mother simply referred to something that the child had just done, leaving her disapproval to be conveyed by her tone of voice and the context, as in *Mata puu shiteru* 'You're farting again' (M 2;1). Sometimes hints alternated with questions; for example, when Y (2;1) was taking toys that did not belong to him, his mother used both the hint *Kore Yotchan no yo* 'This is yours' and the corresponding question *Yotchan no dore?* 'Which one is yours?' at different points. In the following example (M 2;1), M's mother interweaves questions and declarative hints in trying to get the child to give my assistant a turn in their game, but never tells her what to do directly.

Mother: *Maho yaru no?*
   'Will you do it?'
Child: *Un.*
  'Yes.'

Mother: *Maho bakkari ja nai no. Mahochan furefure to itte ageru, oneesan ni.*
   Gambatte.
   'Not only you. Will you say to older sister, "Go go, try hard"?'
 Child: *Iya. Iya da.*
   'No. No.'
Mother: *Oneesan iya na no? Dooshite? Dare ga suru no?*
   'You don't want her to do it? Why? Who will do it?'
 Child: *Maho suru.*
   'I will do it.'
Mother: *Kondo . . . Maho bakkari da ne. Mahochan bakkari.*
   'This time . . . only Maho, isn't it. Only Maho.'
 Child: *Maho bakkari yo.*
   'Only Maho.'

The most frequent type of hint consisted of a reason why the child should perform an action or a warning of the potential negative consequences of a particular behavior. When used alone, these directives are inexplicit in that they merely state a basis or rationale for the desired behavior, while not actually telling the child what to do or refrain from doing. The most frequently cited reasons had to do with the wishes, needs, and feelings of others and will be discussed below with respect to empathy. Positive reasons for performing actions were often based on "felicity conditions" for the request, such as the presence of the necessary objects or the knowledge or ability to perform an action, as in *Shitteru anata* 'You know it (= So sing the song)' (M 2;1). These were sometimes extremely indirect; for example, once Y told his mother that there was nowhere for him to write on a piece of paper that still had some room, and she replied, *Omeme aru n ja nai* 'You have eyes, don't you' (Y 2;4). Mothers also gave hints intended to suggest that the children stop what they were doing and take an alternative course of action; for example, when Y was looking for a book in one place, his mother said, *Sotchi ehon nai deshoo* 'There's probably no book there' (Y 2;1). The most common rationales with negative directive intent were warnings, either of potential damage to objects, such as breaking, falling, spilling, and colliding, or of possible harm to the child, such as getting hurt, becoming sick, and getting cavities.

From the standpoint of socialization to Japanese patterns of dependency, it is interesting to note that among the more frequent rationales that the mothers used to encourage their children to do something were offers to help the child, to perform the action too, or even just to watch the child perform the action alone. Occasionally a mother referred to the child's social responsibilities. For example, when Y asked his mother to help him put away his toys, she responded, *Mama mo ireru no? Mama irenakute, Yotchan mo ireru. Yotchan ga asonda deshoo?* 'Mama put them in too? You'll put them in, not me. You played with them, didn't you?' (Y 1;11).

These mothers' frequent appeals to various rationales for their directives imply a view of even very young children as rational beings, who will be more willing to cooperate if they understand the basis for an imperative. This view is consistent with the findings of Vogel (1963), who reports that among the urban middle-class Japanese mothers he studied, the basic strategy of child rearing was to establish a close relationship with their children and try to "get them to understand" (*wakaraseru*).[8] The use of rationales indicates to the child, and to the mother herself, that she is not merely trying to impose her will, but rather has a sound basis other than her own wishes for giving the directive.

How does the Japanese child learn to interpret this wide range of directive strategies? As Ervin-Tripp points out, it is extremely difficult to investigate children's comprehension of directives, since failure to comply does not necessarily indicate lack of understanding. Moreover, compliance does not necessarily indicate comprehension of the directive per se, since children could be relying upon context, tone of voice, and their comprehension of mothers' affect, rather than degree of directness, in deciphering imperatives. In the present transcripts, there were many cases of compliance with indirect strategies such as questions, statements of desire, and reasons/warnings that indicated that in one way or another the child had understood the directive.

If a child failed to comply with an indirect request, the mother might try to help by "translating" it into a more direct expression. In one interesting case, my assistant wished to end a game in which M (2;1) kept serving her food, and the following interaction took place:

Adult: *Moo ii desu.*
    'It's already good.' (= I've had enough.)
Child: [Continues serving]
Mother: *Moo ii tte oneesan.*
    'Older sister said, "It's already good."'
Child: [Continues serving]
Adult: *Hai. Moo onaka ippai desu.*
    'All right. My stomach is already full.'
 Child [serving]: *Mii.*
    'Milk.'
Adult: *Doomo gochisoosama deshita. A, kondo kore wa mii desu ka?*
    'Thank you for the fine meal. Oh, now is this milk?'
Child: *Suupu na no. Suupu. Suupu.*
    'It's soup. Soup. Soup.'
Adult: *Hai, hai, hai.*
    'All right, all right, all right.'
Child: *Jaa, jaa, jaa.*
    'Here, here, here.'
Mother: *Moo oneesan iya tte, moo ii tte mii wa.*
    'Older sister said, "No!"; she said, "It's already good, as for milk."'

At this point, the child discontinued the game. In this sequence, the mother begins by repeating the phrase *Moo ii* (lit. "It's already good") without the polite *desu* form of the copula for the child. When the child ignored this, and continued serving despite the more explicit *Moo onaka ippai desu* 'My stomach is full' and the polite *Gochisoosama deshita* 'It was a fine meal', her mother intervenes again. In her last utterance, the mother quotes my assistant as having said *Iya,* which is a very strong "No" meaning approximately "I don't want." She juxtaposes this with the less direct expression *Moo ii* 'It's already good', my assistant's first utterance, thus clarifying for the child that *Moo ii* should have been interpreted as *Iya.* Obviously, such cases could teach the Japanese child how to interpret the indirect, polite speech of others as expressing the same strong feelings and wishes as more direct utterances.

From the present transcripts it appears that, as the above example suggests, the primary means by which these children could be learning how to interpret indirection is through the pairing of indirect with direct utterances having the same communicative intent. All of the imperative strategies discussed above did, at least occasionally, occur alone. Rationales/warnings, such as *Ochiru yo* 'It will fall' appeared as the only expression of a directive 11.8 percent of the time, and this was the highest frequency among the indirect imperatives. Obviously, most instances of indirect imperatives occurred in a speech turn or sequence of turns in which the same content was also expressed more directly.

Ervin-Tripp (1977) reports that in her data on English there were sequences in which speakers moved to increasingly explicit forms in addressing directives to young children. There were also numerous examples of this in my data. In the following case, the mother begins by questioning the child's current behavior, then moves on to an explicit imperative. *Mata shuukuriimu motsu no? Ja, hayaku tabechainasai yo* 'Do you have a cream puff again? Well, eat it up quickly' (M 2;1). Such sequences could also be important in teaching children the meanings of certain conventionalized indirect forms, such as *X ga ii* 'X is good', a formula for requesting food: *Mama koohii ga ii desu. Koohii kudasai. Koohii oishii no irete kudasai* 'As for me, coffee is good. Please give me coffee. Please pour some delicious coffee' (Y 1;11).

Thus the mothers frequently followed an indirect request with a more explicit imperative, especially if they strongly disapproved of the child's current behavior. Indirect strategies such as rhetorical questions usually occurred alone only when a lengthy preceding context had established a particular directive as given. For example, during one session Y (2;3) repeatedly tried to take the toys of a younger playmate, and his mother used many direct imperatives telling him to stop, suggested alternatives, and reminded him that the toys did not belong to him. When later in the session Y again tried to take a toy, his mother simply exclaimed, *Dooshite hito no mono soo yatte toru no?* 'Why do you take other people's things like that?' Such cases could serve as a kind of bridge between the comprehension of direct and indirect strategies, helping the child to understand indirect imperatives even when they occur alone. One can imagine that, as a child gets older, the mother may increasingly assume that such indirect questions can function alone as directives.

The progression from less to more explicit directives was not the only one. Mothers also frequently began with an extremely direct and explicit imperative, and then added questions, reasons, and warnings that could convey the same message, as in the following example: *A, yamenasai. Oneechan sekkaku tsukutta no. Oneechan ni okorareru yo.* 'Oh stop. After all your sister's trouble making it. She'll get mad at you' (Y 2;0). Once when Y (1;11) was eating tangerines without offering any to his guests, his mother first gave direct imperatives, then added a rhetorical question: *Ja, oneechan mo tabete tte iwanakya. Un? Oneechan mo doozo tabete tte. Yotchan dake pakupaku tabeten no?* 'Well, you must say, "Older sister, eat too." Right? Say, "Older sister, please eat." Is only Yotchan munching away?'

Sometimes direct and indirect imperatives were mixed in a single speech turn, as in the following case: *Mama supagechi ga ii naa. Tsukutte kudasai. Sakki yatte ta n ja nai. Hayaku tsukutte kudasai. Mama onaka suite imasu yo* 'As for mama, spaghetti is good. Please make some. You did it before, didn't you. Please make some quickly. Mama's hungry' (Y 1;11). In this example, the conventional formula *X ga ii* 'X is good' is followed by an explicit imperative, then a rationale implying that the child should be willing and able to comply, then another imperative, and then a "problem statement" (Ervin-Tripp 1977). Sometimes two indirect forms were coupled. In the following example from Y (2;2), a conventionalized question requesting food, *X ga aru?* 'Is there any *x*?', is preceded by the somewhat more obvious desire statement *Mama sooseeji hoshii desu. Sooseeji arimasu ka?* 'I want sausage. Is there any sausage?' In a similar example, M's mother followed a question with a desire statement: *Osakana o yaite kureru? Mama osakana yaite hoshii naa* 'Will you bake a fish for me? I'd sure like to have a fish baked' (M 2;1). Such cases were quite typical and probably play an important part in teaching the child that various formulations of a directive are functionally equivalent.

It seemed clear from the variety of different combinations used that the mothers were not deliberately sequencing direct and indirect imperatives in any set order. There were probably some occasions when, having uttered an indirect form, mothers felt a need to clarify with something more direct to ensure comprehension and compliance. In general, however, self-repetition and paraphrase seemed to be the mothers' habitual mode of speaking to their 2-year-olds. They did not wait for feedback before starting to paraphrase, and used paraphrases even when the child seemed to understand and be complying with the initial formulation. The mothers may also have wanted to show that they intended to persist in their directives until the child complied.

Whatever the motivations for this style, one result was that the children were frequently exposed to both indirect and direct versions of the same imperative in immediate succession. Ervin-Tripp (1977) has proposed that with indirect imperatives, especially questions and hints that do not mention the desired goal state or object at all, comprehension must rest either on active inference or on repeated conjunction with more explicit forms. The present transcripts provide ample evidence that in this early stage of using indirect imperatives, Japanese mothers do in fact almost always combine them with more direct equivalents. This probably provides the children with their major source of information about the meanings of indirect forms.

Although the children in the present study were very young, they were probably already able to understand a significant portion of the indirect imperatives addressed to them. Perhaps the best evidence for this is that they were themselves beginning to use certain of the indirect strategies in their mothers' speech when giving directives of their own. Across the three children's samples, 78 percent of all imperatives were extremely direct: verbs in the *-te* inflection, nouns referring to desired objects, and lexical items such as *choodai* 'please give'. Indirect strategies used by the children included statements of desire, such as *Mame tabetai* 'I want to eat beans' (Y 2;2), and problem statements, such as *Mama dekinai yo* 'Mama, I can't do it' (Y 2;3, when he was trying to play with origami), or *Tapa nai no, tapa* 'There's no trumpet' (M 2;1, when she wanted to play with her toy trumpet). The children also occasionally used requests in question form, such as the conventionalized *X ga aru?* 'Is there any *x*?' for food; for example, *An no?* 'Is there any?' (Y 2;3, when he wanted candy). Of the three children, only Maho regularly used question requests of the form 'Will you do *x*?', such as *Matte kureru?* 'Will you wait for me?' (M 2;2), and made polite suggestions and offers in question form, for example, *Tabenai?* 'Won't you eat?' (M 2;2). Y occasionally used two different rationales as directives: the availability of a desired object, as in *Mama, mada aru yo* 'Mama, there's still some left' (Y 2;3, when he wanted to continue blowing bubbles), and the right of possession, as in *Yotchan no yo* 'It's mine' (Y 2;1), which he said when he wanted a toy, whether it was his or not. Except for these two reasons, which are closely linked to performance of an action in the child's experience, directives calling for inference, such as rhetorical questions and other types of hints, did not occur in the children's speech. Directive strategies that were grammatically complex, such as statements of obligation or suggestions in the conditional, also were not used by the children at this stage, although they seemed to be able to understand them. Although it is not clear what role social factors played in the children's use of imperatives, it is interesting that certain forms that can be used only by social superiors to inferiors, such as the *-nasai* imperative suffix, did not occur; the children used only the polite request form *-te*.[9]

Interestingly, there was no evidence of indirection in the children's speech in contexts other than giving directives. For example, there were no indirect refusals, although the children were also exposed to many of these. From the transcripts, it was evident that whereas a simple "No!" was usually sufficient to silence a mother's unwelcome requests, getting her to comply with the child's requests was a more difficult matter. Thus the children were motivated to attempt a variety of directive strategies to get what they wanted, and indirection in directive contexts was already making its appearance in the first few months of the third year.

Empathy training

In giving directives, Japanese mothers strongly emphasized sensitivity to the needs, wishes, and feelings of others. In fact, such appeals for empathy, both implicit and explicit, constituted 45 percent of all the rationales given by mothers for their directives. As Table 11.1 shows, these included statements of desire, need, and problems, which were very common when the mothers were trying to show their children how to treat guests. In these transcripts, both Y and M often played a game in which their mothers took the role of guest – along with the real guests, my assistant and I – and the child played the part of the host/ess. In these routines, when expressing requests for themselves, mothers frequently used statements of desire, such as the following (Y 1;11):

Mother: *Mama shimbun yomitai naa.*
    'Gee, I want to read the newspaper.'
 Child: *Nainai.*
    'All gone.'

It was often clear from the children's responses that they understood these statements as imperatives, as both the example above and the following example (M 2;2) show.

Mother: *Mama budoo ga ii wa. Kyuuri demo ii wa.*
    'As for mama, grapes are good. Even cucumber is good.'
 Child [giving imaginary food]: *Hai.*
    'All right.'

Mothers also informed their children of the needs/problems of others, as in *Motto hakkiri ohanashi̇ shinai to oneesan wakaranai yo* 'If you don't speak more clearly, older sister won't understand' (M 2;2) or *Oneechan onaka suichatta* 'Older sister is hungry' (M 2;1). Thus Japanese children learn at an early age that the speaker's wish is their command and that they must try to fulfill the wishes expressed by others.

    The mothers in this sample also tried to get their children to empathize with certain emotions that they expressed to encourage or discourage particular behaviors. A frequent theme with Y's mother was the fear of fire, which she sought to instill in her son: *Yotchan achichi itazura shinai no ne. Kowai, kowai ne, kaji ne* 'Yotchan doesn't play with fire, does he. Fires are scary, scary, aren't they' (Y 1;11). In Japanese, subjects are usually omitted from these expressions of feeling (as elsewhere). Thus there is no distinction, for example, between 'I'm afraid of fires' and 'Fires are scary' in Japanese unless an explicit experiencer is mentioned as subject. The same is true of another common expression, *X ga kawaisoo* '*X* is pitiful' or 'I feel sorry for *x*'. The mothers often expressed this emotion when they wanted their children to give better treatment, usually to a toy, as in the following case: *Kawaisoo, darumasan naguttara* (lit. "The daruma is pitiful if you hit him" or "I feel sorry for the daruma if you hit him" – M 2;2). Mothers also tried to encourage kind behavior toward pets and babies by pointing out that they were *kawaii* 'cute/lovable'.[10] In the following case, Y (2;0) had refused to lend his toys to a younger child, saying *Dame!* 'No!', and his mother replied, *Dame tte yuu no? Hirochan ni mo doozo tte kashite agenakya. Takusan aru kara, hitotsu doozo tte kashite agenakya. Akachan kawaii deshoo?* 'Do you say "No!"'? You must lend one to Hirochan, saying, "Help yourself." The baby is cute/lovable, isn't he?' Through such expressions of emotion, the mothers in this sample revealed their own feelings to their children, apparently hoping to make them feel the same emotion themselves, and to act in accordance with it.

Given the Japanese emphasis on indirection and avoidance of imposing on others, it is important to be able to anticipate the needs of others, so that they will not be forced to make a direct request. One might well wonder how Japanese children learn to "read the minds" of other people in this way. Judging from the present transcripts, the answer seems rather simple: Their mothers tell them directly what other people are thinking and feeling in various situations. A common behavior for all three mothers in the sample was to attribute speech to people who had not actually spoken, thereby indicating to the child what might be on their minds. The speech attributed to others ranged from direct requests, such as *Oneechan omocha misete tte* 'Older sister says, "Show me your toys"' (Y 2;0), to statements of desire, need, and emotional reactions. For example, when Y and M played host/ess, their mothers would attribute requests for food to other people as part of the game. They also did this if the children were eating alone, without offering anything to others. Once, when Y (1;11) was eating a tangerine, his mother suddenly said, *Oneesantachi mo tabetai tte* 'The girls also say, "We want to eat"', although we had not said anything. Mothers also frequently attributed feelings of pain to others, especially if the child was responsible but had failed to notice or apologize for causing the pain. For example, when M's toy dishes fell on my assistant, her mother immediately said, *Neechan itai-itai tte* 'Older sister says, "Ouch ouch"' (M 2;1), before anything had been said. Attributing speech to others is one way Japanese mothers teach their children to be sensitive to others.

Empathy is especially important in order to avoid inconveniencing, annoying, or imposing upon others. As the example above suggests, the mothers were quick to point out cases in which a child had caused someone trouble.[11] Again, this was often done by attributing thoughts or speech to someone who might appear to be silently content. When a child imposed upon someone with a direct request, even if the person seemed to comply willingly the mother might indicate that such behavior is not appreciated. For example, when Y (1;11) asked my assistant to peel a tangerine for him, and she was doing this very amiably, his mother said, *Oneechan jibun no muite taberu tte ne* 'Older sister says she'll peel and eat her own'. Such examples may represent the Japanese child's first encounter with the idea that there is sometimes a difference between what people's behavior seems to indicate and what they are really thinking.

Mothers also often attributed speech to others as an indirect way of correcting inappropriate behavior. In such cases, they would typically attribute various negative reactions to people who had not spoken. For example, when M (2;1) was misbehaving, her mother said: *Oneechan akirechau kara tte itteru yo. Mahochan ni wa akirechau* 'Older sister is saying, "I'm surprised. I'm surprised at Maho" '. Negative reactions and feelings were even attributed to inanimate objects. When Y (1;11) repeatedly dropped apples on the floor, his mother said, *Sonna koto suru n dattara ringosan itai itteru wa yo* 'If you do that kind of thing, Mr. Apple says "Ouch!" '. And when MK (2;4) was getting very loud, pretending that he was firing guns, his mother attributed a request that he stop to his stuffed animal, Kikochan: *Kikochan bikkuri shiteru yo. Kikochan yamete kudasai tte. Gomennasai tte. Kikochan ga itai tte* 'Kikochan is amazed. Kikochan says, "Please stop." Say, "I'm sorry." Kikochan says "Ouch!" '. Thus Japanese mothers use attributions of speech to correct their children's behavior, at the same time distancing themselves from the actual imperative. This strategy serves to deemphasize the mother's role as an authority figure, while teaching children to be aware of the effects of their behavior on others.

Consistent with these findings, Azuma et al. (1980) and Conroy et al. (1980) report that "appeals to feeling" function as a control strategy among Japanese mothers, who often invoke the feelings of others as the rationale for a child's good behavior. In a study of fifty-eight Japanese and sixty-seven American mother–child pairs, each mother was given a set of hypothetical situations, such as being in the supermarket with a disruptive child, and was asked to respond as she would if the child were actually present. In analyzing the results, the authors report, the category "appeals to feelings" had to be created because of its frequency among the Japanese mothers, who used this strategy in 22 percent of their responses, as compared with only 7 percent among American mothers. In these responses, the mother would, for example, ask the child to consider how she felt as mother of such a child, or how the child would feel if someone else did the same thing to him or her. As in my sample, this study found that Japanese mothers appealed to the feelings of third parties and even of inanimate objects. Although these appeals to feelings often do function as control strategies, they can also be viewed as providing children with explicit training in empathy, lessons in how to guess what others are thinking and feeling even when they have not spoken. It is consistent with the very different communicative styles in Japan and America that Japanese mothers used this strategy so much more frequently than American mothers.[12]

Conformity training

Although empathy may seem an entirely desirable ideal, it is, in a way, a double-edged sword. On the one hand, the ability to be sensitive to others has many benefits, including the social harmony that the Japanese value. On the other hand, being so attuned to the feelings of others makes the individual extremely vulnerable to public opinion, creating pressure to conform. And in Japanese social structure, with its emphasis on mutual dependency, this pressure is intense. Thus empathy and conformity may be seen as two sides of the same coin, each contributing to the characteristic Japanese communicative style. Indirection, even silence, can be readily understood by those trained in empathy, as long as people generally conform to expected feelings, attitudes, and behavior.

In the present samples, there was considerable evidence for "conformity training." Mothers were actively engaged in teaching their children Japanese norms for speech and behavior, both through subtle pressure and explicit instruction. The latter was especially striking with respect to polite formulas and context-appropriate turntaking. A large number of maternal directives were aimed at teaching children what to say in particular situations. The mothers told their children to use polite expressions, such as *Doozo* 'Please/ go ahead/help yourself', *Arigatoo* 'Thank you', *Hai* 'Yes', *Choodai* 'Please give', *Gomennasai* 'I'm sorry'; greetings such as *Ohayoo gozaimasu* 'Good morning', *Konnichiwa* 'Hello/good day', *Oyasumi* 'Goodnight', *Baibai* 'Goodbye', *Sayoonara* 'Goodbye', *Itte mairimasu* 'I go and will come back' (said when leaving the house), *Irasshai* 'Welcome', *Mata ne* 'Come again'; and formulas for use at the table, including *Itadakimasu* 'I will receive it' (said before eating) and *Gochisoosama* (*deshita*) 'It was a fine meal'.

The mothers seemed to take every opportunity to teach these formulas to their children. They modeled them when appropriate occasions arose; for example, when my assistant picked up something for Y, his mother said, *Hora, ochichatta yo. Arigatoo wa? Oneechan ni arigatoo tte yuu deshoo* 'Look, it fell. What about "Thank you"? You should say "Thank you" to older sister' (Y 1;11). Mothers attributed polite formulas to characters in story books, and, if another adult used a formula, they would repeat it for the child's benefit. More adult forms were taught to replace childish expressions, as in the following case (Y 2;0):

> Child: *Baibai tte itta no.*
> 'He said "Byebye." '
> Mother: *Itta no ne. Papa nante itta? Itte mairimasu tte itta deshoo. Itte mairimasu.*
> 'He said it, didn't he. What did Papa say? He said, "I go and will come back," didn't he. "I go and will come back." '

The finding that these mothers provided so much instruction in verbal formulas to their 2-year-olds is consistent with research reported in Hess et al. (1980). In their study, Japanese mothers expected earlier mastery of social courtesy, such as greetings, than American mothers. The present data are also consistent with Matsumori's findings; these mothers were clearly concerned only with teaching their children to use polite formulas when addressing others, rather than when speaking to the mothers themselves.

The mothers in this sample also provided their children with a considerable amount of instruction in somewhat less stereotyped verbal behavior, such as saying *Asobimashoo* 'Let's play' to friends. In role-playing routines, the children were taught how to speak on the telephone to their grandmothers and how to interact with guests in their homes. For example, in the host/ess game, Y and M were taught to ask what a guest wanted to eat; to offer food, saying *Doozo* 'Help yourself'; to ask if the food was good, whether it was too hot or cold, and whether the guest wanted more to eat. They were also taught the role of the polite diner; for example, M's mother insisted that she say *Oishii* 'It's delicious' after the first few bites. Clearly, a basic goal of mother–child communication in these samples was to prepare the children for a variety of social interactions. The Japanese codification of contexts and appropriate formulas starts being taught and acquired very early.

In training their children to conform to social expectations, an important strategy used by Japanese mothers is appealing to the imagined reactions of *hito* 'other people', who are watching and evaluating the child's behavior. In the present transcripts it was clear that through their training in empathy, the mothers were teaching their children not only to be sensitive to the needs and desires of others, but also to fear their criticism and disapproval. Benedict (1946) has discussed how Japanese children are inculcated with a fear of ridicule or ostracism. Ito (1980) points out that in Japan mothers often tell a misbehaving child, *Hito ni warawareru* 'You will be laughed at by other people'.[13] This approach locates the source of disapproval and constraint outside the mother, in society at large. As Vogel has noted, the fear of ridicule serves to ally mother and child against the outside world; the mother's role is seen as helping the child to avoid the negative sanctions of others.

In reacting to their children's behavior, the mothers in this sample often emphasized the importance of conformity, either directly or indirectly. For example, if a mother disapproved of her child's behavior, she might say that the behavior was *okashii* 'strange' or even *kowai* 'fearsome/scary'. Once when Y's mother asked him to bring some toy cars, he refused, whined, and started to cry; his mother said, *Okashii yo, naitara* 'It's strange, if you cry' (Y 2;1). Mothers sometimes claimed to be frightened by the child's misbehavior, or attributed this reaction to others. For example, a frequent point of contention between Y and his mother was the child's constant eating; when he ate several tangerines in a row during one session (Y 2;0), she said, *Mata taberu no? Osoroshii* 'Are you eating again? It's fearsome'. And when Y (2;1) loudly refused to sing a song for his mother and me, yelling *Dame!* 'No!', she told him that I found him *kowai* 'scary'. (The full example is near the end of the section "Saying no.") Thus the mothers made it clear that behaviors falling outside the range of normal expectations are frightening and repulsive. In the following case, M (2;1) was playing hostess with her mother; when she began pretending to eat one of the toy dishes, the following exchange took place:

Mother: *Sonna koto shite osara taberu to okashii deshoo? Osara tabeteru hito inai deshoo? Ne? Osara dare ga tabeteru no?*
'Isn't it strange to do that kind of thing, if you eat a plate? No one eats plates, do they? Who eats plates?'
Child: *Kore Mahochan.*
'Maho (eats) this.'
Mother: *Mahochan ga tabeteru no? Kaijuu mitai. Kowai. Iya. Kowai, obake mitai. Mama obake kirai yo.*
'You're eating it? Like a beast. It's scary. I don't like it. It's scary, like a monster. I hate monsters.'

As the example above shows, to get their children to behave mothers sometimes explicitly invoked conformity with the expression *X suru hito inai* 'No one does *x*'. Although the example above was surely spoken lightheartedly, M's mother also used this expression quite seriously when M performed some socially unacceptable action, as in the following case (M 2;2):

Adult: *Kore nani iro?*
'What color is this?'
Child: *Een, dame!*
'No!'
Mother: *Nani yutten no! Midori tte yuu n deshoo.*
'What are you saying! You should say, "Green."'
Child: *Midori.*
'Green.'
Mother: *Dame nante yuu hito dare mo inai yo.*
'There is no one who says things like "No!"'

Another strategy Japanese mothers sometimes use to induce their children to conform to expectations is teasing. Benedict (1946) has proposed that maternal teasing, which the child at first takes seriously, contributes to a later fear of ridicule, since children eventually come to realize that they are being laughed at. Japanese mothers often tease children about childish or disapproved behaviors. For example, Y's mother frequently teased him about his eating, comparing his plump body to Winnie-the-Pooh. Once, when he asked for more to eat, she said, *Motto? Koo, oheso, onaka ni kiite goran. "Daijoobu?" tte* 'More? Ask your belly button, your stomach, "Are you all right?"' (Y 1;11). Y did not seem to recognize his mother's teasing as such, since it was done lightheartedly, and at this age he would readily point to pictures of storybook characters who were fat or who were eating a lot and say, *Yotchan mitai* 'Just like me'.

Teasing is also used to enforce certain attitudes and reactions in Japanese children, such as dependence upon their mothers. Benedict reports that Japanese mothers may threaten to give their children away to visitors; in citing a similar example, Vogel proposes that Japanese mothers keep their children dependent by provoking their anxiety about the outside world while at the same time rewarding intimacy. A striking example of this also occurred in my data. Y (1;11) and his mother were engaged in fantasy play with his toy cars, and his mother suggested that he go shopping in one of the cars. The following exchange then took place:

Mother: *Mama ikanakute ii no.*
    'I don't have to go.'
Child: [Whines]
Mother: *Yotchan hitori de ittoide. Hora, buubuu ni notte, ittoide.*
    'You go alone. Look, ride in the car and go.'
Child: *Iya* [whining].
    'No.'
Mother: *Buubuu notte ittoide.*
    'Ride in the car and go.'
Child: *Eeen, mama mo, mama mo.*
    'Waah, mama too, mama too.'
Mother: *Mamo mo? Mama ii no. Mama ii no.*
    'Me too? I'm all right (without going). I'm all right.'
Child: *Iya da! Iya da!* [starting to cry] *Iya da! Een, mama!*
    'No! No! [starting to cry] No! Waah, mama!'
Mother: *Are, okashii naa. Okashii naa.*
    'What, that's strange. That's strange.'

Although they were only playing, this fantasy based on the *amae* or dependence between mother and child seems to have a kind of primal quality for them. The mother may be teasing, but the emotions being invoked are very real and powerful. Although she calls the child's ultimate tears "strange," she must surely have anticipated some such response. Thus teasing can be used to reinforce the kinds of emotions and reactions expected of children in Japanese society.

When faced with the disapproval of other people, the misbehaving child is expected to feel *hazukashii* 'ashamed'. In such cases, the mother will usually simply say, *Hazukashii*. Typically, no subject is used; thus *Hazukashii* 'shameful' conveys both the mother's own feeling and the strong implication that the child should feel the same way. For example, at 2;2 years, M wet her pants when she was about to leave the house with her parents and guests. As her mother was trying to wash her, she ran away; her mother pointed out that everyone was watching, and repeatedly said, *Hazukashii*.

Kasahara (1974) suggests that this aspect of Japanese child rearing may contribute to a fear of eye-to-eye confrontation that is common among young adults in Japan, but virtually unknown in the West. In this neurosis, people experience a phobia about being stared at by others, and in severe cases fear that they cannot control their own eyes and prevent their stares from inflicting undue pain upon others. The strong emphasis on *Hito ga miteru* 'People are watching' from early childhood, Kasahara suggests, may foster the development of personalities that incessantly watch, and dread being watched by, those outside their family circle.

In this light, it is interesting to note that very young children in Japan may at first strongly resist internalizing their mothers' *Hazukashii* and the disapproval of watching eyes. For example, in the case just mentioned, M responded to her mother's *Hazukashii* with a resounding *Hazukashii chigau!* 'I'm not ashamed!' In fact, Japanese adults do not really expect very young children to measure up to adult norms of self-restraint and discipline. To the American observer, Japanese child rearing seems extremely permissive. Vogel (1963:244) notes that Japanese children are rarely punished, and are allowed to "run, climb, yell, stay up late, eat large amounts of sweets, keep their mother occupied away from company, hit bigger children, and climb up on parents' laps and backs almost with no limit." I can testify that an American's blood will boil to see a child as old as 4 years scream and pummel his mother in the kind of temper tantrum that Benedict describes, while other family members stand patiently by.

From the standpoint of the extreme social constraints on Japanese adults, this early permissiveness may seem mysterious. Benedict claims that the "arc of life" in Japan is a U-curve, with the greatest freedom and indulgence enjoyed by babies and the elderly, and the low point of greatest restriction falling during the prime of life, especially just before marriage. Vogel insists that although Japanese mothers do become stricter as their children grow, they do not suddenly apply a strictness that did not exist before. Rather, he claims, early training appears lenient because it is carried out largely by establishing a close relationship in which few sanctions except a vague feeling of approval or disapproval are required to get the child to behave. This view is supported by the present data. In their comments and attitudes toward their children's unrestricted or selfish behaviors, the mothers in this sample were already sowing the seeds for the social constraints to be imposed later by the watching eyes of *hito* 'other people'. In fact, the permissiveness of the early years increases mothers' opportunities to present the types of reactions described above over a long period of time before any negative sanctions are actually imposed. Thus as Azuma et al. have proposed, early permissiveness in Japanese child rearing probably has the effect of preparing young children for future conformity. The present data suggest that, by the time the period of early indulgence is over, Japanese children will be quite familiar with which behaviors are *okashii* 'strange' to those around them, and which behaviors should make them feel *hazukashii* 'ashamed'. Early training in empathy and conformity thus leads Japanese children to understand the feelings and expectations of others, and also to experience the expected feelings themselves. This helps set the stage for the successful functioning of the Japanese indirect, intuitive mode of communication.

Saying no

One result of Japanese conformity training is the wish to avoid conflict, which leads, in turn, to an avoidance of saying no directly. Since any overt conflict between speaker and hearer could jeopardize the harmony of an interaction if expressed directly, the Japanese rely upon various indirect strategies for saying no, the most extreme of which is simply saying yes. Americans tend to regard such behavior as irresponsible or dishonest, but it can be traced to the Japanese ideal of concern for others that makes it so difficult for them to risk angering or hurting the feelings of the addressee by a direct no. Since the values involved are so basic to Japanese culture, it is interesting to examine the present data to discover how these Japanese mothers said no to their children.

As Table 11.2 showed, prohibitions were quite frequent in the early Japanese mother–child interactions in this sample. This can be readily understood by recalling the rationales the mothers gave for their directives. Prohibitions were used to prevent the children from hurting themselves, damaging objects, causing others trouble; in short, they function to protect children and to teach them socially appropriate behavior. Therefore it is not only acceptable, but even mandatory, for a good mother to use prohibitions, and avoidance of these noes does not occur.

However, it is worth noting that the typical form of prohibition in Japanese is, in fact, indirect. The negative inflection *-naide* 'don't' was quite rare; by far the most common expression of prohibition was V-*cha dame* 'Doing *x* is no good'. This expression is very forceful in tone, and is probably not felt to be indirect by those who use it. Yet these and certain other conventional prohibitions are indirect in their literal readings; they give the reasons for not performing an action, rather than actually saying not to perform it, e.g., *Abunai* 'It's dangerous' (= "Watch out/Stop") or *Ii* 'It's good/all right', which means approximately "It's good as is (without your doing *x*)"; therefore, "Stop doing/don't do *x*." Thus conventionalized Japanese forms of prohibition show a replacement of imperatives with rationales (It's good, bad, dangerous to do *x*) that may once have been motivated by the wish to avoid a more direct "don't."

Whereas prohibitions reflect a conflict concerning the addressee's behavior, contradictions express a clash of opinions between speaker and hearer. The mothers in this sample were generally very direct in contradicting their children. Typically a mother used the expressions *X ja nai* 'It is not *x*', *Chigau* (lit. "It differs"), and occasionally *uso* 'lie' (more similar in tone to English "not true"), and/or presented her own opinion as a corrected version of the child's statement. For example, when Y (2;0) called a picture of an airplane *shinkansen* 'bullet train', his mother responded, *Shinkansen ja nai, kore hikooki deshoo* 'It's not a bullet train, this is an airplane, isn't it'.

Again, if we consider the function of contradictions in the mothers' speech, it becomes clear why such direct clashes of opinion were not avoided. The great majority of maternal contradictions were intended to correct a word used or pronounced incorrectly by the child, as in the example above. Thus the mothers were not contradicting the children to assert their own views on matters of opinion, but rather to help them learn vocabulary. Occasionally contradictions were also used to correct socially inappropriate speech, as when Y (2;0) offered my assistant something to eat saying *Motte tte* 'Take it', and his mother immediately said, *Motte ja nai deshoo. Doozo* 'Not "Take it. Help yourself" '. Thus, as with prohibitions, the contradictions in these mothers' speech were intended for the children's own good, and therefore can be regarded as desirable behavior for the good mother.

Refusals, however, show a very different pattern, with obvious avoidance of the direct no. The mothers very frequently complied with their children's wishes, but, as in other cultures, there was an obvious relationship between the "demand value" of a request (cf. Ervin-Tripp 1977) and compliance. The mothers were more likely to obey commands to look at the child or at a picture than to get up and do or get something for the child. When mothers did refuse requests, they rarely did so directly. This is immediately apparent from Table 11.3, which summarizes the strategies used by the three mothers in this sample in refusing their children's requests.

The first five strategies in Table 11.3 are delaying or avoidance tactics. The mother might ignore the request, promise to comply later, distract the child by changing the topic or offering food, make a countersuggestion, or recycle the

Table 11.3. *The frequency of different strategies for refusing children's requests*

	Y's mother	M's mother	MK's mother
Ignore	0.07 (22)	0.21 (5)	0.16 (3)
Recycle	0.30 (95)	0.38 (8)	0.37 (7)
Promise "later"	0.06 (20)	0.05 (1)	0.11 (2)
Distract	0.05 (15)	—	0.05 (1)
Countersuggestion	0.16 (50)	0.24 (5)	0.21 (4)
Complain	0.01 (3)	—	—
Rationale	0.22 (72)	0.05 (1)	0.11 (2)
Lie	0.06 (20)	—	—
Appeal to feelings	0.02 (7)	—	—
Attribute refusal	0.01 (4)	—	—
Direct refusal	0.07 (22)	0.24 (5)	—
Total refusals	(330)	(25)	(19)

request by asking questions about it. For example, when Y (2;4) demanded that his mother draw a truck with a siren on it, she said, *Sonna no an no?* 'Does it have that kind of thing?' If the child was adamant, recycling strategies served only to buy a little time, but often a child seemed to lose interest in the demand if the mother could delay compliance even very briefly. The most common countersuggestion offered by these mothers was that the child should be the one to perform the desired action; for example, Y's mother responded to a request that she draw for him by saying *Yotchan jibun de kaku n deshoo* 'You'll draw it yourself, won't you' (Y 2;4). Occasionally, a mother might try to get a child to drop a request by complaining, e.g., *Mata dakko? Omoi no ni naa. Omoi no ni naa* 'Sit on my lap again? But you're heavy. You're heavy' (Y 2;1), or by teasing or criticizing the child for making the request. The mother might also simply tell the child not to make the request; for example, when Y (1;11) complained that he had no toy cars, his mother said, *Sonna koto iwanai de. Bubu nakute mo ii tte?* 'Don't say that kind of thing. Will you say "It's all right if there are no cars"? '

As with directives, the mothers frequently refused requests by giving reasons why they could not or would not comply. And again, the reasons often had to do with the "felicity conditions" for the request. For example, the mothers might point out that the desired action was unnecessary or impossible. When Y (2;0) wanted candy, his mother said, *Asa omochi takusan tabeta ja nai* 'Didn't you eat a lot of *mochi* this morning?' Mothers also called for empathy, citing the feelings, rights, and needs of others when refusing requests. When Y (2;3) asked his mother to give him his friend's toy truck, she replied, *Sore wa Daichan no deshoo* 'That's Daichan's, isn't it', and when he wanted to play with his toy ambulance, she pointed out that my tape recorder was on (Y 2;3).

Of the three children, Y was by far the most demanding, at least during the present recordings. He made the most requests, and was the most persistent in repeating them despite his mother's various avoidance tactics. Clearly Y taxed his mother's imagination and patience, and she sometimes responded as the Japanese may do under pressure – by lying. Sometimes a "white lie" served as an excuse for getting Y to perform an action himself, as in the following example (Y 2;3):

Child: *Mama, Yotchan no hikooki.*
    'Mama, my airplane' [repeated three times].
Mother: *Yotchan no hikooki mama shiranai yo. Sagashite kite.*
    'I don't know about your airplane. Go look for it.'

In other cases, she was simply trying to get Y to abandon his request by pretending that it was impossible to fulfill. In a striking example when Y was 1;11 years old, he insisted on playing with his toy ambulance, which he was unable to wind himself. His mother engaged in an elaborate subterfuge lasting several pages of transcript, pretending that she couldn't wind up the toy, that it was broken, asking Y to try himself, and giving it to my assistant to show that she couldn't make it work either.

Why do Japanese mothers bother to give reasons for refusing requests when, at the age of 2 years, the children do not seem to understand or to care what the reasons might be? In addition to their more general wish to avoid a direct refusal, an important factor is probably the mothers' wish to maintain their status as rational adults in going against their children's wishes. Simply refusing requests with *Iya* 'No/I don't want to', as the children usually did, would bring a mother down to the same level as her 2-year-old, making her sound selfish and childish. It would also reduce the exchange to a battle of wills, bringing the mother into direct conflict with her child. In contrast, giving reasons for her refusal puts the mother in a superior position and helps mitigate the conflict. To the extent that the child understands the mother's reasons, the basis for making the demand will be undermined; the child can neither hope for compliance by persisting nor blame the mother for refusing. In any event, reasons can at least serve as yet another delaying tactic, eventually leading the child to abandon the request without forcing the mother to give a direct refusal.

There were, of course, a certain number of direct refusals, which were typically made with the words *Ii* 'It's good/all right (as is)', *Iranai* 'I don't need it', and, very rarely, *Dame* 'It's no good/won't work'. The strongest and most personal expression of refusal in Japanese, *Iya* 'I don't want to', was never used by these mothers as a single-word exclamation. When *Iya* did occur, it was used as a predicate more similar in tone to "unpleasant" or "dislike" than to "No!" For example, when MK (2:4) repeatedly pretended to be firing guns, his mother said, *Mata teppo. Nani de Maachan? Teppo wa moo mama iya da ne. Itai ne* 'Guns again. Why, Maachan? Mama is tired of guns (lit. "Mama already doesn't like guns") It hurts'. Mothers also sometimes attributed a refusal with *iya* to some third party. For example, in her attempts to get Y to stop eating, his mother sometimes attributed refusals of food to his stomach. At 1;11 years, when Y had been eating tangerines and asked for his mother's too, she said, *Futatsu tabeta deshoo moo. Koko ippai da tte itteru mon, onaka ga. Hora. Iya ne, iya ne* 'You've already eaten two. Your stomach is saying, "I'm full" here. Listen. "No, no"'. Thus the directness of refusals, like the force of imperatives, could be mitigated by attributing them to others.

The children in this sample typically obeyed their mothers quite readily, and when they refused their mothers usually did not try to force compliance. But although the three mothers readily accepted an emphatic *Iya!* 'I don't want to!' or *Dame!* 'It's no good!' from their children, either without comment or with a mild *Dooshite iya na no?* 'Why don't you want to?', they were quick to express their disapproval if the children spoke this way to me or to my assistant. In the following examples, the children experienced what may have been among their earliest lessons in avoiding a direct refusal. When Y loudly refused to sing a song for his mother and me, yelling *Dame!* 'No!', his mother attributed a negative response to me: *O, kowai, Yotchan, oneechan kowai tte. Yotchan kowai naa, Yotchan dame nante yuu kara, kowai, kowai* '"Oh, I'm afraid of Yotchan," older sister says, "I'm afraid. Oh, I'm afraid of Yotchan because he says 'No!' I'm afraid. I'm afraid"'. And when Maho (2;2) refused to cooperate in answering my assistant's questions, saying *Dame!* 'No!', her mother immediately corrected her, and told her, *Dame nante yuu hito dare mo inai* 'There is no one who says things like "No"'. (The full example is in the section "Conformity training.") Thus the present data suggest that negative sanctions against saying no directly are first experienced with respect to people outside the child's family. This is consistent with Ueda's (1974) finding that Japanese adults reported using direct refusals more frequently within their family circle than with outsiders. Apparently this pattern is already being taught to children as young as 2 years of age.

The finding that these Japanese mothers so rarely gave direct refusals to their 2-year-olds, and were even teaching them not to refuse others directly, shows how basic this avoidance is to Japanese culture. Given the general permissiveness of Japanese child rearing, and the importance of the mother–child relationship as the ideal embodiment of *amae* or dependency, it is probably difficult for the Japanese mother to refuse her child without undermining her self-image as a good mother. The pressure to avoid refusing the child must have been even greater in the present case, since the mothers were being observed by outsiders. As the years pass, this reluctance to refuse requests will not only shape the children's view of the mother–child relationship but will provide them with a model for using indirection when refusing others. If, as Doi (1973) has suggested, the mother–child relationship in Japan serves as the prototype for later social relationships, it becomes easier to understand the motivation for the characteristic Japanese reluctance to say no and the resilience of this aspect of communicative style even when dealing with blunt naysayers from the West.

Summary and conclusions

It has long been recognized that language is an important part of culture, and this is especially true of communicative style. The particular communicative style of a culture arises from shared beliefs about people, what they are like, and how they should relate to one another, and is an important means of perpetuating those beliefs. In Japan, the individual is seen primarily as a member of a social group, with a responsibility to uphold the interests of that group. Thus arises the need for empathy and conformity, which help to preserve group harmony and group values. The importance of empathy and conformity in Japanese culture gives rise, in turn, to certain characteristics of Japanese communicative style, such as the use of indirection both in giving and refusing directives.

The present study has shown that these aspects of Japanese communicative style can be found in mothers' speech from an extremely early stage in their children's development. As Ochs and Schieffelin (1984) point out, the content of early mother–child verbal interactions plays an important role in the process of socialization. In the present transcripts, it was obvious that an important goal of the mothers in talking to their 2-year-olds was to instill cultural values. For example, by telling their children what other people were thinking and feeling, the mothers encouraged their children to empathize with others; by warning them that certain behaviors were strange, frightening, or shameful in the eyes of others, they indicated the importance of conformity. Another important means by which these mothers imparted cultural values was through "lessons" in communicative style, which were given by example, e.g., using indirection in making and refusing requests, and by direct instruction in how to use and interpret language appropriately in context.

Since studies of linguistic socialization are still so few, it is difficult to evaluate the present findings from a cross-cultural perspective. For example, it is not clear to what extent the communicative strategies discussed here, such as indirection, are used by mothers in other cultures; Matsumori (1981) found that there were few statistically significant differences in the frequency of directive types between the Japanese and American mothers in her study. Much further research is necessary on the particular features of communicative style in different languages and how they relate to cultural values (the same feature might serve different functions in different cultures). One thing, however, is already clear: the study of early mother–child interactions can yield a wealth of information about communicative style and the role it plays in transmitting cultural values to children.

Notes

This research was supported by a postdoctoral fellowship from the Social Science Research Council (Japan Program) held at the University of California, Berkeley, and by a Sloan Foundation postdoctoral fellowship held at the Center for Cognitive Science, Brown University. The data for the study were collected with the support of a Fulbright–Hays Doctoral Dissertation Research Abroad fellowship. This paper is a revised and expanded version of section 11.5, "Communicative Style," of "The Acquisition of Japanese" in D. I. Slobin (ed.), *The Crosslinguistic Study of Language Acquisition* (Hillsdale, N.J.: Erlbaum, 1986).

I would like to express my gratitude to the mothers and children who participated in this study. I sincerely appreciate the assistance of Kazuko Harada, who introduced me to the mothers, of Akiyo Asano, who helped at many of the early recording sessions, and of Kiko Yamashita, who patiently answered my many questions as I wrote this paper. I am especially grateful to Sachiko Ide, who first explained to me many of the mysteries of Japanese communicative style.

1 In Japanese, the term *oneesan* 'older sister' is used to refer to young women and girls, who are not necessarily family members of the speaker. The mothers in this study referred to me and to my assistant with this term.

2 Imperative force is determined partly by the syntactic form of the utterance, which is what Table 11.1 is intended to capture, but also by various other factors, such as intonation. In Japanese, most of the directives presented in Table 11.1 can be made more emphatic by adding the assertive particle *yo,* or made less forceful by adding the assent-seeking particle *ne,* which in such cases is rather similar to the English tag *okay?* The presumptive form of the copula, *deshoo,* is also frequently added to directives. With rising intonation, it functions much like *ne;* with falling intonation, it often expresses the mother's disappointed expectation that the child meet a certain standard (cf. Johanning 1982). Imperatives with the verb inflected in *-te* may be softened by using rising intonation, and suggestions in *-oo* by adding the question particle *ka* and/or rising intonation. Since all these options are available for changing the strength of directive force, there is a much wider range of different degrees of force than Table 11.1 suggests, and also a good deal of potential overlap in force among the directive strategies presented there.

3 Table 11.1 is quite similar in many respects to Matsumori's (1981) analysis of Japanese directives, since both studies were inspired by Ervin-Tripp (1977). However, since I did not read Matsumori's paper until completing my own, and

since my primary interest was in different forms of indirection, there are also certain differences. For example, my category of "Question" directives includes both fairly explicit requests, which Matsumori gives under "Requests," and rhetorical and other indirect questions, which Matsumori lists under "Inferred directives."

4   Since the classification of directives used here is different from Matsumori's, it is difficult to compare the frequencies of directive types across the two studies. However, there are at least two basic similarities: Matsumori also found that direct imperatives were the most frequent directive type (57.6%) in natural conversation and that there was a notable percentage of directives calling for some degree of inference (10%).

5   The extremely forceful imperative inflection V-*e/ro* did not occur in the mothers' speech and had not been acquired by any of the children.

6   In Japanese, the nonpast tense is used for both future actions and generic truths; since subjects are also omitted from these directives, it is often extremely difficult to be certain whether the mother is giving a context-specific instruction or citing a general rule of behavior. Therefore these two categories have been combined in Table 11.2.

7   Matsumori (1981) also treats directives with the verb inflected in -*te goran* as suggestions. Here they have been included under "Imperative forms" with other -*te* forms, such as V-*te kudasai* and V-*te choodai* 'please V'.

8   Lanham (1966) also notes that *wakaraseru* is emphasized over obedience and punishment by Japanese mothers, who patiently try to explain why their children should do as they say.

   Vogel (1963) emphasized that the mothers in his sample wanted their children to go along with their suggestions automatically, and claimed that the mothers did not, therefore, reason with small children or try to explain things to them until they were of school age. If the rationales for directives in the present samples of speech may be regarded as explanations, it appears that some Japanese mothers begin to reason with their children when they are as young as 2 years of age.

9   Certain forms that the mothers used to make indirect requests occurred in the children's speech, but not as directives. For example, declarative sentences expressed actions that the child intended to perform, rather than ones requested of the addressee, e.g., *Yotchan mo yaru* 'I'll do it too' (Y 2;3, when blowing bubbles with his mother). Similarly, the inflection used to convey "cohortatives" in the mother's speech, -*oo,* was used as a "volitional" by the children, to express their own intentions rather than suggestions addressed to the listener, e.g., *Terebi tsukeyoo* 'I'm turning on the television' (Y 1;11). (This usage is grammatically correct and also occurs in adult speech.) M occasionally used the form V-*te ii* 'all right to V', but only when requesting permission, not when proposing a particular course of action to the addressee. These utterances were requests in the sense that they seemed to mean approximately "Let me do *x.*"

10   The word *kawaisoo* 'pitiful' is based upon *kawaii* 'lovable'; fragile, vulnerable things in need of care or protection readily evoke the emotion of "feeling sorry for" and are felt to be lovable.

11   Lanham (1966) also reports that Japanese mothers train their children to be sensitive to the attitudes and feelings of others, and instruct them not to trouble others.

12   It is perhaps worth noting that M's mother appealed to empathy with the feelings, needs, and wishes of others much more frequently than the other two mothers, whose children were boys. In fact, M's mother used appeals based on empathy

69.1% of the time when giving rationales for directives, compared with 31.3% for Y's mother and 35.6% for MK's mother. Of course it is impossible to draw any conclusions from a sample of this size, but it would be interesting to investigate whether Japanese mothers of girls emphasize empathy training more than the mothers of boys. To the extent that empathy is at the heart of Japanese politeness, such a finding would be consistent with Okuda (1979), who found that Japanese mothers of girls claimed to be concerned about the acquisition of politeness more frequently than the mothers of boys. In this light, it is also interesting to note that M was the only child of the three who was starting to use polite verb inflections spontaneously, and who used polite question requests and offers.

13   Lanham (1966) found that 67% of the 255 mothers who responded to a questionnaire on child-rearing practices reported using this threat to make their children behave.

References

Azuma, H., Hess, R. D., Kashigawa, K., & Conroy, M. 1980. Maternal control strategies and the child's cognitive development: a cross-cultural paradox and its interpretation. Paper presented at the International Congress of Psychology, Leipzig.

Barnlund, D. C. 1975. *Public and private self in Japan and the United States: communicative styles of two cultures*. Tokyo: Simul.

Benedict, R. 1946. *The chrysanthemum and the sword: patterns of Japanese culture*. New York: New American Library.

Brown, P., & Levinson, S. 1978. Universals in language usage: politeness phenomena. In E. N. Goody, ed., *Questions and politeness: strategies in social interaction*. Cambridge: Cambridge University Press, pp. 56–311.

Caudill, W. & Weinstein, H. 1974. Maternal care and infant behavior in Japan and America. In T. S. Lebra & W. P. Lebra, eds., *Japanese culture and behavior: selected readings*. Honolulu: University Press of Hawaii, pp. 225–276.

Clancy, P. M. 1980. Referential choice in English and Japanese narrative discourse. In W. L. Chafe, ed., *The pear stories: cognitive, cultural, and linguistic aspects of narrative production*. Norwood, N.J.: Ablex, pp. 127–202.

    1986. The acquisition of Japanese. In D. I. Slobin, ed., *The crosslinguistic study of language acquisition*. Hillsdale, N.J.: Erlbaum, pp. 373–524.

Conroy, M., Hess, R. D., Azuma, H., & Kashigawa, K. 1980. Maternal strategies for regulating children's behavior. *Journal of Cross-Cultural Psychology* 11:153–172.

Cross, T. C. 1977. Mother's speech adjustments: the contribution of selected child listener variables. In C. E. Snow & C. A. Ferguson, eds., *Talking to children: language input and acquisition*. Cambridge: Cambridge University Press, pp. 151–188.

Doi, T. 1973. *The anatomy of dependency*, trans. J. Bester. New York: Harper & Row. Originally *Amae no koozoo*. Tokyo: Kodansha.

    1974. Some psychological themes in Japanese human relationships. In J. C. Condon & M. Saito, eds., *Intercultural encounters with Japan: communication – contact and conflict*. Tokyo: Simul, pp. 17–26.

Dore, J. 1978. Variations in preschool children's conversational performances. In K.

E. Nelson, ed., *Children's language,* vol. 1. New York: Gardner Press, pp. 397–444.

Ervin-Tripp, S. 1977. Wait for me, roller skate! In S. Ervin-Tripp & C. Mitchell-Kernan, eds., *Child discourse.* New York: Academic Press, pp. 165–188.

Gleason, J. B. 1977. Talking to children: some notes on feedback. In C. E. Snow & C. A. Ferguson, eds., *Talking to children: language input and acquisition.* Cambridge: Cambridge University Press, pp. 199–205.

Hess, R. D., Kashigawa, K., Azuma, H., Price, G., & Dickson, P. W. 1980. Maternal expectations for mastery of developmental tasks in Japan and the United States. *International Journal of Psychology* 15:259–271.

Hymes, D. 1972. On communicative competence. In J. B. Price & J. Holmes, eds., *Sociolinguistics.* Harmondsworth: Penguin Books, pp. 269–293.

Ito, K. 1980. Towards an ethnopsychology of language: interactional strategies of Japanese and Americans. *Bulletin of the Center for Language Studies* (Kanagawa University, Yokohama) 3:1–14.

Johanning, Y. K. 1982. The role of the sentence-final copula "deshoo" in Japanese socialization. Unpublished paper. Graduate School of Education, University of Pennsylvania.

Kasahara, Y. 1974. Fear of eye-to-eye confrontation among neurotic patients in Japan. In T. S. Lebra & W. P. Lebra, eds., *Japanese culture and behavior: selected readings.* Honolulu: University Press of Hawaii, pp. 396–406.

Lanham, B. 1966. The psychological orientation of the mother–child relationship in Japan. *Monumenta Nipponica* 26,3/4:321–333.

Loveday, L. J. 1982. Communicative interference: a framework for contrastively analyzing L2 communicative competence exemplified with the linguistic behavior of Japanese performing in English. *International Review of Applied Linguistics* 20,1 (February).

Matsumori, A. 1981. Hahaya no kodomo e no gengo ni yoru koodoo kisei – yookyuu hyoogen no nichibei hikaku. In F. C. Peng, ed., *Gengo shuutoku no shosoo* [Aspects of language acquisition]. Hiroshima: Bunka Hyoron, pp. 320–339.

Newport, E. L., Gleitman, H., & Gleitman, L. R. 1977. Mother, I'd rather do it myself: some effects and non-effects of maternal speech style. In C. E. Snow & C. A. Ferguson, eds., *Talking to children: language input and acquisition.* Cambridge: Cambridge University Press, pp. 109–149.

Ochs, E. & Schieffelin, B. 1984. Language acquisition and socialization: three developmental stories and their implications. In R. Shweder & R. LeVine, eds., *Culture theory: essays on mind, self and emotion.* Cambridge: Cambridge University Press, pp. 276–320.

Okuda, A. 1979. Kodomo to taiguu hyoogen. Unpublished master's degree thesis, Tsukuba University.

Reddy, M. 1979. The conduit metaphor – a case of frame conflict in our language about language. In A. Ortony, ed., *Metaphor and thought.* Cambridge: Cambridge University Press, pp. 284–320.

Scollon, S. 1982. Reality set, socialization, and linguistic convergence. Unpublished doctoral dissertation, University of Hawaii, Honolulu.

Scollon, R. & Scollon, S. 1981. *Narrative, literacy, and face in interethnic communication.* Norwood, N. J.: Ablex.

Ueda, K. 1974. Sixteen ways to avoid saying "no" in Japan. In J. C. Condon & M. Saito, eds., *Intercultural encounters with Japan: communication – contact and conflict.* Tokyo: Simul, pp. 184–192.

Vogel, E. 1963. *Japan's new middle class: the salary man and his family in a Tokyo suburb.* Berkeley: University of California Press.

Wetstone, J. & Foster, L. 1982. From passive to active communicative competence: carrying one's own conversational weight. Paper presented at the Seventh Annual Boston University Conference on Language Development, Boston.

Whorf, B. L. 1956. *Language, thought, and reality: selected writings of Benjamin Lee Whorf.* Cambridge: MIT Press.

12. From feelings to grammar: a Samoan case study

ELINOR OCHS

Introduction

In 1822, after traveling throughout the Pacific, the Reverends Tyerman and Bennett reported a certain problem that many Christian families were experiencing. Writing to London, they referred to the head of one such family:

As a Christian parent, he [Mr. Chamberlain] is naturally very anxious to preserve the minds of his offspring from the moral contamination to which they are liable from the inevitable exposure to the society (occasionally at least) of native children of their own ages, whose language they understand, and whose filthy talk they cannot but hear at times. The abominable conversation (if such it may be called) of infants as soon as they begin to lisp out words, is such a jargon of grossness and obscenity as could not be imagined by persons brought up even in those manufacturing towns of our country where manners are the most depraved. And, so far from reproving the little reprobates, their fathers and mothers, both by voice and example, teach them what they are most apt to learn, the expression and indulgence, at the earliest possible period, of every brutal passion. The subject is one of great delicacy and perplexity to faithful Missionaries in all stations among uncivilized heathen, but particularly in these islands. (1822:465–6)[1]

Without the particular moral interpretation of the good Reverends Tyerman and Bennett, emotional intensity among Pacific peoples, particularly among Polynesians, has been noted and expressed in art, literature, and numerous ethnographic descriptions. The Pacific has often been treated as a haven of passion, a romantic alternative to Victorian repression and morality.

When I began a longitudinal study of language acquisition in a Western Samoan village, I had in mind a documentation of the morphologically and syntactically interesting features of Samoan as they emerged in children's speech over developmental time.[2] I was concerned with those features that have been described for adult Samoan, such as the ergative case-marking system and a word order of verb–subject–object. I had an idea of the conceptual categories and processes that have been related to grammatical relations. I would be looking at notions such as the expression of agent, patient, action, change of state, object undergoing change of state, and the like. I would also be looking at the way in which given and new information are expressed and interact with word-order patterns. These are the bases of grammar that have been considered over the years among those interested in language acquisition and they are the legitimate topics of most grant proposals in this area.

When I began transcribing the tapes of children's speech, however, I was struck by many of the things that impressed the Reverends Tyerman and Bennett. So much of the talk was intensely emotional. Caregivers and children talked *about* feelings and emotional states a great deal, as in the following examples:

(1) Mother to N, 3;4
   Mo: N! Don't do like that again, otherwise I'll be angry at you. Otherwise I'll be angry at you and I won't give you another milk biscuit.

(2) Mother speaking to family members about infant when she cries
   Mo: Oh! Oh! Her willfulness is exceptional!

(3) N, 3, to older sister, M, after M does not give a biscuit to N or to infant sister
   N: M, (?), give something
      give something/
      okay, M, the baby is angry/
      [laughs]
      the baby/

(4) Mother telling other children that N, 3, is behaving badly
   Mo: N is conceited. Let's shame, let's shame N. He is conceited.

(5) Mother to daughter M, 4;10
   Mo: Are you upset, M? What is the thing that upsets you?
   M: I'm angry only with you because I said "Let's us play," but you refuse.

In addition, most of the speech acts engaged in were affect-loaded, such as appeals, rejections, refusals, teasing, accusations, bluffing, shaming, cursing, expressions of respect, sympathy, shock, disappointment, fear, and pleasure. It was clear that display and recognition of emotion were terribly important to these families in this community. This appraisal was reinforced when I looked at caregivers' speech and found that caregivers frequently provoked or elicited the expression of particular affect-loaded speech acts. Caregivers would, for example, ask children to repeat phrases to a third party to convey feelings, as illustrated below.

(6) M, 4;4, has previously called to her friend V to come, but V goes elsewhere. M's mother, L, instructs M what to tell V
   M. ((softly)) L, there's V/

      .

      .

      .

      Why does she go there?/

Mo: Say "Don't come here again!"
M: DON'T COME HERE AGAIN!
Mo: "If you come now, (I) will smack your eyes."
M: IF YOU COME NOW, (I) WILL SMACK YOUR EYES!

Or a caregiver would elicit a challenge from one sibling towards another, socializing the children explicitly into confrontation:

(7) N, 3, accuses other kids of stealing shoes the night before. Mother turns to N's sister M

N	*Others*
	Mo: Is that true, M?
	M: No, (he) is lying/
	(?)/
(she) is lying/	
	M: (he) is lying (emphatic particle)/
	M: he's like X, always lying/

And, if this in itself was not enough to convince me of the role of affect in language acquisition, there was an additional body of material, a veritable treasure trove of emotional riches. Emotional feelings can be encoded at all levels of Samoan grammar – phonological, morphological, and syntactic. Surely, even in the most conservative of perspectives on language development, to understand the acquisition of Samoan grammar one would need to document the evolving production and comprehension of feelings through language.

At this point, a string of questions came to mind demanding answers: How do we talk about emotions and feelings? How do we talk about the linguistic encoding of these phenomena? With their overwhelming concern with the logical dimensions of language, both anthropological and psychological linguistics provided me with insufficient tools to carry out the task of relating affect to language. Fortunately, psychologists and anthropologists have recently revived the interest in emotions. Several Social Science Research Council seminars and American Anthropological Association symposia as well as a series of workshops at the Australian National University have generated or drawn attention to a number of papers on the interface of culture, cognition, and emotional experience. I am considerably in debt to these materials in the formulation of my ideas on Samoan expression of emotion. In the following discussion, I draw from these sources as well as from research on affect in Samoa carried out by Gerber (1975), Mead (1928), and Shore (1977, 1982).

The expression of emotion

Affect: a working definition

Many of the recent research papers on emotion have considered emotion as a physiological process associated with the nervous system. Several researchers have argued for the universality of a core set of emotional states, including fear, anger, grief, and embarrassment (Scheff 1977). Other research has focused on the expression and conceptualization of emotions within particular cultures. All human beings experience a core set of emotions sometime in their lives, but how they interpret and manifest those experiences differs across cultures. Levy (1984), for example, suggests that certain emotions may be objects of considerable attention and knowledge. They are what Levy calls "hypercognized," richly expressed within the culture. Other emotional responses may be underplayed or "hypocognized." Often a hypocognized emotion will be repressed and/or reinterpreted as some other experience such as physical illness.

The concern with expression of emotion has led to an interest in a wide range of emotional processes, structures, and concepts; for example, feelings, moods, dispositions, attitudes, character, personality, masking, double binds, undercutting, and the like (see Irvine 1982 for a review of this domain). To generalize, this semantic domain is often referred to as *affect,* and this is the term I will be using in the remainder of this discussion. *My particular concern will be with linguistic conventions associated with affect in Samoan and how young children acquire knowledge of these conventions over developmental time.* To pursue this question, let us turn to Samoan itself and consider those dimensions of affect that are richly encoded or, as Levy would say, hypercognized.

Affect: child development

In the introduction to this chapter, I indicated that Samoan caregivers are concerned with the child's affective competence, particularly with the child's capacity to produce and recognize conventional expressions of emotions, both verbal and nonverbal. This concern is of course not limited to Samoan society, as is evidenced by the current literature on socialization and social development (Bowlby 1969; Bretherton & Beeghly 1982; Dunn & Kendrick 1982; Eibl-Eiblesfeldt 1970; Heath 1983; Hoffman 1981; Levy 1973; Lutz 1981; Much & Shweder 1978; Schieffelin 1979; Seymour 1980; Super & Harkness 1982; Zahn-Waxler, Radke-Yarrow & King 1979). The concern is universal, and apparently children quite early in their lives attend to, recognize, and act on displays of emotion by others in their social environment. Klinnert et al. (1983) report that by 9 months of age infants can monitor the facial expression of affect of mothers and will act differently towards some third object according to the affect displayed. Through this type of monitoring, termed *social referencing* (ibid.), infants are socialized into associating particular events (e.g., the co-presence of a particular object, a change of state, etc.) with particular feelings on the one hand and particular expressions on the other.

Infants come to know for particular situations what they should feel and how to display or mask that feeling (Schieffelin 1979). These frames lay the groundwork for attitudes, opinions, values, and beliefs that evolve in one's lifetime.

EVENT → AFFECT i → DISPLAY AFFECT i
     → DISPLAY AFFECT ii (MASK AFFECT i)

Recognition and use of lexical and grammatical structures for conveying feelings are a more sophisticated extension of this early form of production and appraisal of affect expression. The work of Bretherton & Beeghly (1982), Dunn & Kendrick (1982), and Zahn-Waxler, Radke-Yarrow & King (1979) demonstrates that verbal competence in this domain is regularly displayed before the age of 2 (as early as 18–20 months). This research concerns primarily children's acquisition of lexical terms of emotion (in English only). If we include prosody, we can see conventional linguistic expression of affect through intonation even before a child's first words, and it is certainly widely in evidence throughout the single-word stage (Cruttendon 1982; Halliday 1973; Peters 1977).

An important difference between the use of lexical terms of emotion and intonation is that typically the lexical terms assert or predicate a quality of self or others whereas intonation presupposes or implies that quality. Relative to intonation, the adjectives of affect such as "afraid," "angry," "mad," "happy," etc. indicate more explicitly the nature of the affect communicated. These adjectives have considerable interest for developmental psychologists, because their use displays to a high degree an awareness among young children of their own and others' feelings. Dunn & Kendrick (1982), for example, have documented the capacity of 2- and 3-year-old children to notice and even anticipate the feelings of their younger siblings:

> The important point on the issue of perspective-taking is that the children commented on the baby's behavior in a way that certainly did not always represent a projection of their own feelings about their own situations. Sometimes the difference between the perspective of the child and the baby was made quite explicit. One boy watching his baby brother playing with a balloon, commented to the observer: "He going pop in a minute. And he going cry. And he going be frightened of me too. I LIKE the pop." (p. 46)

The interest in affect among development psychologists is growing by leaps and bounds, for it seems that a great deal can be learned about children's cognition from observing affective behavior of children and others engaged in face-to-face interaction. These behaviors indicate the extent to which children can take a sociocentric perspective, their understanding of cause and effect, and their concept of person as distinct from other entities in their environment. It is apparent from existing studies that attitudes, emotions, moods, feelings, and the like are communicated and perceived in the first year of life and that this system expresses an understanding of the world, i.e., a world view.

Affect: linguistic dimensions

Research in adult processing indicates further the essential role of affect in communication (see, for example, Mandler 1975; Norman 1979; Zajonc 1979). Among other phenomena, the processes of attention, memory, and recognition can be facilitated or impeded by an individual's emotional state. We have every reason to believe from this growing literature as well as from the writings of Burke (1962) and Hymes (1974) that such a fundamental component of human nature will find its place in language beyond prosody and the lexicon. Speakers' affective dispositions are expressed through syntactic, morphological, and phonological structures, such as verb voice (Hopper 1979; Hopper & Thompson 1980), word order (Givon 1979; Halliday 1967; Kuno 1972; MacWhinney 1977, 1984), sentential mood (Searle 1969), right and left dislocation (Chafe 1976; Duranti & Ochs 1979), tense/aspect (Hopper 1979; Smith 1983), deictics and other determiners (Clancy 1980; Duranti 1984), quantifiers (Lakoff 1972; Brown & Levinson 1978), focus particles (Dixon 1972; Hawkinson & Hyman 1974), phonological simplification, reduplication (Ferguson, 1977), and phonological variation (Blom & Gumperz 1972; Ferguson 1977; Labov 1966).

In most arenas of daily communication, speakers convey not only information concerning some state or event but their feelings about some state or event as well, and languages will have varying structures for encoding this level of information. Much as in the social referencing of facial expressions discussed in the infant-development literature, adult listeners will attend to these linguistic structures as keys (Goffman 1974; Hymes 1974) to an affective proposition a speaker is conveying. In certain contexts, the speaker is more highly constrained as to the affective frame he can communicate. Both the affect and the grammatical structures to convey that affect will be tightly bound to registral norms (Andersen 1977; Ferguson 1977). This is the case for many formal communicative contexts, such as certain formal meetings, certain religious services, and certain literate genres such as scholarly writing and front-page news articles in American society.

An important stand taken in this chapter is that all sentences expressed in context will have an affective component. In certain contexts, the affect conveyed will be one of "distance" from some proposition conveyed. Thus, a speaker or writer may convey an impersonal attitude or indifference or objectivity in expressing information. As noted, such an affect may be a registral defining feature. Indeed, much of current scientific communication is consumed with the idea that objectivity is an ideal disposition and means a formal style. It would be naive to see this disposition as the absence of affect. The impersonal, objective style reflects and expresses cultural assumptions about the relation between the communicator (scientist), the topic of the message (scientific research), and the audience of that message. This style renders the communication more valid and "factual," deemphasizing the subjective dimensions of the proposition(s) conveyed.

In other contexts, the personal, subjective response of the communicator to the information conveyed is more overtly expressed. As will be discussed in the following section, on Samoan, the personal feelings of speakers are presupposed or asserted in a wide variety of informal and formal contexts.

Distinct from the dimension of impersonal to personal is the notion of markedness of affect (see Irvine 1982). Speakers in different speech communities have expectations regarding the type of affect expression associated with particular events, settings, and social status of communicator. For example, speakers have expectations concerning the expression of affect by women to women, women to men, men to women, men to men, parents to children, judges to members of the jury, members of a funeral party to each other, and so on. When these communicators display a more marked form of affect, more complex interpretations of the psychological states and intentions of the communicator may be generated.

Whereas both our own experience and scholarly research validate that affect does indeed penetrate the linguistic code, the precise nature of this penetration has not been clarified. Until recently, affect has not been a topic of concern among psychologists pursuing research into information theory. Shweder (1984) has argued that the concept of "man" as a rational being, while having a long history in Western thought, has become the foremost concern of the social sciences generally since World War II, as evidenced by the emergence of cognitive psychology, cognitive anthropology, cognitive sociology. Linguistics has followed this pattern as well, with Chomsky's attachment to cognitive psychology as a theoretical paradigm. Now that the prominent figures in information processing have renewed the interest in affect and incorporated affect in their models of communication, perhaps linguistics will follow suit and begin to ascertain the grammatical structures associated with affect and the pragmatic and sociolinguistic systems in which they participate.

The linguistic expression of affect in Samoan

The semantic domain

The structures to be discussed here are drawn from family interactions in which young children participate. In addition, I will be relying on research on affect in Samoa carried out by Gerber (1975), Mead (1928), and Shore (1977,

1982). As discussed by Gerber (1975), Samoans have no word exactly corresponding to the English term "emotion," but rather refer to the notion of "feeling" (*lagona*). Certain feelings corresponding to emotional feelings originate inside the chest (*loto*).

The concept of feeling is bound to the concept of self in all societies. As discussed in considerable detail by Shore (1977, 1982), Samoans see persons as not having much control and as often not responsible for their feelings and actions. Feelings are seen as reactions. This is encoded in the morphology of constructions using verbs of feeling. The objects of these verbs are marked with the preposition *i*, which also is a case marker indicating instrumental semantic role. Thus, a sentence such as *Fiafia Sina i le mea alofa*, lit. 'happy Sina instrument/middle verb object proposition the gift', can be loosely understood as "Sina is happy because of the gift." These constructions are also translated as "Sina likes the gift," but this captures more the English than the Samoan concept of affect. In line with the orientation towards external origins of feelings, in Samoan conversation there is explicit talk about the origins of a feeling in some person. However, there does not appear to be much talk about feelings as origins of behavior. One's actions are seen as evidence of one's feelings rather than as consequences of one's feelings. Thus, for example, from the Samoan point of view generosity, the giving of food and money and labor, indicates *alofa* 'love' more than it follows from *alofa*. Indeed, the meaning of verbs of feeling is more action- (or reaction-)like than in a language like English. Caregivers will often control small children by warning them that they or others will not love them (if they act in some undesirable way). This is usually understood as meaning that they will not give things to or do things for the child. Withdrawal of love means in the most fundamental sense withdrawal of goods and services. In English-speaking Western communities, withdrawal of love is seen more as the origin or reason for withdrawal of goods and services. The latter behaviors are usually seen as indicators that a change of affective state has taken place.

In household interactions with small children, four major feelings dominate Samoan talk and behavior. These are the feelings of *alofa* (love), *'ita* (anger), *fa'a'aloalo* (respect), and *tautalaititi* (impudence, disrespect). These affects are topics of talk in themselves, as discussed earlier, and are associated with a range of grammatical structures. When put to use, these structures signal or key that a particular affect or intensity of affect is in play much the same way as do body postures and facial gestures. Indeed, a semiotic grammar would specify the ways in which nonverbal and verbal expressions of affect systematically cooccur in Samoan.

Linguistic encoding of affect

Table 12.1 displays some of the ways in which Samoan encodes affect. There are special affect particles, affect first person pronouns, and affect determiners. In addition, there are interjections, affect-loaded terms of address and reference, and a long list of affect descriptors. Like many other languages, Samoan uses prosody as well to encode feelings, e.g., loudness, intonation. More language-specific, as noted by Shore, is the use of the front and back of the oral cavity to convey distinct affects, namely delicacy/properness (in a Christian sense) versus earthiness/coarseness. Additionally, Samoans may switch back and forth between two different phonological registers and two lexical registers (respect vocabulary and unmarked vocabulary) to indicate a shift in mood or in intensity of feeling.

Pragmatic functions

Affect specifiers and affect intensifiers. I have found it useful to analyze the linguistic features that encode affect in terms of two semantic roles. The first role is that of indicating *the nature of the affect being conveyed*. When a feature carries out this role, I will refer to it as an *affect specifier*. The second role is that of indicating the *intensity of the affect being conveyed*. Linguistic features that carry out this role are *affect intensifiers*. All of the features listed in Table 12.1 are affect intensifiers in the sense that they are affect-loaded alternatives to more neutral features. However, the features differ in the degree to which they function as affect specifiers as well. For example, the particles *a, ia,* and *fo'i* are unmarked with respect to type of affect. They can be used to intensify over a range of positive and negative affects. On the other hand, the affect particle *e* is more specifically associated with negative feelings such as anger, irritation, disapproval, or disappointment. Other features even more narrowly specify affect, such as the first person pronoun *ka ika* 'poor me' and the determiner *si* 'the dear', both of which denote sympathy for the referent.

Speech-act function. In many cases, the affect specifier or intensifier may color the interpretation of the sentence as a whole, much like a sentence adverb. Among other effects, the feature may indicate to the hearer which speech act is being performed. For example, the particle *e*, as just discussed, typically denotes anger, disappointment, displeasure, or irritation. Adding this particle to an assertion or imperative utterance usually signals that the utterance is a threat or warning. For example, the imperative *Fa'akali!* 'Wait!' constitutes a neutral directive out of context. When the particle *e* is added, as in *Fa'akali e!* 'Wait + neg. affect', the utterance is interpreted as a warning, with a gloss something like "You just wait!" Similarly, the declarative utterance *Laku i 'oo* 'I'm going over there' is a neutral assertion out of context. The utterance with the particle *e*, *Laku i 'oo e* 'I'm going over there + neg. affect', will usually be heard as a warning or a threat that the speaker is going to the specified location. We can also carry out this analysis

Table 12.1. *Linguistic expression of affect in Samoan*

Particles	Interjections	Pronouns	Articles	Phonology
ia (intens.)	*ota* ⌉ pos./neg. sur- prise	*ta* ⌉ 1st person	*si* (sing.) ⌉ 'the dear'	loudness ⌉ (intens.)
a (intens.)	*ola*	*ta ita* ⌉ sympathy pronouns	*nai* (plur.) ⌋	lengthening
e (intens.)	*uoi*	*lota*		stress
fo'i (intens.)	*uoia* ⌋	*lata*		glottal stop ⌋
		etc.		
	auoi – pos./neg. surprise; sympathy			reduplication (± intens.)
				backing (earthiness)
	tafiolaē ⌉ neg. surprise/ *otafefe* ⌋ sympathy			fronting (refinement, distance)
	uisa			switching registers between /t/ & /k/ (indicates abrupt mood change)
	oki			
	tch			
	i			
	'isa ⌉ annoyance *sē* ⌋			
	a'e ⌉ disapproval *a'a* ⌋			
	talofae – sympathy			
	tae 'shit'			

Address/reference terms	Adjectives of affect
maile 'dog'	*ita* 'angry'
pua'a 'pig'	*lotoleaga* 'jealous'
mataomo 'smallpox'	*lotomalie* 'agreeable'
moepī 'bedwetter'	*fiafia* 'happy'
moeti'o 'bedshitter'	*mimita* 'proud'
lima pipilo 'smelly hand'	*fiapoto* 'conceited'
lou aitae 'your shittiness'	*fiamatua* 'acts like bigshot',
pū tele 'big hole' (to woman)	acts like boss'
Sapina (name of woman, used	*fiasiō* 'showoff'
to effeminate man; man	*fiapepe* 'babyish'
who fumbles in sport)	*fiu* 'fed up, bored'

ali'i 'master'/'little devil'	*ofo* 'surprised'
(to child)	*fa'aaloalo* 'respectful'
sole 'mate'	*fa'amaoni* 'faithful'
toea'ina 'dear old man'	*popole* 'worried'
si 'dear' + ref. term, e.g.,	*fefe* 'afraid'
si tama 'dear boy'	*pala'ai* 'cowardly'
suga 'lassie'	*maualalo* 'humble'
Evalina (name of woman	*maualuga* 'show pride'
who is crazy)	*tautalaiti* 'cheeky'
avilu 'baby face' (look	*ulavale* 'naughty'
young for age)	*taea* 'disgusting'
lou alelo 'snake/eel eyes'	

Respect vocabulary

afio mai 'come (of a chief)
maliu mai 'come (of an orator)'

Nicknames (*gao*)

ma'ila 'scarface'
vaepi'o 'polio'
lafa 'ringworm'
o laulauati 'lisper'
etc.

261

for the first person sympathy pronouns. When the neutral first person is used in the imperative utterance *Mai ma a'u!* 'Give (it) for me!', the utterance will usually be heard as a demand. When the sympathy pronoun is used, as in *Mai ka 'ika!* 'Give (it) for dear me!', the imperative will usually be heard as begging.

I have introduced here only the bare bones of the system. As more of the same types of affect specifiers appear, with or without affect intensifiers, the interpretation of the speech act changes. For example, warnings become threats and acts of begging become acts of pleading.

Speech-genre function. At this point, I suggest that affect features function to signal not only speech acts but *speech genres* and *speech events* as well. The use of these features over continuous discourse (indeed, their absence as well!) defines that discourse as a type of talk. Certainly in Samoan the extended use of respect vocabulary is a key (Bauman 1977; Duranti 1983; Hymes 1972) to the fact that the speaker is delivering a formal speech rather than engaged in some other type of activity. Similarly, the use of affect features in narrative discourse distinguishes that discourse as *personal narrative* rather than as a narrative that might appear in a newspaper article. These features are not incidental to the genre or event. The use of affect in personal narrative, for example, is tied to the purpose of these discourses. They are primarily told to express a feeling and, if possible, to secure an empathetic response from the audience (Langness & Frank 1981). For Samoans at least (and I suspect for most people in most societies), a telling of a personal experience without affect is a story without a point and a speaker without competence.

Constraints across turns and speakers. In examining personal narratives exchanged among adult speakers of Samoan, I have found that the domain of influence of affect features extends even beyond the discourse of a single speaker. To put this more precisely, *there is a sequential organization of affect across turns and speakers.* A narrator will use one or more affect features that will indicate the attitude or feelings of the narrator toward the events discussed. These features clue the addressee as to the appropriate feedback response. Thus, in the course of a personal narrative, one can isolate sets or pairs of affect-linked turns. The existence of such an organization reinforces the notion that the point of telling stories is to express feelings and elicit sympathy. The selection of the appropriate empathetic response will be guided by the narrator's initial selection of affect specifiers and intensifiers. An illustration of the sequential organization of affect is provided in Ex. 8.

(8) Women weaving and talking about the funeral of another woman's mother
F: uhmm [pause] sa'o ā   le   mea ga ka   popole
                right emph. ART thing that I-dear worry

ai   le   lo'omakua   le   tagi.
PRO ART old woman ART cry
"It's true that the thing poor me worried about was the old
woman crying."
L: Kagi kele si   lo'o⫽ /makua
    cry   much the dear old woman
    "The old woman cried a lot"

F: Kagi ia   le   lo'oma/ /kua
                                      cry emph ART old woman
                                      "The old woman really cried"

L: Kalofa e! sh!
                                      pity   emph
                                      "What a pity"

F: Le mafai– kau alu aku   ia [pause] falekua   gei fo'i
    not able– try go deixis emph   chief's wife this emph
    ma le   solosolo [pause] solosolo   fo'i o le
    with ART handkerchief   handkerchief emph of ART

keige [pause]
girl
"The chief's wife was not able– tried to give the
handkerchief–the handkerchief of the girl [= older woman
whose mother had died]."
E   alofa ā   i   si   oga kigā
pres love emph OBJ ART-dear her mother
"(She) really loves her dear mother"

In this example, one woman is telling two other women about a funeral. In the
narrative, several features associated with feelings of sympathy are used. The
narrator refers to herself with the first person sympathy pronoun *ka* in the
phrase *le mea ga ka popole ai* 'the thing that poor me worried about'. The
narrator refers to the woman whose mother had died with the sympathy
reference term *lo'omakua* 'dear old woman'. The intensity of this feeling is
heightened by the narrator switching phonological register on the word *tagi*
'cries'. This word is spoken in the register that uses /t/ in contrast to the
previous discourse, which is in the register /k/.

All of this conveys to the hearers what the narrator's attitudes are and
suggests the appropriate response. The first response by L is a more intensive
repetition of the narrator's description. L uses the sympathy determiner *si* as
well as the sympathy reference term *lo'omakua* in referring to the grieving
woman. The crying is emphasized not by code switching, which the narrator
had used, but by the use of the adverbial intensifier *kele* 'a lot'. The narrator
subsequently paraphrases what L has just said, using the intensifier particle *ia*
to emphasize the crying of the woman. This particle typically occurs in
escalations or second sayings of utterances. After three utterances that focus
on the poor woman's crying, L responds with the appropriate interjection of
pity and sympathy *Kalofa e!* In these lines and subsequently, the turns are

systematically organized in terms of conventional expressions of affect. Each turn constrains the affect expressed in the next turn.

To summarize the points made so far, affect is richly encoded at many levels of Samoan grammar and discourse. The linguistic features that express affect fall into two nonexclusive functional categories – those that *specify* affect and those that *intensify* affect. These features enter into the literal meaning of propositions. Further, they signal the speech act performed by an utterance. Finally, there are cooccurrence restrictions on the use of affect specifiers and intensifiers within and across utterances and turns.

Acquisition of affect expression in Samoan

Affect once encoded is a powerful means of securing some desirable response from others, constraining what will be said next and what will be done next. Young children understand this cause–effect relation quite early in rural Western Samoa and use language to this end from the very beginning.

Developmental span

In this section, the order of emergence of grammatical forms expressing affect is presented. The data on which this ordering is based are drawn from utterances that express either anger (*'ita*) or sympathy/love (*alofa*). Table 12.2 presents the construction type or area of grammar and the time of its first appearance in the acquisition corpus. It does not indicate order or appearance of different forms within the same grammatical category (e.g., different interjections, focus particles, etc.).

One of the most general developmental patterns to emerge from the data is that most of the grammatical forms for expressing positive and negative affect are acquired before the age of 4.

The expression of affect through linguistic structures begins at the single-word stage. At the single-word stage, the children in the study used a variety of curses and vocative insults, switched back and forth between two phonological registers for rhetorical effect, and used the affect first person pronoun ('poor I', 'poor me'). All this was supplemented by a variety of prosodic strategies for conveying affect. These prosodic strategies are recognized and named in Samoan. For example, there are terms for shouting (*e'e*), screaming (*i'i*), speaking softly (*leo vaivai*), speaking loudly (*leo kele*), whining (*fa'a'u*), and so on, each conventionally linked to types of affect.

From a Samoan perspective, the acquisition of verbal affect expression begins not only in the single-word stage, but at the very first word, the beginning of recognizable Samoan itself. Every Samoan parent we questioned

Table 12.2. *First appearances of grammatical forms of affect*

Age of child	Grammatical forms (anger)	Grammatical forms (sympathy)
1;7	Prosody Phon. alternation of t/k Interjection (*tae* 'shit')	Prosody Phon. alternation of t/k 1st pers. poss./obl. pronoun (*ta/ta ita*)
1;10	Neg. existential (*leai*)	Focus particles (*a, ia*)
1;11	Neg. imperative (1st deg. intens.: *aua*)	
2;0	Vocative (*ise*)	Vocative (*sole*)
2;2	—	3rd pers. ref. term Pred. adj. (*fiu* 'weary') Diminutive suffix
2;4	Neg. imperative (2nd deg. intens.: *soia*)	—
2;5	Pred. adjective ('*ita* 'angry')	—
2;11	3rd pers. ref. term (*le alelo*)	—
3;7		Sing. determiner (*si*)

said that their child's first word was *tae,* a term meaning "shit." The term is a curse, a reduced form of '*ai tae,* meaning "eat shit." This conventional interpretation of a child's first word reflects the Samoan view of small children as characteristically strong-willed, assertive, and cheeky. Indeed, at a very early point in their language development, children use the curse frequently and productively to disagree, reject, and refuse and to prevent or stop some action from being carried out.

Presupposition and predication

As might be predicted from other developmental studies (Cruttendon 1982), linguistic forms that presuppose affect seem to be acquired before forms that predicate affect in the form of an assertion. Thus, like English-speaking children, Samoan children use prosodic devices for conveying affect at the earliest stage of language development. Further, for both anger and sympathy, the explicit predication of these affects through predicate adjectives of affect (e.g., *fiu* 'weary/fed up', '*ika* 'angry', *fiafia* 'happy') is a relatively late development. Rather than saying "I am angry," for example, children at first convey their anger through increased loudness, through a negative interjection, or through a vocative. Similarly, before children state, "I am happy (about something or towards some person)," they will convey their feelings through phonological code switching, through a referential term of positive affect for self (*ka ika* 'dear me'), or through a vocative of endearment (*sole* 'mate/brother', *suga* 'lassie', etc.).

I note here that the children predicate feelings associated with their own and others' physiological conditions (hunger, thirst, tiredness, etc.) far more often than they predicate/assert affective feelings. These predications are formed by prefixing the verb *fia* 'want/feel like' to a verb denoting a physical action or activity, such as *'ai* 'eat' (*fia 'ai* = "want to eat" or "hungry"), *'inu* 'drink' (*fia 'inu* = "want to drink" or "thirsty"), and so on. The predication of these feelings begins at 25 months among the children in our study.

Speech-act context

Somewhat parallel to the results of the section "Presupposition and Predication," children use the grammatical forms of affect first and more often in directives than in assertions. In the domain of sympathy/love, for example, first person sympathy pronouns first appear in the course of begging for objects. Whereas the affect pronoun is used in begging at 19 months (when our recording began), this pronoun is not used in assertions until 29 months.

Just as an adult uses these affect pronouns to obtain sympathy from the audience in the telling of a narrative, young children use them to obtain sympathy from someone who has some desired good. As discussed earlier, from a Samoan perspective sympathy/love is manifest when the audience-/addressee offers the desired good (in the case of begging) or the desired verbal expression of support and appreciation (in the case of a narrative about "poor me"; see Ex. 8).

Referents and subjects

Despite the sociocentric orientation of socialization, Samoan children show a decided egocentrism in their use of affect terms, determiners, and adjectives. Looking at Table 12.2, we can see that young children acquire or at least produce terms referring sympathetically to ego (first person pronoun of affect) before terms referring sympathetically to others (third person reference terms such as *koeiga* 'old man') and before noun-phrase constructions that contain the sympathy determiner *si* 'the dear' (e.g., *si kama* 'the dear boy', *si keige* 'the dear girl'). When children first use these third person forms, they use them to refer to themselves and much later apply them to other referents. For the domains of both anger and sympathy/love, reference to addressee, i.e., vocatives, precedes third person forms of reference. Finally, the egocentric bias is seen in subject referents of predicate adjectives. These predicates all refer to the speaker, i.e., the child, in our corpus of children under the age of 4.

Affect-marked versus neutral constructions

Perhaps the most interesting developmental pattern is that there is a strong tendency for affect constructions to be acquired before the corresponding neutral constructions. With the exception of the acquisition of determiners, whenever there are two alternative forms of carrying out a semantic function, the affect-marked form is acquired before the neutral form.

The best example of this is seen in the acquisition of first person full pronoun forms. As noted earlier, Samoan has an affect full pronoun *ta ita* ('poor I', 'poor me'). In addition, it has a neutral full pronoun *a'u* ('I', 'me'). Both terms can appear in a variety of syntactic roles. As possessive and genitive constituents, they may both be inflected for what may be roughly called inalienable and alienable possession. The two systems are presented in Table 12.3.

The first uses of the first person pronoun in the children's speech are as benefactives ("for me"), corresponding to indirect objects in adult speech, and as possessive adjectives. In both roles, the affect pronoun appears in children's speech several months before the neutral pronoun appears. For example, for one child the affect pronoun appeared as a benefactive at 19 months, whereas the neutral first person benefactive appeared four months later at 22 months. For a second child, the possessive affect form appears at 21 months, whereas the neutral first person possessive forms appear at 24 months. Examples of the affect pronoun taken from a child at the single-word stage and a child at the multiword stage are presented below.

(9) K, 1;7, asking mother for food

K	*Mother*
[Crying] / /mai/	/ /(Leai.) Leai.
bring	(no) no
"bring it/"	(No.) No.
[Calls name of mother]	
	'O le ā
	topic ART what
	"What is it?"

(i)ta/
dear me
"for dear me/"

(10) P, 2;5, asking mother for water
P: mai   ua vai   deika [= ta ita *or* ka ika]
   bring ?   water poor me
   "bring water for dear me/"

Table 12.3. *First person pronouns*

Category	Neutral form ("I, me, my")	Affect form ("Poor I, poor me, poor my")
Full pronoun[a]	*a'u*	*ta ita*
Subject clitic	*'ou*	*ta*
Poss. adj., sing., specific, inalienable	*lo'u*	*lota*
Poss. adj., sing., specific, alienable	*la'u*	*lata*
Poss. adj., sing., nonspecific, inalienable	*so'u*	*sota*
Poss. adj., sing., nonspecific, alienable	*sa'u*	*sata*
Poss. adj., plural, specific, inalienable	*o'u*	*ota*
Poss. adj., plural, specific, alienable	*a'u*	*ata*
Poss. adj., plural, nonspecific, inalienable	*ni o'u*	*ni ota*
Poss. adj., plural, nonspecific, alienable	*ni a'u*	*ni ata*

[a]These forms behave, syntactically, like nouns and can be used to express different grammatical functions, viz. subject, direct object, indirect object, oblique object.

A very similar pattern is found if we look at the acquisition of negation. In this case, we find young Samoan children using their official first word *tae/kae* (the interjection meaning "eat shit") to express negation in the way in which English speaking children use "No" and "Don't!" The Samoan child at the single-word stage and later as well will use the negative affect term *tae/kae* to disagree, to reject, to refuse, and to prevent or stop some action from being carried out. The use of this form for these functions appears long before the more neutral negative particle *leai* 'No' and the negative imperative *aua!* 'Don't!' As stated earlier, the youngest children in our sample are using the affect term *tae/kae* at 19 months. The use of the negative particle *leai* 'No' does not appear in the speech of one child until 22 months and for the other young child not until 24 months. The use of the negative imperative *aua!* 'Don't!' appears at 23 months for one child and 25 months for the second child. An illustration of how young children use *tae/kae* to refuse and reject is presented in the example below:

(11) K, 1;7, refusing to comply with his mother's wishes

K	Mother
	'ai muamua le talo
	eat first ART taro

"Eat first the taro"
ā?
okay
"Okay?"

tae
shit
"shit/"

'ai muamua le   talo lea.
eat first   ART taro this
"Eat first the taro here."

u tae/
? shit
"(?) shit/"

'a'a
neg. affect
"Don't!"
Se   'ai muamua le   talo lea
please eat first   ART taro this
"Oh please eat first the taro here."

tae/
shit
"shit/"

The basis for children's preference of the affect form over the neutral form appears to be rhetorical. As noted earlier, for example, the affect first person pronoun expressing sympathy for oneself is used to elicit sympathy from others for oneself. In adult speech, one finds this pronoun in narratives of complaint, for example, where minimally some sort of commiseration is desired. As discussed earlier, in the children's corpus the most common environment for the pronoun is in the course of asking for some good or service. In using the affect pronoun, the speaker appeals to the addressee to provide what is desired out of love or sympathy for the speaker. The neutral first person pronoun does not have this rhetorical force. Children apparently are sensitive to these rhetorical differences. The affective forms can "buy" something that the neutral pronoun cannot.

Implications of acquisition patterns

These and other findings strongly support the idea that children can express affect through conventional linguistic means from a very early point in developmental time. The Samoan materials indicate that small children are concerned with the rhetorical force of their utterances and that rhetorical strategies may account for certain acquisition patterns.

Affect strategies and goals, then, should be considered along with others that have been proposed as underlying children's emerging grammar. No matter to what use you put words – whether to request, to assert, or to question – you need to get the hearer to recognize your disposition with respect to those elocutionary acts and their propositions. All languages have conventional means of encoding this information. We can turn to the historian, the drama critic, and the clinical psychologist to tell us this. But we can also turn to our transcripts and our recordings of infants, small children, and caregivers. These materials reveal the patterned and conventional ways in which affect pervades both form and meaning in language.

Notes

The research on which this paper is based was supported by the National Science Foundation (1978–80), the Australian National University Research School of Pacific Studies (1980–1), and the Gardner Howard Foundation (1982–3).
1   I am grateful to Dotsy Kneubuhl for discussing the role of affect in the lives of Samoan children and for sending me this excerpt.
2   For a description of the field research methods used in collecting these data as well as an overview of Samoan social organization, see Platt paper in this volume.

References

Andersen, E. 1977. Learning how to speak with style. Unpublished Ph.D. dissertation, Stanford University.
Bauman, R. 1977. *Verbal art as performance*. Rowley, Mass.: Newbury.
Blom, J.-P. & Gumperz, J. 1972. Social meaning in linguistic structures: code-switching in Norway. In J. Gumperz & D. Hymes, eds., *Directions in sociolinguistics*. New York: Holt, Rinehart & Winston, pp. 407–434.
Bowlby, J. 1969. *Attachment and loss,* vol. 1: *Attachment*. New York: Basic.
Bretherton, I. & Beeghly, M. 1982. Talking about internal states: the acquisition of an explicit theory of mind. *Developmental Psychology* 18,6:906–921.
Brown, P. & Levinson, S. 1978. Universals in language usage: politeness phenomena. In E. Goody, ed., *Questions and politeness*. Cambridge: Cambridge University Press, pp. 56–289.
Brown, P. & Levinson, S. 1978. Universals in language usage: politeness phenomena. In E. Goody, ed., *Questions and politeness*. Cambridge: Cambridge University Press, pp. 56–289.
Burke, K. 1962. *A grammar of motives/a rhetoric of motives*. Cleveland, Ohio: Meridian Books.
Chafe, W. 1976. Givenness, contrastiveness, definiteness, subjects, topics and point of view. In C. Li, ed., *Subject and topic*. New York: Academic Press, pp. 25–56.
Clancy, P. 1980. Referential choice in English and Japanese narrative discourse. In W. Chafe, ed., *The pear stories: cognitive, cultural and linguistic aspects of narrative production*. New York: Academic Press, pp. 127–202.
Cruttendon, A. 1982. How long does intonation acquisition take? Paper delivered at the Stanford Child Language Forum, Stanford University, Stanford.

Dixon, R. M. 1972. *The Dyirbal language of North Queensland.* Cambridge: Cambridge University Press.

Dunn, J. & Kendrick, C. 1982. The speech of two and three year olds to infant siblings. *Journal of Child Language* 9:579–595.

Duranti, A. 1984. The social meaning of subject pronouns in Italian conversation. *Text* 4:277–311.

Duranti, A. & Ochs, E. 1979. Left-dislocation in Italian conversation. In T. Givon, ed., *Syntax and semantics,* vol. 12: Discourse and syntax. New York: Academic Press, pp. 377–416.

Eibl-Eiblesfeldt, I. 1970. *Ethology: the biology of behavior.* New York: Holt, Rinehart & Winston.

Ferguson, C. 1977. Baby talk as a simplified register. In C. Snow & C. Ferguson, eds., *Talking to children.* Cambridge: Cambridge University Press, pp. 209–235.

Gerber, E. 1975. The cultural patterning of emotions in Samoa. Unpublished Ph.D. dissertation, University of California, San Diego.

Givon, T. 1979. *On understanding grammar.* New York: Academic Press.

Goffman, E. 1974. *Frame analysis.* New York: Harper & Row.

Halliday, M. 1967. Notes on transitivity and theme in English: II. *Journal of Linguistics* 3:199–244.

  1973. *Explorations in the functions of language.* London: Arnold.

Hawkinson, A. & Hyman, L. M. 1974. Hierarchies of natural topic in Shona. *Studies in African Linguistics* 5:147–170.

Heath, S. 1983. *Ways with words: language, life and work in communities and classrooms.* Cambridge: Cambridge University Press.

Hoffman, M. 1981. Perspectives on the difference between understanding people and understanding things: the role of affect. In J. Flavell & L. Ross, eds., *Social cognitive development: frontiers and possible futures.* Cambridge: Cambridge University Press, pp. 67–81.

Hopper, P. 1979. Aspect and foregrounding in discourse. In T. Givon, ed., *Syntax and semantics,* vol. 12: *Discourse and syntax.* New York: Academic Press, pp. 213–241.

Hopper, P. & Thompson, S. 1980. Transitivity in grammar and discourse, *Language* 56:251–299.

Hymes, D. 1972. On communicative competence. In J. B. Pride & J. Holmes, eds., *Sociolinguistics.* Harmondsworth: Penguin Books, pp. 269–285.

  1974. *Foundations in sociolinguistics: an ethnographic approach.* Philadelphia: University of Pennsylvania Press.

Irvine, J. 1982. Language and affect: some cross-cultural issues. In H. Byrnes, ed., *Contemporary perceptions of language: interdisciplinary dimensions.* Georgetown Round Table on Languages and Linguistics. Washington, D.C.: Georgetown University Press, pp. 31–47.

Klinnert, M. D., Campos, J. J., Sorce, J. F., Emde, R. N., & Svejda, M. 1983. Emotions as behavior regulators: social referencing in infancy. In R. Plutchnik & H. Kellerman, eds., *Emotions: theory, research and experience,* vol. 2: *The emotions.* New York: Academic Press, pp. 57–86.

Kuno, S. 1972. Functional sentence perspective: a case study from Japanese and English. *Linguistic Inquiry* 3:161–195.

Labov, W. 1966. *The social stratification of English in New York City.* Washington, D.C.: Center for Applied Linguistics.

Lakoff, G. 1972. Hedges: a study in meaning criteria and the logic of fuzzy concepts. In *Papers from the Eighth Regional Meeting of the Chicago Linguistics Society.* Chicago: University of Chicago Press, pp. 183–228.

Langness, L. & Frank, G. 1981. *Lives: an anthropological approach to biography*. Novato, Calif.: Chandler & Sharp.

Levy, R. 1973. *Tahitians: mind and experience in the Society Islands*. Chicago: University of Chicago Press.

1984. Emotion, knowing and culture. In R. Shweder & R. A. LeVine, eds., *Culture theory: essays on mind, self and emotion*. Cambridge: Cambridge University Press, pp. 214–237.

Lutz, C. 1981. Talking about "our insides": Ifalukian conceptions of the self. Paper presented at the meetings of the Association for Social Anthropology in Oceania, Symposium on Folk Psychology in Pacific Cultures.

MacWhinney, B. 1977. Starting points. *Language* 53:152–78.

1984. Grammatical devices for sharing points. In R. Schiefelbusch & J. Pickar, eds., *The acquisition of communicative competence*. Baltimore: University Park Press, pp. 323–374.

Mandler, G. 1975. *Mind and emotion*. New York: Wiley.

Mead, M. 1928. *Coming of age in Samoa*. New York: Morrow.

Much, N. & Shweder, R. 1978. Speaking of rules: the analysis of culture in breach. In W. Damon, ed., *Moral development*. San Francisco: Jossey-Bass, pp. 19–39.

Norman, D. 1979. Twelve issues for cognitive science. Center for Human Information Processing Report 87. University of California, San Diego.

Peters, A. 1977. Language learning strategies. *Language* 53:560–573.

Scheff, T. 1977. The distancing of emotion in ritual. *Current Anthropology* 18,3:483–505.

Schieffelin, B. 1979. How Kaluli children learn what to say, what to do, and how to feel. Unpublished Ph.D. dissertation, Columbia University.

Searle, J. 1969. *Speech acts*. Cambridge: Cambridge University Press.

Seymour, S. 1980. Household structure and status and expressions of affect in India. Paper presented at the 79th Meeting of the American Anthropological Association, Symposium on Socialization of Affect, Washington, D.C.

Shore, B. 1977. A Samoan theory of action: social control and social order in a Polynesian paradox. Unpublished Ph.D. dissertation, University of Chicago.

1982. *Sala'ilua: a Samoan mystery*. New York: Columbia University Press.

Shweder, R. 1984. Anthropology's romantic rebellion against the enlightenment; or there's more to thinking than reason and evidence. In R. Shweder & R. A. LeVine, eds., *Culture theory: essays on mind, self and emotion*. Cambridge: Cambridge University Press, pp. 27–66.

Smith, C. 1983. A theory of aspectual choice. *Language* 59,3:479–501.

Super, C. & Harkness S. 1982. The development of affect in infancy and early childhood. In D. Wagner & H. W. Stevenson, eds., *Cultural perspectives on child development*. New York: Freeman, pp. 1–19.

Tyerman, D. & Bennett, G. 1822. *Journal of voyages and travels*, vol. 1., comp. J. Montgomery. London: Frederick Westley and A. A. Davis, Booksellers to the London Missionary Society.

Zahn-Waxler, C., Radke-Yarrow, M., & King, R. 1979. Child-rearing and children's pro-social initiations toward victims of distress. *Child Development* 50:319–330.

Zajonc, R. B. 1979. Feeling and thinking: preferences need no inferences. Invited address to the American Psychological Association.

Index